TOURIST TRAINS
GUIDEBOOK
✛ FOURTH EDITION ✛

KALMBACH BOOKS

Kalmbach Books
21027 Crossroads Circle
Waukesha, Wisconsin 53186
www.Kalmbach.com/Books

First edition published in 2007. Fourth edition in 2013.

Published in 2013
17 16 15 14 13 1 2 3 4 5

Manufactured in China

ISBN: 978-0-87116-771-2

Front cover photo: Georgetown Loop by Jim Wrinn
Back cover photo: Mount Washington Cog Railway by Karl Zimmermann

Editor: Randy Rehberg
Art Director: Tom Ford

Publisher's Cataloging-In-Publication Data

Tourist trains guidebook / [from the publishers of Trains magazine ; editor: Randy Rehberg]. -- 4th ed.

p. : ill. (chiefly col.) ; cm. -- (Trains books)

Includes index.
ISBN: 978-0-87116-771-2

1. Railroads--United States--Guidebooks. 2. Railroads--Canada--Guidebooks. 3. Railroad museums--United States--Guidebooks. 4. Railroad museums--Canada--Guidebooks. 5. Railroad travel--United States--Guidebooks. 6. Railroad travel--Canada--Guidebooks. I. Rehberg, Randy. II. Kalmbach Publishing Company. III. Title: Trains magazine.

HE2727 .T68 2013
917.304/025

Winter Photo Shoots

Time Travel! Set your watch back a century, and experience world class photographic opportunities. Witness railroading as it was in the last century. Photograph century-old original steam locomotives pulling vintage freight and passenger cars that are original to the railroad! An incredible event!

Winter Photo Shoot

2½ Days...$450
Both weekends.............................$835
Members:
2½ Days.
B................................$395

Railroad Reality Week

Work on the Railroad! Learn, hands-on what it takes to run a 19th century railroad. You will work in a machine shop, crew a train, repair track, operate a diesel locomotive. For one week you will have the greatest adventure of your life!

Adult Session........................*...$995*

Dates: J............6 or...A............17...

Sleep in a Caboose
Sleep in a Bunkhouse

Unique Opportunity! Spend the night in the 19th century! Sleep in a Caboose or in the Crew Bunkhouse in a National Historic Landmark Railroad Yard. Then ride the train!

Caboose Overnight........................$115
Members: $80
Caboose Overnight & Train Ride.......$165
Member: $139
Bunkhouse Overnight....................$135
Members: $95
Bunkhouse Overnight & Train Ride..$185
Members: $150
(Accommodations: 2 adults and a child)

Be the Engineer

Operate a Locomotive! You are the Engineer - Instruction included.

Be the Engineer - 14 Mile Trip
Diesel....$645   Steam....$845
Members: Diesel $545; Steam $745
Ultimate Engineer Package - 2 Trips
Both Steam & Diesel....$1,095 (28 miles)
Members: $945
Be the Engine....

Contributors

The following people provided reviews of the tourist train sites: Kevin Andrusia, Bryan Bechtold, Marvin Clemons, Dave Crosby, Steve Glischinski, John Godfrey, Martin Hansen, Mike Harbour, Scott Hartley, Patrick Hiatte, David Hoge, Tom Kline, Kathi Kube, G. Wayne Laepple, Robert LaMay, Elrond Lawrence, David Lustig, Rob McGonigal, Jackson McQuigg, Alexander Mitchell IV, Tom Murray, Don Nickel, Steve Patterson, Mark Perri, Mark Perry, Ralcon Wagner, Bob Withers, Jim Wrinn, and Karl Zimmermann.

Contact us

To improve future editions of the guidebook, we would like to hear from you. Let us know about the sites you visited, your experiences, and if our descriptions were accurate. Please send your comments to *Tourist Trains* editor, Kalmbach Books, 21027 Crossroads Circle, PO Box 1612, Waukesha, WI 53187-1612.

Contents

Introduction

This guidebook is about adventures that feature steel wheels on steel rails. Within these pages, you'll find historic trains across North America that will take you on a journey of discovery. On the railroads listed here, you'll find wilderness, tall timber, ocean views, and dazzling vistas. You'll also find unique experiences: the chance to ride a train to see bald eagles, go rafting, or enjoy a concert at a mountaintop venue. You'll find museums that keep alive our rich railway history—from the days of steam locomotive power to sleek streamlined diesels. You'll also find railroading's most sacred shrines: historic sites that mark where history was made—and often still is today.

The *Tourist Trains Guidebook* is an essential tool that takes you into the exciting world of heritage railroading. This guide is designed to spur your imagination and spark your curiosity to go and explore. It's packed with useful information. You'll learn where to find real operating steam locomotives. You'll discover trains that run within sight of, or right through, some of our land's greatest national parks. You'll find trains that take you to see wildlife up close, relive history, or provide the chance to zipline through the trees.

You'll discover where you can step inside a genuine 1920s roundhouse, learn about narrow gauge trains that once went in search of riches in rugged territory, and find places that tell the story of man and machine vs. mountains. Some museums even have programs that allow you to run a locomotive.

Planning a vacation? This guide is your perfect resource. Pick a destination, flip through the pages, and learn about the exciting trains nearby. I encourage you to do as I do and let this book steer you to the tracks where adventure and excitement are always just around the next bend.

Jim Wrinn

Jim Wrinn, Editor
Trains magazine

Using the guidebook

Tourist Trains Guidebook describes 495 excursion trains, dinner trains, trolley rides, railroad museums, and historical depots across the United States and Canada. The sites are described in either full-page reviews or in shorter listings. In this fourth edition of the guidebook, you'll find more than 35 exciting new sites.

Trains magazine staff and contributors reviewed 198 of the top attractions. Their reviews provide an in-depth look at each location. They describe what each train ride or museum offers and gives you an idea of when to go for the best experiences. They also point out nearby activities that are worth doing and what you shouldn't miss to make your visit most enjoyable.

Almost 300 other unique attractions are presented in capsule descriptions that offer a concise look at each site and provide contact information.

We have included the most up-to-date details possible for every attraction. However, due to the many factors that can affect a tourist train or museum, we recommend that you contact any site before planning your visit. Steam engines may not be running, schedules and prices may change, and museums may be under renovation.

While almost every attraction has a website, many of them post their most current information and upcoming events on Facebook. We will also list updates and any corrections to the guidebook on www.TrainsMag.com.

You can browse the listings by state or province, where you'll find the shorter entries first followed by the full-page reviews. Each grouping is listed in alphabetical order. You can also look for an individual site using the index at the back of the book.

ALABAMA

Foley Railroad Museum

Housed in a former Louisville & Nashville depot, the museum contains photos and artifacts relating to railroads, the City of Foley, and Baldwin County history. It displays an L&N diesel switch engine, several boxcars, and a caboose. The museum is open Monday through Friday.

LOCATION: 125 E. Laurel Avenue, Foley
PHONE: 251-943-1818
WEBSITE: foleyrailroadmuseum.com
E-MAIL: foleymuseum@gulftel.com

Fort Payne Depot Museum

Located in northeast Alabama, the museum is a former passenger station built in the late 1800s of pink sandstone, and it displays railroad artifacts in a caboose. It also includes local historical, military, and Native American items. The museum is open Mondays, Wednesdays, and Fridays.

LOCATION: 105 Fifth Street NE, Fort Payne
PHONE: 256-845-5714
WEBSITE: fortpaynedepotmuseum.com
E-MAIL: depotmuseum@bellsouth.net

Huntsville Depot & Museum

Built in 1860, the depot is the oldest in Alabama and is listed on the National Register of Historic Places. You can read graffiti left by Civil War soldiers and climb aboard several steam locomotives for an up-close look. The museum is open Tuesday through Saturday March through December. The annual WhistleStop festival takes place in early May.

LOCATION: 320 Church Street NW, Huntsville
PHONE: 256-564-8100
WEBSITE: earlyworks.com
E-MAIL: form on website

Leeds Historic Depot

Built in 1884 by the Georgia Pacific Railway, the Leeds depot was restored in 1984. It serves as headquarters for the Mid-South Chapter of the Railway & Locomotive Historical Society. The agent-operator's office has been authentically restored, and a small exhibit dedicated to the local legend of John Henry is available for viewing by appointment. The Leeds Downtown Folk Festival & John Henry Celebration takes place in September.

LOCATION: 933 Thornton Ave NE, Leeds
PHONE: 205-699-0440
WEBSITE: midsouth.rlhs.org

Heart of Dixie Railroad Museum

LOCATION: 1919 Ninth Street, Calera
PHONE: 205-757-8383 or 205-668-3435
WEBSITE: hodrrm.org
E-MAIL: info@hodrrm.org

Marvin Clemons

The museum features exhibits housed in a restored depot from Wilton, Ala. It operates two trains and displays a variety of locomotives and rolling stock. The Heart of Dixie has been designated as the official railroad museum for the state of Alabama.

CHOICES: The museum's Calera & Shelby Railroad operates over 5.5 miles of the Louisville & Nashville's former Alabama Mineral branch line through the forested countryside. Two one-hour, diesel-powered excursions run every Saturday. The two-foot gauge Shelby & Southern steam train operates short rides on select days. The museum is open Tuesdays, Thursdays, and Saturdays mid-March through mid-December. Admission to the depot museum and outdoor exhibits is free (donations are welcome). A pavilion is available for picnics.

WHEN TO GO: With comfortable temperatures and lower humidity, spring and autumn are ideal seasons for a visit, as well as the best times to enjoy the colorful foliage along the heavily wooded Calera & Shelby right-of-way. For family outings, the museum regularly operates a number of theme-related excursions including the Cottontail Express, Day Out with Thomas, Steam Days, Pumpkin Patch Express, Santa Special, and the ever-popular North Pole Express.

GOOD TO KNOW: The Ozan Winery offers wine-tasting train excursions aboard the Calera & Shelby Railroad on Saturday afternoons. Trains board at the winery.

WORTH DOING: Located only a 15-minute drive from the museum, the American Village provides a delightful setting for a Revolutionary-era village, complete with special events and tours.

DON'T MISS: Housed in an early 20th century L&N freight house, the museum's Boone Library contains an extensive archive of books, periodicals, maps, and other local railroadiana. It is open on Saturdays.

GETTING THERE: The museum is located 30 miles south of Birmingham, just one mile off I-65 at Exit 228. Drive towards Calera and turn left onto Ninth Street to the museum.

North Alabama Railroad Museum

LOCATION: 694 Chase Road, Huntsville
PHONE: 256-851-6276
WEBSITE: northalabamarailroadmuseum.com
E-MAIL: narm-mail@comcast.net

Ralcon Wagner

Combining a nicely restored country depot with a surprising variety of early diesel motive power and vintage rolling stock, the North Alabama Railroad Museum is a hidden jewel tucked away in the scenic Tennessee Valley.

CHOICES: The museum's depot and 35-piece collection of rolling stock is open for self-guided tours seven days a week. The museum also runs a diesel-powered, 10-mile round-trip excursion over its Mercury & Chase Railroad. Many trips have a special theme, and excursions operate primarily on select Saturdays April through December. Santa and Easter Bunny rides are shorter than other excursions. One-hour guided tours are available when the excursion train runs.

WHEN TO GO: Anytime is a good time to take a self-guided tour of the museum. North Alabama's Tennessee Valley is at its scenic best in the early spring and late fall when the weather is typically ideal for taking one of the museum's themed excursions.

GOOD TO KNOW: The centerpiece of the museum is the Chase depot built by the Chase family in 1937 to serve its nursery business and the community that grew around it. The 1,000-acre nursery was once among the largest in the southeastern United States.

WORTH DOING: No trip to the Huntsville area is complete without a visit to the U.S. Space & Rocket Center. Located a short 10-minute drive from the museum, the center features a replica Saturn V rocket and other space exhibits.

DON'T MISS: The historic Huntsville Depot is located downtown. Built in the 1860s by the Memphis & Charleston Railroad, this building is steeped in Civil War history. It features exhibits on Alabama railroads and the Civil War and displays rolling stock and locomotives.

GETTING THERE: The museum is located near downtown Huntsville within a two-hour drive from Birmingham, Chattanooga, or Nashville. From Birmingham, take I-65 north (from Nashville, take I-65 south) to the I-565 east spur to the Moores Mill Road exit and then left onto Chase Road. From Chattanooga, take I-24 west to Highway 72 to Moores Mill Road and then left onto Chase Road.

ALASKA

Museum of Alaska Transportation & Industry

The museum is home to the trains, planes, and other machines that helped develop the state. It features a train yard with locomotives, railcars, and a renovated section house. The museum is open daily mid-May to September.

LOCATION: 3800 W. Museum Drive, Wasilla
PHONE: 907-376-1211
WEBSITE: museumofalaska.org
E-MAIL: form on website

Tanana Valley Railroad Museum

The museum runs a restored 1899 Porter 0-4-0 steam locomotive around the perimeter of Pioneer Park on select days during the year. The museum is open daily Memorial Day through Labor Day, and visitors may see restoration activity as well as learn about the railroad. Pioneer Park contains several other interesting museums and operates a narrow gauge train through the site.

LOCATION: 2300 Airport Way, Fairbanks
PHONE: 907-459-7421
WEBSITE: ftvrr.org
E-MAIL: ftvrr.inc@gmail.com

Alaska Railroad

LOCATION: 411 W. First Avenue, Anchorage
PHONE: 800-544-0552 or 907-265-2494
WEBSITE: alaskarailroad.com
E-MAIL: reservations@akrr.com

Tom Murray

Completed in 1923, the Alaska Railroad was built to link the Pacific seaport of Seward with the resource-rich interior long before there were highways. Passenger service offers breathtaking excursions into rugged back-country terrain that is often inaccessible by car.

CHOICES: The flagship *Denali Star* operates daily between Anchorage and Fairbanks with stops at Talkeetna and Denali National Park. A local favorite, the *Coastal Classic* goes to Seward, where boat tours provide access to Kenai Fjords National Park. Each of these trains includes a refurbished "lower 48" heritage dome car, coach, and bistro car, as well as a GoldStar (first class) dome car sporting open-air viewing decks. Adventure class (coach) passengers can watch the Alaskan landscape roll by from open Dutch doors. The *Hurricane Turn* provides flag-stop service for campers and fishermen along the Susitna River. The *Glacier Discovery* runs from Anchorage to Whittier for glacier cruises and to Spencer Glacier and Grandview whistle-stops for kayaking, rafting, and hiking.

WHEN TO GO: Most trains operate mid-May to mid-September when the weather is warm and the days are long. Early in the season, when there is still snow on the mountains and little rain, is best. The Aurora winter train operates between Anchorage and Fairbanks on weekends from mid-September to mid-May, and various special trains also run during this time of year.

GOOD TO KNOW: The railroad works closely with major cruise lines, offering cruise passengers Grandview service (using former Florida Fun Train cars) to connect the ports of Seward and Whittier with the Anchorage airport. The cruise lines also operate their own double-decker domes on the *Denali Star*. However, the railroad's own equipment provides more flexibility, including the ability to move from car to car.

WORTH DOING: The *Hurricane Turn* provides an escape from sightseeing and tourism overload and a chance to visit with friendly Alaskans on their way to remote cabins.

DON'T MISS: Try either the *Coastal Classic* or *Glacier Discovery*. The scenery south of Anchorage is more varied and breathtaking than most of the Denali route.

GETTING THERE: Alaska Airlines has the most flights, but Anchorage and Fairbanks are also served by other major airlines. Cruise ships from Vancouver and Seattle that dock at Seward, Whittier, and Anchorage are another option.

White Pass & Yukon Route

LOCATION: 231 Second Avenue, Skagway
PHONE: 800-343-7373 or 907-983-2217
WEBSITE: wpyr.com
E-MAIL: info@wpyr.com

Karl Zimmermann

The White Pass & Yukon's 67.5 route miles make it the longest operating narrow gauge railroad in North America. More importantly, virtually every one of those miles is knockout beautiful—a potpourri of lakes, rivers, and snow-capped mountains. Completed in 1900, the railroad was built to link the Yukon and other booming gold-mining districts with tidewater at Skagway.

CHOICES: There are many options for riding. The most popular is the half-day, 40-mile round trip to White Pass Summit. Other possibilities include going seven miles farther to Fraser and continuing on to Whitehorse by motor coach. Even better are the twice-weekly, six-hour trips along the full length of the line, Skagway to Carcross, available in either direction with motor-coach return.

WHEN TO GO: The White Pass & Yukon operates from early May to late September, and any time in that window is fine for a visit—though it is likely to be bracingly chilly early and late. As compensation, the snow-capped mountains will be more scenic.

GOOD TO KNOW: One of the railroad's two steam locomotives, either Mikado No. 73 or Consolidation No. 69, operates on Mondays and Fridays. Unique and colorful diesels—modernized, shovel-nose General Electric units and newer low-nose road switchers built by Alco and then MLW—handle all the other trains.

WORTH DOING: The few hotels and handful of B&Bs in Skagway are best booked in advance. You can tour Skagway, the Yukon, and other scenic areas by Jeep, raft, horseback, or dogsled.

DON'T MISS: Although the entire line is spectacular, pay particular attention to the first 20 miles to White Pass Summit. Here, the railroad uses grades of up to 3.9 percent to climb 2,865 feet. For the best views, grab seats on the left side of the train.

GETTING THERE: Most passengers arrive at Skagway by cruise ship, but the railroad successfully caters to independent travelers as well. You can get to Skagway from Bellingham, Wash., or Prince Rupert aboard the comfortable ferries of the Alaska Marine Highway. For motorists, Skagway is 110 miles south of the Alaska Highway via the South Klondike Highway. A commuter airline serves Skagway from Juneau.

ARIZONA

Arizona Railway Museum

The museum restores and displays railroad equipment of the Southwest and has more than 30 pieces of equipment including locomotives, freight cars, passenger cars, and a PCC trolley. It is open weekends September through May, with work sessions taking place on Saturdays. Several passenger cars and a caboose are usually open for visitors to view. All cars are open on National Train Day.

LOCATION: 330 E. Ryan Road, Chandler
PHONE: 480-821-1108
WEBSITE: azrymuseum.org
E-MAIL: info@azrymuseum.org

Southern Arizona Transportation Museum

You can tour the former Southern Pacific Railroad depot Tuesday through Sunday, and take in a newer exhibit that features oral history accounts of railroaders. The centerpiece of the museum is steam locomotive No. 1673, which was built in 1900. On Saturdays, you can learn more about No. 1673 with a visit to the locomotive's cab.

LOCATION: 414 N. Toole Avenue, Tucson
PHONE: 520-623-2223
WEBSITE: tucsonhistoricdepot.org
E-MAIL: contactus@tucsonhistoricdepot.org

Tucson Modern Streetcars

Tuscon's new streetcar system is scheduled to open in late 2013. The 3.9-mile line will connect the downtown area with the Fourth Avenue Business District and the University of Arizona. The all-electric streetcars will operate during the day and at night.

LOCATION: Congress Street to Helen Street, Tucson
PHONE: 520-624-5656
WEBSITE: tucsonstreetcar.com
E-MAIL: info@tucsonstreetcar.info

Grand Canyon Railway

LOCATION: 233 N. Grand Canyon Boulevard, Williams
PHONE: 800-843-8724 or 928-635-4253
WEBSITE: thetrain.com
E-MAIL: info@thetrain.com

Jim Wrinn

This train doesn't take passengers into the canyon, or even along the rim, except for a short distance, but it offers a unique way to reach one of the great scenic wonders of North America in style. Diesel-powered (and a few steam) trains take riders from Williams on a 65-mile journey to the Grand Canyon's South Rim through high desert and pine forests. An exceptional ride, the trip is also a great value in that it saves you time in trying to find a parking space at the ever-popular South Rim.

CHOICES: Grand Canyon offers five levels of service: coach, first class, dome, luxury dome, and parlor. Service and attention are hallmarks of this railroad. Coach passengers won't be disappointed with the strolling musicians and attentive service, while those in cars with higher levels of service will be pampered with extra room, private bars, and exceptional views.

WHEN TO GO: Traveling this area any time is fascinating. Christmas Day is the only day the railroad doesn't run. The summer's heat is foiled by air-conditioned cars.

GOOD TO KNOW: You can ride from Williams, spend the night at South Rim, and return on the next day's train. The railroad has its own hotel, restaurant, RV park, and pet-sitting service available at Williams, which is a charming western town with plenty of shops and restaurants worth checking out. The Williams depot, built in 1908, was originally home to a Harvey Hotel and is listed on the National Register of Historic Places.

WORTH DOING: At South Rim, the train arrives at an old Santa Fe Railway depot. Walk up the hill to El Tovar, the historic railroad hotel, and you'll stand in awe of nature at its finest.

DON'T MISS: The railroad offers steam operations on special days during the year behind Burlington Route 2-8-2 No. 4960. The engine uses recycled vegetable oil. Plan ahead and enjoy a steamy adventure. The Cataract Creek Rambler is a short steam-train ride that also operates several times during the year.

GETTING THERE: Williams is 32 miles west of Flagstaff. Take I-40 to Exit 163 and follow Grand Canyon Boulevard to the depot.

Verde Canyon Railroad

LOCATION: 300 N. Broadway, Clarkdale
PHONE: 800-582-7245
WEBSITE: verdecanyonrr.com
E-MAIL: info@verdecanyonrr.com

Verde Canyon Railroad

On the Verde Canyon Railroad, you'll ride a former copper mining spur down a lush green valley where eagles often soar. Ride across bridges, around rock formations, and through a 680-foot tunnel.

CHOICES: The four-hour, historic route from Clarkdale to the deserted Perkinsville Ranch travels between two national forests and into Verde Canyon, which is accessible only by rail. Narration describes the history, archaeology, geology, and wildlife of the area. Two levels of service are available. Coach seating features traditional Pullman-style seats with a snack bar. First-class passage provides more spacious seating, panoramic windows, and complimentary appetizers. All cars access open-air viewing cars equipped with shaded canopies. A caboose is also available for small private parties.

WHEN TO GO: Trains run year-round, but summer can be exceptionally hot. In winter, you can view nesting bald eagles in their natural habitat.

GOOD TO KNOW: The railroad's pair of streamlined diesel locomotives from the 1950s features a special eagle paint scheme. Located in Clarkdale, the Verde Canyon Railroad depot opened in 1997 on the same site of two previous depots.

WORTH DOING: Visit the Tuzigoot National Monument, where an ancient Sinagua pueblo was built. The 42-acre site includes guided tours of the pueblo ruins and hiking trails.

DON'T MISS: At the depot, a short walk takes you to the John Bell Museum, a renovated boxcar that contains Verde Canyon Railroad history displays.

GETTING THERE: The railroad is about 40 minutes from Sedona and two hours from Phoenix. From Sedona, go southwest toward Cottonwood on Highway 89A to Mingus Avenue. Turn right on Mingus Avenue and go two miles to Main Street. Turn right on Main Street and travel through Old Town Cottonwood. Look for the sign and turn right on Broadway. From Phoenix, take I-17 north to Exit 287. Go west on Highway 260 and then turn left at Main Street through Old Town Cottonwood. Look for the sign and turn right on Broadway.

ARKANSAS

Fort Smith Trolley Museum

Visit this museum and you can see its collection of railroad, streetcar, and transportation exhibits, including Frisco steam locomotive 4003. Board No. 224, a restored Fort Smith streetcar at the Fort Smith Museum of History on Rogers Avenue for an enjoyable trolley ride. The museum is open weekends year-round, and trolleys run daily May through October and on weekends the rest of the year.

LOCATION: 100 S. Fourth Street, Fort Smith
PHONE: 479-783-0205
WEBSITE: fstm.org
E-MAIL: info@fstm.org

Frisco Depot Museum

This restored Victorian depot was built in 1886 and operated by the Frisco Railroad. Take a self-guided tour and hear the stories of 14 figures representing passengers, station workers, and train crew. You can also examine a Frisco caboose. Located in Mammoth Spring State Park, the depot is closed on Mondays.

LOCATION: Highway 9 and Highway 63, Mammoth Spring
PHONE: 870-625-7364
WEBSITE: arkansasstateparks.com/mammothspring
E-MAIL: mammothspring@arkansas.com

Arkansas & Missouri Railroad

LOCATION: 306 E. Emma Street, Springdale
PHONE: 800-687-8600 or 479-751-8600
WEBSITE: amrailroad.com
E-MAIL: brenda@amrailroad.com

Arkansas & Missouri Railroad, Dick Hovey

Arkansas

From the highest point to down in the hollers, the Arkansas & Missouri operates excursion trains powered by its all-Alco roster of diesels. Rebuilt air-conditioned coaches transport riders through some of the most rugged terrain between the Appalachians and the Rockies. The A&M operates 139 miles of former St. Louis-San Francisco trackage from Monett, Mo., to Fort Smith, Ark., through the Boston Mountains of northwest Arkansas.

CHOICES: The longest ride is a 134-mile round trip from Springdale to Van Buren with a three-hour stop in Van Buren, where passengers can shop or dine near the 1901 Frisco depot. Another ride is a 70-mile round trip from Van Buren to Winslow with a ride over 100-foot trestles and through the 1,702-foot-long Winslow tunnel. A third trip takes you from Fort Smith over the Arkansas River to Winslow.

WHEN TO GO: With its schedule of special events, trains run all year. Fall offers the best scenery, and fall trips sell out quickly, but spring is also popular because everything is blooming.

GOOD TO KNOW: Three classes—first class, club, and coach—are offered on all trips, with lunch or snacks offered for first class and club but not coach. Fares increase for trips during the fall foliage season. If you join the A&M fan club, members receive a 20 percent discount.

WORTH DOING: The A&M excursion fits in nicely with a trip to Branson or to the William J. Clinton Presidential Library in Little Rock. Eureka Springs offers shopping, and the nearby Buffalo and Mulberry Rivers provide camping, canoeing, and hiking opportunities. Two Civil War battlefields are nearby.

DON'T MISS: For a old-time railroading experience, you can purchase a ticket for the restored B&O cupola caboose, which holds about a dozen passengers.

GETTING THERE: Various airlines offer flights into Northwest Arkansas Regional Airport. Travel over I-540 and I-40 gives the area quick access, making the A&M easily accessible for a day of fun.

Arkansas Railroad Museum

LOCATION: 1700 Port Road, Pine Bluff
PHONE: 870-535-8819
WEBSITE: arkansasrailroadmuseum.org
E-MAIL: info@arkansasrailroadmuseum.org

Arkansas Railroad Museum

The Arkansas Railroad Museum is the state's largest railroad museum. The museum is located in the machine shop built in the later part of the 19th century for the St. Louis Southwestern Railway, or Cotton Belt. The machine shop was part of a large complex of buildings and shops once located at Pine Bluff.

CHOICES: The museum's most famous tenant is the last steam locomotive built for the St. Louis Southwestern. No. 819 was assembled in the building that now houses the museum and was placed in service in early 1943. Along with No. 819, SSW No. 336 is also housed at the museum. Several diesel Alcos are also on display along with some passenger cars, a complete SSW work train, cabooses, and a Jordan snowplow. The museum features a large collection of memorabilia from the Cotton Belt and other Arkansas and East Texas railroads.

WHEN TO GO: The museum is open Mondays through Saturdays. Most exhibits are located inside, but much of the museum is not climate-controlled and therefore subject to the heat and cold. Operating hours can be affected by extreme temperatures.

GOOD TO KNOW: Engines 819 and 336 are the only surviving Cotton Belt steam locomotives, and both are on the National Register of Historic Places.

WORTH DOING: While in Pine Bluff, you can take in the historical museum, which is located in a restored union station that is also listed on the National Register of Historic Places.

DON'T MISS: The museum holds an annual railroadiana show the first Saturday in April.

GETTING THERE: The museum is easily accessible from Little Rock, which has a daily Amtrak stop and an airport served by several airlines. The museum lies just a short distance off I-530, which connects Little Rock and Pine Bluff.

Eureka Springs & North Arkansas Railway

LOCATION: 299 N. Main Street, Eureka Springs
PHONE: 479-253-9623
WEBSITE: esnarailway.com
E-MAIL: form on website

Patrick Hiatte

Spend a pleasant hour on one of the last remnants of the Missouri & North Arkansas Railroad, from Eureka Springs north to Junction and back. Along the way, enjoy the natural beauty of the Ozarks and Leatherwood Valley.

CHOICES: For the 4.5-mile, round-trip excursion, you can ride an ex-Rock Island commuter coach (complete with straps for standees) to Junction, where the locomotive turns and runs around the train for the return trip to Eureka Springs. Other options include trying the noon lunch train or the evening dinner train. The train is powered by a 1942 vintage diesel locomotive.

WHEN TO GO: From April through October, there are multiple daily departures Monday through Saturday. The train also operates the entire Memorial Day and Labor Day weekends. Eureka Springs is a year-round resort area, but most visitors arrive during the summer months and autumn, when the thickly wooded surrounding hills are ablaze with fall color. The tourist tide ebbs briefly in late August.

GOOD TO KNOW: The *Eurekan* dining car is climate-controlled, but the coaches are not, except for the pot-bellied stove and ceiling fans. Coach windows can be opened to catch the Ozarks breeze on warm days.

WORTH DOING: Explore Eureka Springs, as the entire city was designated as a historic district. In about two square miles, almost 500 buildings have historic significance. Wander the steep, winding streets and browse the art galleries and boutiques. Visit the many springs that were promoted because of their healing powers. View classic Victorian hotels, including The Crescent and the Basin Park, which has ground-level access to each of its eight stories (the hillside on which it's built is that steep).

DON'T MISS: Look through the Eureka Springs depot, which was built in 1913, and the rail equipment displayed outside. Gems include steam locomotive 201, built for service in Panama, and a station wagon equipped to run on rails as an inspection car, as well as a turntable and water tank.

GETTING THERE: Eureka Springs is about an hour northeast of Fayetteville along Highway 62 or an hour southwest of Branson, Mo., via Highways 65, 86, and 23.

River Rail

LOCATION: East Third Street, Little Rock
PHONE: 501-374-5354
WEBSITE: cat.org/rrail
E-MAIL: info@cat.org

Ralcon Wagner

River Rail is a heritage trolley line operated by the Central Arkansas Transit Authority between Little Rock and North Little Rock using replica vintage electric cars. The 3.4-mile route connects historical districts and tourist attractions in both cities.

CHOICES: Trolleys stop at 20 designated stations along the route. River Rail operators provide information on historic sites and attractions during the leisurely ride through a variety of unique neighborhoods. All cars are climate-controlled and handicap accessible. Fares are reasonable; however, exact fare is required. If you intend on riding more than once, a one- or three-day pass is your best bet. Passes are available from car operators and at select locations.

WHEN TO GO: The River Rail trolleys operate year-round except on major holidays. Service from North Little Rock to downtown Little Rock and the Clinton Presidential Center (Blue Line) operates daily from morning until evening with extended hours Thursday through Saturday. Additional service is provided over the downtown loop (Green Line), Monday through Saturday until early evening.

GOOD TO KNOW: The current roster of replica trolleys was built specifically for River Rail. All of the cars were designed to resemble the Birney-type streetcars that were once used in Little Rock until the late 1940s.

WORTH DOING: Little Rock has many attractions that appeal to the entire family. You can tour the State Capitol Building or the Clinton Presidential Center, shop and enjoy a meal in the River Market District, watch boats cruise down the Arkansas River as you stroll through Riverfront Park, or visit the kid-friendly Museum of Discovery.

DON'T MISS: Take time to walk or bike across the former railroad vertical lift bridges spanning the Arkansas River. Both have been converted to pedestrian use as part of the impressive River Trail network. You can view the ornate 1899 Choctaw & Memphis depot, now restored as part of the Clinton Presidential Center campus.

GETTING THERE: Follow I-30 into downtown Little Rock, take Exit 141A (Second Street), and proceed west. There is ample parking (free and paid) adjacent to the trolley along both Second Street and President Clinton Avenue around the River Market District.

CALIFORNIA

Colma Depot

This former Southern Pacific depot was built in 1865 and is part of the Colma Historical Association's museum, which also includes a blacksmith shop and freight shed. The second stop between San Francisco and San Jose, the depot was built to shelter passengers at Colma, where farmers and teamsters stopped on the way to San Francisco. The museum is open Tuesday through Sunday.

LOCATION: 1500 Hillside Boulevard, Colma
PHONE: 650-757-1676
WEBSITE: colmahistory.org
E-MAIL: colmahist@sbcglobal.net

Edward Peterman Museum of Railroad History

A restored former Southern Pacific depot houses the museum's collection of artifacts that highlights Western railroads with a focus on signaling. Along with the depot, which dates to 1863, the site features a restored 1926 tower, a section tool house, a speeder shed, and OWR&N business car No. 184. The museum, operated by the South Bay Historical Railroad Society, is open Tuesday evenings and Saturdays.

LOCATION: 1005 Railroad Avenue, Santa Clara
PHONE: 408-243-3969
WEBSITE: sbhrs.org
E-MAIL: form on website

Fort Humboldt State Historic Park

The park includes a logging museum that displays historic, steam-powered redwood-logging equipment, including two 0-4-0 locomotives and a steam donkey. On select summer Saturdays, the Timber Heritage Association steams up the equipment and provides short train rides. The park also includes a historical museum on the site where Ulysses S. Grant briefly served.

LOCATION: 3431 Fort Avenue, Eureka
PHONE: 707-445-6567
WEBSITE: parks.ca.gov/default.asp?page_id=665
E-MAIL: info@parks.ca.gov

History Park

History Park contains 27 original and reconstructed historic buildings including a trolley barn. Operated by the California Trolley & Railroad Corporation, the barn contains trolleys, a horse-drawn streetcar, and other historic vehicles. Trolley rides take place on park grounds on weekends.

LOCATION: 1650 Senter Road, San Jose
PHONE: 408-287-2290
WEBSITE: historysanjose.org or ctrc.org

Lomita Railroad Museum

This museum is a replica of the Boston & Maine station at Wakefield, Mass. You can climb into the cab of Southern Pacific No. 1765, a 2-6-0 Baldwin built in 1902, and look inside a 1910 UP caboose. Several freight cars and a wooden water tower are also displayed. The museum exhibits lanterns, china, and other artifacts. It is open Thursday through Sunday.

LOCATION: 2137 W. 250th Street, Lomita
PHONE: 310-326-6255
WEBSITE: lomita-rr.org
E-MAIL: f.bilyeu@lomita.com

Millbrae Train Museum

The museum contains photos, artifacts, and documents related to the area's railroad history. Housed in a former Southern Pacific train station, the museum displays a 1941 Pullman sleeper from the *City of San Francisco* streamliner. The museum is one of 10 historical landmarks on a self-guided walking tour. It is open on Saturdays, as is the nearby Millbrae History Museum.

LOCATION: California and Murchison Drives, Millbrae
PHONE: 650-333-1136
WEBSITE: millbraehs.org
E-MAIL: form on website

National City Depot

Still in its original location, the National City Depot, built in 1882, is the oldest railroad-related structure in San Diego County. Operated by the San Diego Electric Railway Association, it exhibits several trolleys, railroad items, and local historical displays. The depot is open Thursday through Sunday.

LOCATION: 922 W. 23rd Street, National City
PHONE: 619-474-4400
WEBSITE: sdera.org/depot.php
E-MAIL: webmaster@sdera.org

Nevada County Narrow Gauge Railroad and Transportation Museum

The museum's collection features NCNGRR engine No. 5. The 1875 Baldwin hauled timber, passengers, and freight. Other narrow gauge equipment and wooden railcars are on display as are a 1901 steam-powered carriage and other historic transportation pieces. Docent-led tours of the museum are available. It is open Friday through Tuesday during summer and on weekends in winter.

LOCATION: 5 Kidder Court, Nevada City
PHONE: 530-470-0902
WEBSITE: ncngrrmuseum.org
E-MAIL: contact@ncngrrmuseum.org

Niles Depot Museum

The museum focuses on the Southern Pacific and Western Pacific, the early railroads of Fremont, Newark, and Union City. It also includes Union Pacific and Amtrak artifacts. Exhibits include railroad signals, model railroads, and a WP caboose. Housed in a passenger depot and a freight depot, the museum is open on Sundays.

LOCATION: 37592 Niles Boulevard, Fremont
PHONE: 510-797-4449
WEBSITE: nilesdepot.org
E-MAIL: museum@nilesdepot.org

Poway-Midland Railroad

You can ride a variety of railroad equipment on this railroad. It operates a 1907 Baldwin 0-4-0 steam locomotive, a trolley car, and a speeder. You'll also see historic buildings, restored rolling stock, and a gallows turntable. Special events are scheduled throughout the year.

LOCATION: 14134 Midland Road, Poway
PHONE: 858-486-4063
WEBSITE: powaymidlandrr.org
E-MAIL: pmrr-info@cox.net

Railway & Locomotive Historical Society, Southern California Chapter Museum

Featuring classic gingerbread architecture, a former AT&SF 1887 depot was moved to the Los Angeles Fairplex. Now a museum, it houses rail exhibits. Outdoor displays of rolling stock and locomotives include a Union Pacific Big Boy. You can visit the museum during the county fair in September or during monthly open house weekends.

LOCATION: 1101 W. McKinley Avenue, Pomona
PHONE: 909-623-0190
WEBSITE: railgiants.org
E-MAIL: form on website

California

Roots of Motive Power

Roots of Motive Power collects and restores rail and other equipment used for logging. The organization gets steamed up at various events during the year, both on and off the site, including the Roots of Motive Power Festival at the Roots facility and Frontier Days in Willits. Visitors can also tour the collection during scheduled work days each month.

LOCATION: 400 E. Commercial Street, Willits
WEBSITE: rootsofmotivepower.com
E-MAIL: mail@rootsofmotivepower.com

San Bernardino History and Railroad Museum

Located in a restored 1918 Santa Fe depot, the museum contains a replicated 1910 railroad station, a variety of railroad inspection and work vehicles, artifacts, and photographs. It also features objects of local historical value including antique vehicles. The museum is open on Saturdays.

LOCATION: 1170 W. Third Street, San Bernardino
PHONE: 909-888-3634
WEBSITE: sbdepotmuseum.squarespace.com
E-MAIL: sbrrdays@me.com

San Francisco Municipal Railway

The San Francisco Municipal Railway operates city transit services, historic streetcars, and cable cars. Cable cars run on three lines: Powell and Hyde, Powell and Mason, and California. Streetcars run regularly on the F Market and Wharves Line that connects the downtown area with Fisherman's Wharf. The San Francisco Railway Museum, which features a replica of a motorman's platform of a 1911 streetcar and other interactive exhibits, is at the F Market Steuart Street stop, just across from the Ferry Building.

LOCATION: 1145 Market Street, San Francisco
PHONE: 415-701-2311 or 311
WEBSITE: sfmta.com/transit

Society for the Preservation of Carter Railroad Resources

Visit this museum on a work day and you'll see restoration efforts of wooden cars completed using hand tools and 19th century techniques. Most cars the society preserves were built by Carter Brothers in Newark. For a one-of-a-kind experience, you can ride a train car pulled by Belgian draft horses. Special train rides operate at various times during the year.

LOCATION: 34600 Ardenwood Boulevard, Fremont
PHONE: 866-417-7277
WEBSITE: spcrr.org
E-MAIL: curator@spcrr.org

<mark>26</mark>

South Coast Railroad Museum

The museum's centerpiece is the historic Goleta depot, a Victorian-styled Southern Pacific country station. The museum features hands-on exhibits and a SP bay window caboose. Special events are scheduled throughout the year, and handcar rides are offered. In the Gandy Dancer Theater, you can view railroading and travel films. It is open Wednesday through Sunday.

LOCATION: 300 N. Los Carneros Road, Goleta
PHONE: 805-964-3540
WEBSITE: goletadepot.org
E-MAIL: form on website

Tehachapi Depot Railroad Museum

Built as a Southern Pacific type 23 depot, the building replaces the 1904 depot, which burned down in 2008. Among the museum's artifacts is a collection of railroad signals. The depot also schedules a variety of events during the year. It is open Thursday through Monday.

LOCATION: 101 W. Tehachapi Boulevard, Tehachapi
PHONE: 661-823-1100
WEBSITE: tehachapidepot.com
E-MAIL: fotd@tehachapidepot.com

Waterfront Red Car Line

The Red Car Line runs along the Port of Los Angeles waterfront as it did in the 1900s. It operates a restored car, No. 1058, as well as several replicas. You can board at World Cruise Center, Downtown, Ports O' Call, and Marina stations. Cars run Friday through Sunday and during some special events.

LOCATION: Sixth Street at Harbor Boulevard, San Pedro
PHONE: 310-732-7678
WEBSITE: portoflosangeles.org/recreation/waterfront_rcl.asp

Western America Railroad Museum

Housed in the restored Casa Del Desierto, a 1911 Harvey House, the museum features railroad art, artifacts, and memorabilia. Its outdoor displays include locomotives, cabooses, and other equipment. Highlights include Santa Fe FP45 No. 95 in classic warbonnet scheme, a 1938 horse car, and an experimental A-frame container. It is open Fridays, Saturdays, and Sundays.

LOCATION: 685 N. First Street, Barstow
PHONE: 760-256-9276
WEBSITE: barstowrailmuseum.org
E-MAIL: warm95@verizon.net

Cable Car Museum

LOCATION: 1201 Mason Street, San Francisco
PHONE: 415-474-1887
WEBSITE: cablecarmuseum.org

David Lustig

Of all the transportation systems in the United States, one—the cable car—is forever linked to the City by the Bay, San Francisco. Here's a museum that tells the history of the cable car in the city, from its start in 1873. The museum houses several historic cable cars. Also on display are photos, tools, and models.

CHOICES: As part of the Washington-Mason Line powerhouse and carbarn, the museum isn't static. You'll see cable cars come and go all day. Make sure to descend the steps from the museum deck into the winding room to see the cables that pull the cars along the city streets. You can also view three antique cable cars from the 1870s: the No. 46 grip car and the No. 54 trailer from the Sutter Street Railway and the Clay Street Hill Railroad No. 8 grip car.

WHEN TO GO: The museum is open every day (except New Year's Day, Easter, Thanksgiving, and Christmas). There is never a bad time to visit San Francisco, but be sure to take a jacket no matter what time of year it is!

GOOD TO KNOW: Admission to the museum is free. During the 1980s, the cable car system was completely overhauled. Track and cables were replaced on 69 city blocks. The powerhouse was rebuilt, and the cable cars were repaired and updated.

WORTH DOING: There is always plenty to see and do in San Francisco. You can walk through the Presidio, tour Alcatraz, visit Chinatown, or just hang out at Fisherman's Wharf.

DON'T MISS: Take in the cable car bell-ringing contest in Union Square, which has been an annual tradition since 1949.

GETTING THERE: No question about it—ride a cable car there! Both the Powell-Hyde and Powell-Mason Lines stop right at the museum. From the California Line, get off at Mason Street and walk three blocks north to the museum. Tickets can be purchased as you board the cable car.

California State Railroad Museum

LOCATION: 125 I Street, Sacramento
PHONE: 916-445-6645 or 916-323-9280
WEBSITE: csrmf.org
E-MAIL: form on website

Jeff Terry

This is among the best interpretive museums about railroading. The museum mixes a magnificent large-artifact collection with plenty of details and a sense of drama that bring them to life. Displays, hands-on exhibits, and human interaction all combine to produce an excellent experience for everyone, from those with a passing interest in railroads to those with a deep appreciation for railroading. And if you want the real thing, the museum operates its Sacramento Southern Railroad, a short train ride.

CHOICES: Made up of several buildings, the museum offers guided tours. The Railroad History Museum, at 100,000 square feet, is the largest exhibit space and contains 21 restored cars and locomotives. Be sure to climb the stairs that take you into the cab of one of the largest preserved steam locomotives, a rare Cab Forward with its crew compartment in front of the boiler.

WHEN TO GO: Weekends, April through September, are when the museum offers its Sacramento Southern train rides behind Granite Rock No. 10, a rebuilt 1943 tank engine. The 40-minute, six-mile round trip travels over the levees of the Sacramento River. The museum also runs special events and excursions throughout the year.

GOOD TO KNOW: The museum is situated in the Old Sacramento district of the state capital near where the first transcontinental railroad was launched eastward in the 1800s. The district is a 28-acre National Historic Landmark District and state historic park. Over Labor Day weekend, 200 tons of dirt transforms the historic district into a mining camp during Gold Rush Days.

WORTH DOING: The Old Sacramento State Historic Park contains a variety of museums, landmarks, and historical buildings.

DON'T MISS: When you board the Sacramento Southern, which is celebrating 30 years of service in 2013, take a look at the reconstructed Central Pacific freight depot, where you'll see displays highlighting the freight transportation industry.

GETTING THERE: When driving to Sacramento, take I-80 from San Francisco or I-5 from Reno. If you want the full rail experience, take an Amtrak train. The station is adjacent to Old Sacramento. The museum is at the corner of Second and I Streets.

California

Fillmore & Western Railway

LOCATION: 364 Main Street, Fillmore
PHONE: 805-524-2546
WEBSITE: fwry.com
E-MAIL: info@fwry.com

David Lustig

Operating over a segment of a former Southern Pacific branch line, the Fillmore & Western Railway is a well-run combination of weekend scenic excursion trains, murder mystery dinner trains, and special trains. It is also one of the premier movie location sets. Billing itself as the "Home of the Movie Trains," from wrecks to shootouts, Hollywood has used this scenic little Southern California line to represent Washington D.C., Florida, the Pacific Northwest, and just about every place in between.

CHOICES: On some passenger runs, the F&W operates ex-Duluth & Northeastern 2-8-0 steam engine No. 14. On weekend excursion trains, you can ride in an open-air railcar or in restored vintage passenger coaches. The train stops in downtown Santa Paula for an hour, letting you visit the historic Southern Pacific depot, the amazing rotating water ball in Railroad Plaza Park, the Santa Paula Art Museum, the California Oil Museum, or the Ventura County Agriculture Museum.

WHEN TO GO: Weekend excursions run on Saturdays January through March and on Saturdays and Sundays April through September and in November.

GOOD TO KNOW: The railroad hosts several different dinner train options for families including some murder mystery trains.

WORTH DOING: Farther north up the California coast is Santa Barbara, San Luis Obispo, and the Hearst Castle, the ultimate in opulence and home of the man who ran the Hearst newspaper and radio empire.

DON'T MISS: Explore the healthy roster of passenger and freight equipment in various states of repair found on the property.

GETTING THERE: Fillmore is about 60 miles northwest of downtown Los Angeles and about 25 miles east of Ventura. The nearest large-scale commercial airport is the Bob Hope Airport in Burbank. Flights also originate in Santa Barbara.

Knott's Berry Farm

LOCATION: 8039 Beach Boulevard, Buena Park
PHONE: 714-220-5200
WEBSITE: knotts.com
E-MAIL: info@knotts.com

Dave Crosby

Knott's Berry Farm is a Southern California theme park that has morphed from its 1952 western-style operation to a world-class attraction with rides and events designed for every age. Part of the theme park is the original three-foot-gauge Ghost Town & Calico Railroad.

CHOICES: The railroad is just one part of this large theme park operation that rivals any other attraction in the United States. Most trains are powered by one of two Denver & Rio Grande Western 2-8-0s, either No. 41 (former Rio Grande Southern No. 41 and originally Denver & Rio Grande Western No. 409) or No. 340 (also a former D&RGW of the same number). There is also a Rio Grande Southern Galloping Goose and a number of authentic narrow gauge coaches, a parlor car, and a caboose.

WHEN TO GO: Southern California is enjoyable almost any time of the year, although summers can get very hot.

GOOD TO KNOW: If you're bringing the family, plan to stay all day. Like other theme parks in the area—Universal Studios and Disneyland—this is a kid-friendly destination with everything you need in one giant arena to tucker out even the hardiest person by the end of the day. New attractions opening in 2013 in the Boardwalk section are the Coast Rider, Surfside Glider, and Pacific Scrambler rides.

WORTH DOING: Southern California abounds in attractions, restaurants, and activities for everyone. Spend a week or a weekend.

DON'T MISS: Good news for the railroad fan is that, by carefully selecting your photographic spots, you can come away with images that make it look like you snapped them in Colorado 60 years ago.

GETTING THERE: Buena Park is part of the greater Los Angeles area in Orange County and is near a number of local commercial airports. A vehicle is a must. Freeway exits are clearly marked.

Laws Railroad Museum

LOCATION: Silver Canyon Road, Bishop
PHONE: 760-873-5950
WEBSITE: lawsmuseum.org
E-MAIL: lawsmuseum@aol.com

David Lustig

The 11-acre Laws Railroad Museum is home to the largest collection of equipment that operated on the Southern Pacific's narrow gauge empire, which at one time stretched almost 300 miles from Nevada to the Lone Pine area of Owens Valley.

CHOICES: Museum displays include SP 4-6-0 No. 9, one of the last three steam engines to operate on the line, various freight cars, a caboose, a turntable, and the original station. By the time the railroad was abandoned, Laws existed pretty much in name only with the station being the only major building still standing. The museum has built a number of structures to show what Laws looked like in its heyday. A former Death Valley Railroad gas-electric doodlebug operates on select summer weekends.

WHEN TO GO: The museum is open all year with a few exceptions. It is closed on several major holidays such as New Year's Day, Easter, Thanksgiving, and Christmas. It also may close due to severe weather, and some buildings close during winter.

GOOD TO KNOW: The nearest city with restaurants and accommodations is Bishop. If you drive up from the south on Highway 395, there are numerous towns with hotels and eateries, starting with Lone Pine, Independence, and Big Pine. During the ski season, Highway 395 is the main route to and from the various resorts north of Bishop, so you might consider making reservations well in advance.

WORTH DOING: Owens Valley is known for the many motion pictures, mostly westerns, that have been filmed there over the years. A number of small nonrail museums dot the area. The remains of the Manzanar Relocation Center, one of the places where Japanese-Americans were interned during World War II, is now part of the National Park Service and open to the public.

DON'T MISS: The area from Keeler to Laws is littered with narrow gauge artifacts, ranging from the remains of trestles and buildings to 4-6-0 No. 18 in Independence. The former SP standard gauge Lone Pine depot is intact as a private residence.

GETTING THERE: Laws is truly in the middle of nowhere, and the trip to the museum is half the fun. The museum is 4.5 miles north of Bishop on Silver Canyon Road, just off Highway 6.

Napa Valley Wine Train

LOCATION: 1275 McKinstry Street, Napa
PHONE: 800-427-4124 or 707-253-2111
WEBSITE: winetrain.com
E-MAIL: form on website

Napa Valley Wine Train, Trenton McManus

When you think of Napa Valley, you think of wine. And if you want a unique wine experience, take this ride through one of the world's most famous grape-growing valleys. You'll ride in elegant style onboard a fashionable train on a three-hour, 36-mile round trip while enjoying gourmet food and a glass of wine while watching the vineyards roll by as you travel to St. Helena and back.

CHOICES: Ride in a heavyweight passenger car or a vista dome, each with a different dining experience. Both lunch and dinner trains operate. You can also take part in many scheduled events such as onboard wine tastings, murder mysteries, vintner lunches, and moonlight escapes. Special trains also run around select holidays, and tours at several wineries are available.

WHEN TO GO: Any time of the year is good, but the September grape-harvesting season is among the most popular. Daily service begins in March and goes through November, with Friday through Sunday service the rest of the year. During summer, the *Silverado* car offers barbecue-style meals.

GOOD TO KNOW: Attire is generally casual depending on the time of year or type of event. Dinner may be more dressy, and cocktail-party attire is acceptable. As Phil Collins might say, "No jacket required," but they are suggested for cool nights. One bit of advice: no blue jeans.

WORTH DOING: Napa Valley is filled with hundreds of wineries to visit as well as having numerous special events.

DON'T MISS: Enjoy the wine. The train's wine bar offers a selection of 40–50 wines for tasting. Its wine shop carries almost 300 different wines. All entrees are prepared in the kitchen cars, and you are welcome to sneak a peek inside to watch the action.

GETTING THERE: From San Francisco, take I-80 east to Exit 19. Follow Highway 29 north and exit at Napa/Lake Berryessa. Take Highway 221, which becomes Soscol Avenue, into Napa. Turn right on First Street and then turn left on McKinstry Street. Ferry service from San Francisco makes for a fun day.

Niles Canyon Railway

LOCATION: 6 Kilkare Road, Sunol
PHONE: 925-862-9063
WEBSITE: ncry.org
E-MAIL: pla_ncry@ncry.org

Niles Canyon Railway, Al Siegwarth

This museum railroad, a project of the Pacific Locomotive Society, provides a magnificent ride through a dramatic canyon at the edge of the San Francisco Bay area. An outstanding collection of equipment and beautiful scenery make this an excellent day trip in central California.

CHOICES: The railway runs 75-minute round trips through scenic Niles Canyon between Sunol and Niles. Departures are scheduled at both stations. On all trains, you can select from open cars, covered cars, or enclosed coaches. Trains are powered by either a diesel or a steam locomotive, when available, from the railway's impressive collection that also includes a variety of passenger cars, freight cars, and cabooses.

WHEN TO GO: The railroad operates the first and third weekends April through August and on the first and third Sundays the remaining months, except November and December, when the holiday schedule for the nighttime Train of Lights offers rides four days a week.

GOOD TO KNOW: The line through Niles Canyon was the last completed link of the transcontinental railroad.

WORTH DOING: While in Fremont, you can visit the Niles Essanay Silent Film Museum and even take in a silent Saturday night flick. You can also visit the nearby Niles Depot Museum.

DON'T MISS: The restored Sunol depot was originally built in the 1880s, and the Niles depot, which features colonnade-style architecture and houses railroad exhibits, was built in 1901.

GETTING THERE: The Niles Canyon Railway is situated between Oakland and San Jose. From San Jose, you can take I-880 to Fremont and exit on Highway 84 east. Turn left onto Mission Boulevard and continue three blocks west to Sullivan Street, and the Niles station is on the left. To reach the Sunol depot from San Jose, just take I-680 to Highway 84. Travel west on Highway 84 one mile and turn right onto Main Street to Kilkare Road. From Oakland, take I-880 to Highway 84 east to get to either location.

Orange Empire Railway Museum

LOCATION: 2201 S. A Street, Perris
PHONE: 951-943-3020
WEBSITE: oerm.org
E-MAIL: info.oerm@gmail.com

Dave Crosby

The Orange Empire Railway Museum was organized in 1956 by trolley and electric railway enthusiasts to preserve a fast disappearing way of transportation. Visitors can ride on classic trolleys, passenger trains, and other railroad equipment from Southern California's past.

CHOICES: Two trolleys run on a half-mile loop line, and one is usually an early Los Angeles streetcar. Another train, pulling freight or passenger cars, operates on the 1.5-mile standard gauge main line. On the freight train, you can ride in either a caboose or open gondola. The cars and locomotives are rotated from the museum's collection, which contains more than 180 vintage pieces. You also have the opportunity to run a locomotive.

WHEN TO GO: The museum is open 363 days a year and special events occur during the year. Trains run on weekends and some holidays. The weather is usually bearable during most of the year; however, summertime temperatures can reach triple digits.

GOOD TO KNOW: The museum, situated on 100 acres of land, is about 20 miles south of Riverside. It has preserved, and is restoring, an eclectic mix of more than 225 pieces of railroad equipment that includes electric, steam, and diesel power as well as a variety of freight and passenger rolling stock.

WORTH DOING: The surrounding area, from Riverside to Temecula, is well developed with all the amenities a traveler would expect. For military aircraft fans, the March Field Air Museum has an extensive collection of aircraft adjacent to March Air Reserve Base in Riverside.

DON'T MISS: A 1922 steam engine, Ventura County Railway No. 2, operates excursions the third weekend of every month from September to May and during certain special events and major holidays.

GETTING THERE: Perris is about an hour's drive from either San Diego or Los Angeles. In Perris, exit at Route 74. Follow Route 74 (Fourth Street) west for one mile and turn left onto A Street.

Pacific Southwest Railway Museum

LOCATION: 750 Depot Street, Campo
PHONE: 619-465-77766 or 619-478-9937 (weekends)
WEBSITE: psrm.org
E-MAIL: webmaster@psrm.org

Pacific Southwest Railway Museum, John Wright

The Pacific Southwest Railway Museum operates in two locations near San Diego. The main collection is at Campo, just north of the U.S.–Mexico border. The other location is at La Mesa, about 10 miles east of downtown San Diego.

CHOICES: At Campo, visitors can enjoy several train-riding options, including a 12-mile, diesel-powered trip on a mountain railroad to Tunnel No. 4, and locomotive cab rides are available on the trip. Another shorter ride takes you to the Campo Stone Store and through scenic Campo Valley. The 40-acre site displays more than 80 pieces of equipment including diesel locomotives (among them, several interesting military switchers), steam locomotives, freight cars, passenger cars, and cabooses. Also featured is a fully restored "Jim Crow" passenger car. The La Mesa site displays railroading exhibits, freight cars, and a steam locomotive.

WHEN TO GO: The Campo facility is open most weekends throughout the year. The museum offers a variety of special events, including some tailored to kids, such as pumpkin and North Pole trains. The La Mesa site is open on Saturday afternoons.

GOOD TO KNOW: The restored La Mesa depot is the only surviving San Diego and Cuyamaca Railway station.

WORTH DOING: The greater San Diego area is brimming with places to visit, including Old Town. Sea World is just north of the city, and the coastline is tourist friendly. If you have always wanted to tour a U.S. Navy aircraft carrier, the decommissioned USS *Midway* is open to the public, with many types of aircraft positioned on its flight deck.

DON'T MISS: Now a history museum, the Campo Stone Store was also a military outpost, bank, and post office. Another Campo museum to visit is the Motor Transport Museum with its large collection of vehicles and industrial equipment.

GETTING THERE: The Campo site is 50 miles east of San Diego. From San Diego, take Highway 94 to Campo and turn right onto Forrest Gate Road and then left onto Depot Street. Take the Spring Street exit off Highway 94 into La Mesa to reach the La Mesa depot, which is at 4695 Nebo Drive.

Railtown 1897 State Historic Park

LOCATION: Fifth Avenue at Reservoir Road, Jamestown
PHONE: 209-984-3953
WEBSITE: railtown1897.com
E-MAIL: form on website

Dave Crosby

Railtown 1897 State Historic Park is considered by many as the premier place for seeing California railroad history. It was originally part of the Sierra Railroad, arguably one of the best-known railroads in the world due to its extensive use in movies and television shows. You can also enjoy a train ride over these historic rails.

CHOICES: The historic shops and roundhouse have been operating as a steam locomotive maintenance facility for more than 100 years. One of the highlights of any visit is taking the roundhouse tour and experiencing for yourself what a working facility looks, feels, and smells like. On the six-mile, 40-minute round trip through California's Gold Country, you can ride in coaches or open-air observation cars. Special theme trains also run during the year.

WHEN TO GO: The park is open Thursday through Monday year-round. Guided roundhouse tours take place each day of the summer schedule but are more limited during the rest of the year. Excursions run every weekend April through October with limited service in November and December. Steam-powered train rides behind Sierra No. 3 usually take place on Saturdays and with other locomotives on Sundays.

GOOD TO KNOW: The state of California purchased the station, shops, and roundhouse facilities in 1982 to create Railtown 1897. With more than 200 credits, it is one of the most-filmed railroad locations. The first known filming was in 1919 for a silent movie, and scenes for *High Noon, Back to the Future Part III,* and *Unforgiven* were filmed here.

WORTH DOING: This area, up through Sutter's Mill, is where people settled during the gold strikes, so history abounds. If you like the outdoors and learning western history, this is a great place to explore.

DON'T MISS: On the guided tour of the roundhouse, be sure to examine the props that were used in the movies filmed on the railroad.

GETTING THERE: From any direction, you have to drive to get to the Jamestown area. but California's Gold Country is almost universally seductive, so you'll enjoy the trip. It is about a 90-minute drive from Stockton.

Roaring Camp Railroads

LOCATION: 5401 Graham Hill Road, Felton
PHONE: 831-335-4484
WEBSITE: roaringcamp.com
E-MAIL: form on website

Elrond Lawrence

Located in coastal wooded mountains, Roaring Camp runs two unique trains that offer the best of California scenery. The steam-powered Roaring Camp & Big Trees operates a narrow-gauge line through redwood forests, while the Santa Cruz, Big Trees & Pacific runs diesel-powered trips down a scenic river gorge to the ocean.

CHOICES: The Roaring Camp & Big Trees operates 1880s-era Shay, Heisler, and Climax locomotives on a winding route up Bear Mountain. The route passes through Welch Big Trees Grove, the state's first redwood forest preserve. The 75-minute excursions feature open-air coaches, and passengers can detrain at the summit to tour the forest. Santa Cruz boardwalk trains employ 1920s-era passenger coaches and open-air cars pulled by an ex-Santa Fe CF7 diesel. The three-hour round trip runs through Henry Cowell Redwoods State Park, down the San Lorenzo River Gorge, and through an 1875 tunnel before arriving at the historic Santa Cruz boardwalk.

WHEN TO GO: While crowds can be thick, summer is still the best time to visit. The higher altitude and close proximity to the ocean bring moderate temperatures. The marine climate also brings cool and foggy days, usually in summer. Special trains include moonlight steam train dinner parties, ghost trains in October, and a Santa Cruz holiday lights train in November and December.

GOOD TO KNOW: In Santa Cruz, six miles away, the century-old seaside boardwalk is a historic gem and features a 1924 wooden roller coaster. Monterey, Pacific Grove, and Pebble Beach are only a short drive away on California Highway 1.

WORTH DOING: Roaring Camp re-creates an 1880s logging town and includes a steam-powered saw mill, period buildings, and picnic grounds. Access to the grounds is free, and picnicking is encouraged, but there is a charge for parking.

DON'T MISS: Seasonal events in Roaring Camp include Civil War battles, mountain men gatherings, a harvest festival, and a musical saw festival.

GETTING THERE: Roaring Camp is located six miles north of Santa Cruz off Route 17. Take Mount Hermon Road which ends at Graham Hill Road. Turn left on Graham Hill Road and drive a half mile to Roaring Camp.

Sacramento RiverTrain

LOCATION: 400 N. Harbor Boulevard, West Sacramento
PHONE: 800-866-1690
WEBSITE: sacramentorivertrain.com
E-MAIL: info@sierrarailroad.com

Sacramento RiverTrain

Just outside of Sacramento, you'll find a uniquely scenic and relaxing train ride through rich farm country and a sprawling wildlife refuge. Operating over a 1911 electric interurban route, the Sacramento RiverTrain rolls between the cities of West Sacramento and Woodland, traveling along the banks of its namesake river and through the Yolo Wildlife Area, which is home to nearly 200 species of birds.

CHOICES: The railroad operates dinner, brunch, and lunch trains year-round, mostly on weekends. Passengers can board in either Woodland or West Sacramento for a leisurely 28-mile round trip that lasts more than three hours. Powered by Sierra Northern 131, a mid-century GP9 diesel in striking yellow and black colors, the train features a combination of vintage coaches, diners, and open-air cars. Interiors boast a relaxed, plantation-style décor.

WHEN TO GO: Trains run all year and are climate-controlled. Those who enjoy riding open-air cars might prefer to visit during the spring or fall, instead of the sweltering summer months that typically exceed 90 degrees. Special events include train robberies and murder mystery excursions, plus beer trains and sunset dinner trains. Seasonal trips include pumpkin trains, valentine specials, a New Year's Eve express, and a popular Christmas train that runs from late November through December.

GOOD TO KNOW: The route is rich with history, originally built by the Woodland and Sacramento Railroad and operated by the Northern Electric Railway. Later owners included the Sacramento Northern, Western Pacific, Union Pacific, and Yolo Shortline.

WORTH DOING: Woodland features a charming historic downtown, surrounded by museums and wineries. Only 15 minutes away, Sacramento is home to the state capital, the California State Railroad Museum, and many other historic attractions.

DON'T MISS: Look for the 8,000-foot Fremont Bridge over the Sacramento River, which the railroad claims is the longest wooden trestle in the western United States.

GETTING THERE: From San Francisco, take I-80 East to West Sacramento and take Exit 83. Turn right on Reed Avenue and then turn left on North Harbor Boulevard. The station is almost underneath the I-80 overpass.

Sierra Railroad Dinner Train

LOCATION: 330 S. Sierra Avenue, Oakdale
PHONE: 800-866-1690 or 209-848-2100
WEBSITE: sierrarailroad.com
E-MAIL: info@sierrarailroad.com

Sierra Railroad

The Sierra Railroad was formed in 1897 to connect the San Joaquin Valley to the Gold Country. Today, the Sierra carries passengers, hauls freight, and makes movies. The Sierra Railroad Dinner Train provides visitors an opportunity to travel on the historic Sierra Railroad while dining and enjoying the passing countryside.

CHOICES: There are a variety of trips to choose from, including those featuring romantic dinners, murder mysteries, lunches, Sunday brunches, and Wild West showdowns. Along the route through the scenic Stanislaus River Valley, you'll pass through distinct western scenery and the scenes of various Hollywood westerns including *High Noon, Bad Girls,* and *Pale Rider.*

WHEN TO GO: The dinner train runs year-round, and any time is a good time to take a train ride through California's historic and fascinating Gold Country.

GOOD TO KNOW: Seasonal trips include a spring wildflower train, Chocolate Festival trip, and the popular Christmas train.

WORTH DOING: Being way out west, you can visit the Cowboy Museum in Oakdale. The museum is housed in a historic Southern Pacific depot.

DON'T MISS: The Sierra Railroad is also a functioning freight operation, so railfans can view more then just passenger cars. To see an historic steam locomotive maintenance facility, you can take in Railtown 1897 Historic Park in nearby Jamestown.

GETTING THERE: The Sierra Railroad is located at the junction of Highway 108 and Highway 120 in the city of Oakdale, which is 90 minutes from Sacramento. The train station, which is made of railcars, is on Sierra Avenue.

Skunk Train

LOCATION: 100 W. Laurel Street, Fort Bragg
PHONE: 866-457-5865 or 707-964-6371
WEBSITE: skunktrain.com
E-MAIL: rjp@mcn.org

Skunk Train

One of the most amazing attributes of the Skunk Train is its ability to make you feel small. Ride the train from the coastal town of Fort Bragg and you'll quickly find out why. The route travels through a scenic wilderness filled with giant redwoods. As the train takes you through the mountain scenery, the giant trees will make your neck sore unless you move to an open car, where you can stand in wonder.

CHOICES: You can ride from either end of the 40-mile line, boarding at Willits or Fort Bragg. Motor cars operate over the line all year, while diesel-powered trains and steam engine No. 45 run mostly during the summer. The line features 30 trestles, two tunnels, and a route that snakes its way up the redwood-covered mountainside. A summer overnight trip from either station allows you to spend one or more nights at the other end before returning. A kayaking and train ride package is also available.

WHEN TO GO: Trains operate all year, but most excursions from Fort Bragg run March through September. Excursions from Willits take place during summer. A variety of special trains operate during the year.

GOOD TO KNOW: The railroad got its nickname from the yellow-painted, self-propelled gas-powered cars of the California Western Railway that provided service starting in 1925 and prompted people to say, "You can smell 'em before you can see 'em."

WORTH DOING: Along the coast between December and April, you have a good chance to see a California gray whale as they migrate south from Alaska and then return. For an up-close experience, you can find a whale-watching excursion operating out of Fort Bragg.

DON'T MISS: Ride the train on days when steam locomotive No. 45 is running. A 2-8-2 Mikado type built by Philadelphia's famous Baldwin Locomotive Works in 1924, the locomotive is among the largest in regular service today.

GETTING THERE: Just over three hours north of San Francisco, the scenic drive to Fort Bragg starts on Highway 101. At Cloverdale, exit onto Highway 128 west, which turns into Highway 1, and continue north to Fort Bragg. The depot is at the foot of Laurel Street.

Travel Town Museum

LOCATION: 5200 Zoo Drive, Los Angeles
PHONE: 323-662-5874
WEBSITE: traveltown.org
E-MAIL: travel.town@lacity.org

David Lustig

Travel Town is a good place to enjoy a couple of hours looking at equipment that has been preserved nowhere else. The museum, part of the Griffith Park complex in Los Angeles County, has a collection of small- to medium-sized steam, diesel, and electric locomotives and a surprisingly diverse roster of rolling stock.

CHOICES: Operated by the Department of Recreation and Parks, the museum is free and kid-friendly. Nevertheless, the diversity of the saved equipment makes Travel Town worth stopping at if you're in the area. Steam equipment includes tank locomotives, 0-6-0s, 2-8-0s, a 2-6-2, a 2-8-2, a Shay, and a Heisler. Other equipment to view includes an operating EMD Model 40 diesel, a Baldwin RS-12, a Santa Fe gas-electric, a Pacific Electric freight motor, plus various pieces of rolling stock.

WHEN TO GO: The museum is open every day except Christmas. During Pacific Daylight Time, weekend hours are extended one hour. On select Saturdays during the year, docent-lead tours through selected historic railroad passenger cars take place. In October, Depot Day features special exhibits and activities.

GOOD TO KNOW: A food concession is inside, but eating and picnic areas are nearby in other parts of Griffith Park. If you would like to have lunch at a historic eatery, you can grab a chili dog at Pink's, which is 15 minutes away on La Brea Boulevard and has been operating since 1939.

WORTH DOING: Explore Griffith Park, a quiet oasis in busy LA, and especially take the time and visit the park's other sites including the famous observatory and world-class Los Angeles Zoo, which is right next to Travel Town.

DON'T MISS: If you want to take a break from walking, a rideable scale train encircles the collection.

GETTING THERE: Travel Town is near the confluence of I-5 and the 134 Freeway. Freeway exits are clearly marked.

Western Pacific Railroad Museum

LOCATION: 700 Western Pacific Way, Portola
PHONE: 530-832-4131
WEBSITE: wplives.org
E-MAIL: info@wplives.org

Western Pacific Railroad Museum

Here at one of the Western Pacific's last diesel locomotive shops is a great collection of rolling stock. The focus is on one of the West's most beloved railroads, which traveled through beautiful mountain scenery and hosted the legendary *California Zephyr*. The setting couldn't be more appropriate.

CHOICES: This 37-acre site displays more than 100 pieces of equipment. Three former Western Pacific streamlined diesels call the museum home, as do locomotives from the Union Pacific and Southern Pacific. Western Pacific 0-6-0 No. 165, a steam switcher currently being restored, is the only steam locomotive in the collection. Rolling stock includes passenger cars, boxcars, cabooses, and maintenance-of-way equipment. The museum is hands-on, so you can climb into cabs and hop onto cars.

WHEN TO GO: The museum is open daily May through September and Friday through Sunday in October. On summer weekends, caboose rides through a pine forest on a one-mile loop of track make for a fun train trip. In December, Santa trains run.

GOOD TO KNOW: Visit in August for the annual Portola Railroad Days festival, which includes train rides, food, music, and a parade.

WORTH DOING: Close by is Lassen Volcanic National Park, where you can see hydrothermal features such as boiling mud pots, steaming ground, and roaring fumaroles.

DON'T MISS: Run a locomotive through the museum's program that puts you in the engineer's seat.

GETTING THERE: Portola is located in the Feather River Canyon between Sacramento and Reno. From the west, take I-80 to Highway 89 and go north to Highway 70, which runs into Portola. From the east, take I-80 to Highway 395 to Highway 70.

Western Railway Museum

LOCATION: 5848 Highway 12, Suisun City
PHONE: 707-374-2978
WEBSITE: wrm.org
E-MAIL: form on website

Western Railway Museum

The Western Railway Museum gives visitors the opportunity to ride historic streetcars and interurban electric trains that once served California and other western states. There are more than 50 cars on display.

CHOICES: A trip to the Western Railway Museum begins in the mission-revival inspired visitor center. After purchasing admission tickets, explore Cameron Hall, a large display and exhibit hall designed in the grand railroad station style. The museum offers 15-minute, one-mile-long streetcar rides around the grounds. Its interurban ride over the former Sacramento Northern Railway main line has been expanded to Birds Landing Road and features views of Suisun Marsh and Mount Diablo. You can ride on San Francisco streetcar No. 1016 or Sacramento Northern interurban No. 1005, which has been restored to its 1934 configuration.

WHEN TO GO: The Western Railway Museum is open Saturdays and Sundays from September to May. From Memorial Day through Labor Day, the museum expands its schedule and is open Wednesday through Sunday. It is closed on some holidays.

GOOD TO KNOW: The museum offers guided weekend tours of two of its car houses. It also features a shaded picnic area that is well suited for family or group outings.

WORTH DOING: During October, special Pumpkin Patch Trains take visitors on a scenic five-mile journey to a pumpkin patch, complete with a hay-bale fort, hay rides, live music, animals, and, of course, pumpkins. In April, the *Scenic Limited* also runs.

DON'T MISS: Visitors can stroll through the museum's large car house or take a guided tour of the building on weekends.

GETTING THERE: The museum is about 45 miles northeast of San Francisco, 12 miles east of I-80 on Highway 12. Public transportation is an option in reaching the museum by train and bus service.

Yosemite Mountain Sugar Pine Railroad

LOCATION: 56001 Highway 41, Fish Camp
PHONE: 559-683-7273
WEBSITE: yosemitesteamtrains.com
E-MAIL: form on website

Yosemite Mountain Sugar Pine Railroad

The Yosemite Mountain Sugar Pine Railroad is a four-mile railroad excursion at Yosemite National Park's south gate. The ride allows you to see what it was like when steam locomotives hauled massive log trains through the Sierra Nevadas. It is a restored segment of the old narrow gauge Madera Sugar Pine Lumber Company Railroad, with a portion of the original right-of-way reconstructed using the same techniques as 100 years ago.

CHOICES: Two geared Shay steam locomotives, formerly used on the West Side Lumber Company, power the excursion trains. A unique experience is riding a Jenny railcar powered by Model A Ford automobile engines. The *Moonlight Special*, which operates Saturday nights in the spring and fall and Saturday and Wednesday nights during the summer, begins with a steak dinner and includes masked bandits, moonlight, and campfire sing-alongs.

WHEN TO GO: The Yosemite Mountain Sugar Pine Railroad operates daily from late March through October. At close to 5,000 feet elevation, it can get chilly at Fish Camp, even in the summertime. At the height of summer tourist season, Yosemite National Park gets extremely crowded.

GOOD TO KNOW: Refurbished railcars, once used to transport logging crews, now carry excursion passengers.

WORTH DOING: You can easily spend an entire day or longer in the area. Other activities in the Fish Camp area include fishing, backpacking, hiking, camping, and mountain biking. You can even try your hand at panning for gold.

DON'T MISS: For a fun and melodramatic evening, partake in a moonlight melodrama, which starts with a steak dinner, continues with music and a steam train excursion, and finishes with a melodrama in the woods.

GETTING THERE: Fish Camp is 40 miles north of Fresno and 60 miles east of Modesto on Highway 41. The nearest big-time commercial airline service is at Fresno and Sacramento.

COLORADO

Cripple Creek & Victor Narrow Gauge Railroad

The four-mile, 45-minute trip takes you through Gold Country over a portion of the old Midland Terminal Railroad. Running south from Cripple Creek, the steam train crosses a reconstructed trestle and passes historic mines near the deserted mining town of Anaconda. The railroad operates three narrow gauge locomotives, and trains operate mid-May to mid-October.

LOCATION: Fifth Street and Bennett Avenue, Cripple Creek
PHONE: 719-689-2640
WEBSITE: cripplecreekrailroad.com
E-MAIL: fun@cripplecreekrailroad.com

Limon Heritage Museum

This museum focuses on local history and the Union Pacific and Rock Island Railroads. Located in a restored 1910 depot, it features a restored office and rail exhibits. A saddle boxcar, dining car, and UP caboose are on display in the adjacent rail park. It is open Monday through Saturday Memorial Day to Labor Day.

LOCATION: 899 First Street, Limon
PHONE: 719-775-8605
WEBSITE: townoflimon.com

Moffat Railway Car

Tours of this 1906 Pullman car are available weekdays through the Moffat County Visitor Center, near where it is on display. The car originally belonged to rail magnate David Moffat and was named for his daughter Marcia. The nearby Museum of Northwest Colorado (590 Yampa Avenue) contains a display of Moffat Road memorabilia.

LOCATION: 360 E. Victory Way, Craig
PHONE: 800-864-4405 or 970-824-5689
WEBSITE: craig-chamber.com
E-MAIL: info@craig-chamber.com

Pueblo Railway Museum

Concentrating on the golden age of railroading, the museum displays steam engines, diesel locomotives, and rolling stock in the yard behind Union Depot. Artifacts and rotating displays are housed in the Southeastern Colorado Heritage Center located across from the depot. Locomotive cab and caboose rides are offered during the year.

LOCATION: 132 W. B Street, Pueblo
PHONE: 719-251-5024 or 719-544-1773
WEBSITE: pueblorailway.org
E-MAIL: info@pueblorailway.org

Ridgway Railroad Museum

The Ridgway Railroad Museum focuses on local railroading history. It displays an assortment of restored railcars, and its indoor collection includes artifacts, photos, and tools. The museum is open daily June through September and Monday through Friday the rest of the year. It holds various special events and monthly work sessions.

LOCATION: Highway 550 and Highway 62, Ridgway
WEBSITE: ridgwayrailroadmuseum.org
E-MAIL: ridgwayrailroadmuseum@ouraynet.com

Rio Grande Southern Railroad Museum

The museum is located in a replica of the original Dolores depot. It is home to the restored Galloping Goose No. 5, which now operates several times during the year on the Cumbres & Toltec Scenic Railroad and the Durango & Silverton Narrow Gauge Railroad. The museum is open Mondays through Saturdays during summer and Tuesdays and Thursdays during winter.

LOCATION: 421 Railroad Avenue, Dolores
PHONE: 970-882-7082
WEBSITE: gallopinggoose5.com
E-MAIL: gghs5@centurytel.net

Windsor Museum

Located in Boardwalk Park, a 1880s Colorado & Southern depot houses an exhibit of local steam-era railroading history. You can walk through a freight room, waiting room, and station agent's room. A caboose, schoolhouse, and church are also on site. The museum is open Thursdays through Sundays. A remote audio tour is available by calling 970-404-3333 or visiting the website.

LOCATION: 100 N. Fifth Street, Windsor
PHONE: 970-674-2443
WEBSITE: windsorgov.com
E-MAIL: cknight@windsorgov.com

Colorado Railroad Museum

LOCATION: 17155 W. 44th Avenue, Golden
PHONE: 800-365-6263 or 303-279-4591
WEBSITE: coloradorailroadmuseum.org
E-MAIL: info@coloradorailroadmuseum.org

Dave Crosby

When you think of Colorado railroading, you think of mountain-climbing, narrow gauge trains of the Denver & Rio Grande Western. And that is exactly what you'll see at this museum just outside Denver in Golden. But that's not all—the museum includes 100 pieces of equipment from many other Colorado railroads.

CHOICES: The museum features narrow gauge and standard equipment, from a steam locomotive once used on the Pikes Peak Cog Railway to a 317-ton Burlington Route steam locomotive and even a set of streamlined 1950s passenger diesels from the Rio Grande. You'll see examples of the famous Galloping Goose self-propelled railbuses that ran on the narrow gauge Rio Grande Southern in southwestern Colorado and the only preserved standard gauge Rio Grande steam locomotive, No. 687, a 2-8-0 built in 1890 and retired in 1955.

WHEN TO GO: The museum is open year-round, except for several holidays. On the third Saturday of each month, a vintage steam or diesel locomotive powers passenger trains on a short ride around the 15-acre property. Better yet, ride Galloping Goose No. 7, which runs on many other Saturdays during the year.

GOOD TO KNOW: New pieces on display include former Denver, Boulder & Western narrow gauge 2-8-0 locomotive No. 30, Denver & Rio Grande Western coach 280, and D&RGW caboose 04990.

WORTH DOING: The MillerCoors Brewery is adjacent to the museum and offers tours on most days throughout the year.

DON'T MISS: Visit the five-stall roundhouse that houses the museum's restoration shop and features an operating turntable. A viewing gallery gives you a peek at the work it takes to maintain the collection.

GETTING THERE: The Colorado Railroad Museum is located 12 miles west of downtown Denver and is easily reached from I-70. Take Exit 265 westbound or Exit 266 eastbound, and it is just off Highway 58 between I-70 and Golden.

Durango & Silverton Narrow Gauge Railroad

LOCATION: 479 Main Avenue, Durango
PHONE: 877-872-4607 or 970-247-2733
WEBSITE: durangotrain.com
E MAIL: form on website

Jim Wrinn

The Durango & Silverton is one of the most spectacular narrow gauge steam train rides in North America. Traveling through the Rockies, coal-fired locomotives pull trains through the rugged Animas River Gorge on a railroad built in the 1880s to reach southwest Colorado silver mines.

CHOICES: The Durango & Silverton offers several options for passengers. During summer, you can live like a president with Presidential class service, which includes seating on the *Cinco Animas*, which features plush seating and outdoor viewing platforms. For great views, try first-class service on the *Silver Vista* or *Knight Sky*, glass-roofed, open-air observation cars with outdoor viewing platforms. First-class service is also available aboard an 1881 parlor car. Deluxe service and standard service provide seating in a coach car or a gondola. The Cascade Canyon winter train travels 26 miles from Durango to the Cascade station and back.

WHEN TO GO: Winter provides incredible snowy vistas. Summer offers the excitement of up to four trains running each way, but it is also the busy season. September has the best nature show when Aspen trees turn a brilliant yellow and quiver in the autumn breeze. Various events take place throughout the year.

GOOD TO KNOW: For a fee, yard tours are available to give you a chance to see the inner workings of the railroad.

WORTH DOING: Take part in the other activities that abound near Durango, such as whitewater rafting, hiking, and fly fishing. A visit to Mesa Verde National Park is a must.

DON'T MISS: There is a two-hour layover in Silverton, which gives you time to visit the freight yard museum in the depot, which is open May through October and displays many pieces of rolling stock. The Durango museum, part of the roundhouse, is open corresponding to the passenger train schedule. There, a baggage car used in *Butch Cassidy and the Sundance Kid* is now a movie theater.

GETTING THERE: The station is located in downtown Durango. The drive to the Four Corners area on Highway 550 is a scenic delight, as long as you don't mind heights.

Forney Museum of Transportation

LOCATION: 4303 Brighton Boulevard, Denver
PHONE: 303-297-1113
WEBSITE: forneymuseum.org
E-MAIL: volunteer@forneymuseum.org

Dave Crosby

An antique auto collection that began with one Kissel Kar is now a transportation museum with more than 500 items. The museum's showroom contains everything on wheels from buggies and bicycles to fire engines and Denver's only cable car.

CHOICES: In the museum's indoor train pit, you'll find a Big Boy locomotive, cabooses, trolleys, passenger cars, and, of course, a Forney locomotive. While the Big Boy may get the most attention, there are a number of other interesting pieces in the rail collection, including a rotary snow plow, a steam crane, and a 4-6-0 locomotive from the Chicago & North Western.

WHEN TO GO: The museum is open Monday through Saturday year-round. It features special exhibits, family activities, and events related to different modes of transportation. On Big Boy Weekend over Father's Day, you can go inside the cab of the world's largest articulated steam locomotive and walk through a 1920s dining car, 1890s coach, and 1905 caboose, which are open only once a year.

GOOD TO KNOW: A founder of the Forney Museum of Transportation, J. D. Forney was a second cousin to Matthais Forney, who designed the steam locomotive that bears his name. Forney-type tank locomotives operated primarily on narrow gauge railroads, elevated railways, and surface passenger lines.

WORTH DOING: There are plenty of things to do in Denver, within 15 minutes of the museum, such as touring the Capitol, the Firefighters Museum, the Botanic Gardens, and the Unsinkable Molly Brown's house.

DON'T MISS: One of eight remaining Big Boy locomotives, Union Pacific No. 4005 was wrecked in 1953 and rebuilt. Also view highlights of the auto collection such as Amelia Earhart's 1923 Kissel Speedster, a 1967 amphibious car from Germany, a 1911 electric car, a Staver, and a Nyberg.

GETTING THERE: The Forney Museum is located northeast of downtown Denver, a short distance off I-70 via Exit 275B.

Fort Collins Municipal Railway

LOCATION: Roosevelt Street and Oak Street, Fort Collins
PHONE: 970-224-5372
WEBSITE: fortnet.org/trolley
E-MAIL: fcmrs@netzero.com

Bryan Bechtold

Fort Collins was the last city in the United States to operate the tiny four-wheel trolley cars known as Birneys, running its trolley system until 1951. A volunteer group of citizens rebuilt the original Mountain Avenue track and restored Car 21 to like-new condition, returning it to operation on its authentic tree-lined route in 1984.

CHOICES: The three-mile, round-trip trolley ride runs along Mountain Avenue from City Park to Howes Street, two blocks west of downtown. A round trip lasts 30 minutes. Other boarding stops are at Shields Street and Loomis Street. There are free rides on special days and for moms on Mother's Day and dads on Father's Day.

WHEN TO GO: The trolley operates on weekend afternoons and holidays from May to September.

GOOD TO KNOW: The original trolley barn is just two blocks north on Howe Street at the downtown end of the line. Inside is Birney Car 25, which is undergoing restoration. Car 25 is one of five remaining cars that ran in Fort Collins.

WORTH DOING: Both ends of the route are family friendly. Downtown Fort Collins has an outstanding variety of restaurants and shopping just a short walk from the trolley. You can also pack a picnic and enjoy the City Park end of the line. For outdoor enthusiasts, Rocky Mountain National Park is less than two hours away by car.

DON'T MISS: For railfans, BNSF freight trains run down the middle of nearby Mason Street for almost a mile providing an opportunity to view mainline action up close.

GETTING THERE: Fort Collins is 65 miles north of Denver on I-25. Exit I-25 at Colorado 14 and then drive west through town to City Park. A small depot is next to the tennis courts at Roosevelt and Oak Streets.

Georgetown Loop Railroad

LOCATION: Loop Drive, Georgetown
PHONE: 888-456-6777
WEBSITE: georgetownlooprr.com
E-MAIL: info@historicrailadventures.com

Jim Wrinn

This railroad shows how engineering overcame mountains when it came to reaching precious minerals in the Colorado Rockies. As the name states, the railroad's highlight is a full loop, where the tracks cross over themselves to gain elevation. The reconstructed Devil's Gate viaduct stands no less spectacular than when it was built in the late 1800s.

CHOICES: You can board at the Devil's Gate station in Georgetown or at Silver Plume. Either way, you experience the same trip, but riding up grade first is always the better show. As you ride the train, scan the mountain slopes for bighorn sheep. Both diesel and steam locomotives operate. A variety of dinner train options, from barbecues to steak and trout, are available on select evenings throughout the season.

WHEN TO GO: The operating season begins in May and continues into November. During much of the season, five trains run on a daily basis. Holiday trains operate in November and December. Beginning in October, the trains are made up of heated coaches pulled by a diesel locomotive. Interstate traffic from Denver over the July 4th holiday can be a major headache.

GOOD TO KNOW: Steam locomotive No. 9, built in 1923 by the Lima Locomotive Works, is a rare Shay geared locomotive with three cylinders on one side.

WORTH DOING: The town of Georgetown is quaint and quiet with little influences of the modern world—with the exception of nearby I-70. Its National Historic Landmark District features unique shops, restaurants, and small museums in restored Victorian buildings.

DON'T MISS: After riding the train, travel on I-70 between Georgetown and Silver Plume and watch another train tackle the mountain, with not only the loop but also with a series of zigzags. At Silver Plume, you can take a guided walking tour through the 1870s Lebanon Silver Mine.

GETTING THERE: The railroad is about 50 miles west of Denver off I-70. Exit 226 takes you to Silver Plume and, a few miles away, Exit 228 takes you to Georgetown.

Leadville, Colorado & Southern Railroad

LOCATION: 326 E. Seventh Street, Leadville
PHONE: 866-386-3936 or 719-486-3936
WEBSITE: leadville-train.com
E-MAIL: form on website

Colorado

Leadville, Colorado & Southern Railroad

In a state with many spectacular scenic railroads, this line doesn't disappoint. Leaving from the charming mining town of Leadville, the LC&S marches up the side of the Rockies near the tree line. Upon departure from the depot, the train leaves the 10,200-foot elevation for a 900-foot climb along the southern side of the upper Arkansas River Valley to a point close to Climax at Fremont Pass. The train passes through forests of lodgepole pine, spruce, and aspen.

CHOICES: On the 22-mile trip, you can ride in an open car or a car with a roof. Especially for train fans, there are several seats available in the locomotive or in the caboose. If it's a beautiful day in Colorado, as it often is, stick to the open cars for unobstructed views. Stay on the right side of the train for spectacular views of the mountains and the molybdenum mine at the end of the line. Along the way, the conductor provides narration and answers questions.

WHEN TO GO: The trains run late May into October, when the aspen trees put on a magnificent show of yellow. In mid-summer, the Wildflower Special lets you view alpine flowers at their peak.

GOOD TO KNOW: Incorporated in 1878, Leadville is the highest incorporated city in the continental United States at 10,152 feet above sea level. Downtown Leadville is home to many shops, galleries, restaurants, and lodging establishments and makes an easy base camp from which to explore the central Rockies.

WORTH DOING: Be sure to explore Leadville's National Historic Landmark District, which includes many buildings built between 1880 and 1905.

DON'T MISS: Raft and ride packages are available that combine a half-day rafting trip along Browns Canyon on the Arkansas River with a scenic train ride.

GETTING THERE: From Denver, take I-70 west and then Highway 91 south to Leadville. From Vail, take I-70 west to Highway 24 and then Highway 24 south to Leadville.

53

Pikes Peak Cog Railway

LOCATION: 515 Ruxton Avenue, Manitou Springs
PHONE: 800-745-3773 or 719-685-5401
WEBSITE: cograilway.com
E-MAIL: info@cograilway.com

Pikes Peak Cog Railway

The Pikes Peak Cog Railway offers a unique Swiss Alpine experience on rails. Diesel-powered, self-propelled passenger cars navigate unbelievably steep grades with the help of a cog to ascend the 14,110-foot high peak. The view at the top is beautiful, but the journey is awe inspiring as well with trains going beyond the timberline.

CHOICES: The railroad offers three-hour round trips that allow you 30 minutes at the summit. It also provides a one-way trip to the top for anyone who would like to hike back down (about six hours). During the first part of the trip, the train travels through boulder fields, where you may see some interesting "faces" in the giant boulders. You'll also see some wildlife and a bristlecone pine forest with trees believed to be 2,000 years old.

WHEN TO GO: The railroad, unbelievably, operates year-round, thanks to a homemade snowplow that operates like a giant snow blower on rails. During summer, the railroad runs up to eight trains a day with departures every 80 minutes. During winter, November through March, the railway runs a limited schedule that is subject to a minimum number of passengers. A Santa train runs halfway up the peak in December.

GOOD TO KNOW: The railroad uses modern Swiss-built trains of a type used in the Alps. These units tackle grades of up to 25 percent.

WORTH DOING: At the base of Pikes Peak, about an hour's drive away, lie the historic gold-mining towns of Cripple Creek and Victor. You may still find gold in Cripple Creek—at the town's casinos—or ride the Cripple Creek & Victor Narrow Gauge Railroad. In Colorado Springs, explore the many red sandstone formations in the Garden of the Gods.

DON'T MISS: At the peak, make sure to walk around the summit and look for Denver. Just be careful. On the north side is a drop-off called the Bottomless Pit.

GETTING THERE: Manitou Springs is six miles from Colorado Springs. Take Exit 141 off I-25 and go west (toward the mountains) on Highway 24 four miles to the Manitou Avenue (Manitou Springs) exit. Go west on Manitou Avenue for 1.5 miles to Ruxton Avenue. Turn left and go to the top of Ruxton Avenue.

Platte Valley Trolley

LOCATION: 15th Street and Platte Street, Denver
PHONE: 303-458-6255
WEBSITE: denvertrolley.org

Platte Valley Trolley, Darrell Arndt

The Platte Valley Trolley is often referred to as one of Denver's best-kept secrets. The trolley runs through the South Platte River Greenway Park linking several of the city's most popular attractions. The trolley is a faithful replica of a turn-of the-century, open-air breezer, which is ideally suited for enjoying the sightseeing trip.

CHOICES: The route starts at Confluence Park beside the REI store. The riverfront ride lasts 25 minutes. Stops are made at the Downtown Aquarium, Children's Museum, and Sports Authority Field at Mile High. The trolley only makes intermediate stops southbound, and runs end-to-end northbound.

WHEN TO GO: The trolley operates Friday, Saturday, and Sunday afternoons starting in April and going through October. It departs continuously every half hour from REI. During Denver Bronco home games, fans can catch a shuttle to the game.

GOOD TO KNOW: Confluence Park is the site of Denver's original settlement and is now a hub for paved bicycle trails that serve the city.

WORTH DOING: The Platte River area is a great place to take the family. Combine a trolley ride with nearby attractions, such as the Children's Museum, Elitch Gardens Theme Park, or the aquarium. You can also take a tour of Sports Authority Field and the Colorado Sports Hall of Fame.

DON'T MISS: The flagship REI store is housed in the former Denver Tramway powerhouse building. The Starbucks there has a collection of photos showing the interior as it looked in 1901, quite a difference from the three-story climbing rock there now. Give it a try!

GETTING THERE: The route is located in downtown Denver. By car, take I-25 to Exit 211 (23rd Street), turn east on Water Street, and follow the signs to the Children's Museum or continue straight to the REI store for your best parking options. RTD buses operate within a short walk. The trolley is about a 15-minute walk from Amtrak and RTD light rail service at Union Station.

Rio Grande Scenic Railroad

LOCATION: 601 State Avenue, Alamosa
PHONE: 877-726-7245 or 719-587-0509
WEBSITE: coloradotrain.com
E-MAIL: questions@coloradotrain.com

Dave Crosby

The Denver & Rio Grande built an incredibly scenic route into the San Luis Valley and its biggest city, Alamosa, in the late 1880s. The standard gauge line of today replaced a much more difficult narrow gauge line but lost nothing as far as its engineering marvels or trackside splendor.

CHOICES: The railroad offers a variety of train rides. The regular excursion train crosses famous La Veta Pass to let you view the Rockies. On Fridays, Saturdays, and Sundays, a steam train winds through a variety of scenery, from flat farmland to mountains, on its trip from Alamosa to La Veta. Also on those days, a diesel-powered train runs from La Veta to Fort Garland. For an extended rail adventure, you can ride through the San Luis Valley to Antonito, where a connection can be made to the Cumbres & Toltec Scenic Railroad.

WHEN TO GO: Regular excursions run late May through September. In addition to the summer concerts, other special events take place.

GOOD TO KNOW: Seating choices vary by route and train. They include dome, coach, and open-air cars. The newest option is seating aboard restored club cars that ran on the fabled *City of New Orleans*.

WORTH DOING: Explore the Spanish Peaks country. It is filled with hiking trails, scenic roads, and natural wonders such as the tallest sand dunes in North America, which are found in Great Sand Dunes National Park.

DON'T MISS: Between June and August, the railroad presents its summer music festival in a mountain setting that is accessible by excursion trains. You can enjoy music under the stars, surrounded by aspen and pines, in a natural meadow amphitheater.

GETTING THERE: Located in south-central Colorado, Alamosa is about 200 miles south of Denver and 90 miles west of Pueblo. Highway 160 is the key route in and out of the San Luis Valley. The highway becomes Main Street in Alamosa, and the depot is just off Main Street on State Avenue.

Royal Gorge Route Railroad

LOCATION: 401 Water Street, Cañon City
PHONE: 888-724-5748 or 719-276-4000
WEBSITE: royalgorgeroute.com
E-MAIL: reservations@royalgorgeroute.com

Royal Gorge Route, Jeff Shane

Nowhere else in America can you ride a train through a very narrow mountain gorge with a fast-flowing river and look straight up at one thousand feet of cliff. The railroad offers a range of services on its 24-mile round trip through the Royal Gorge.

CHOICES: Service classes on the two-hour excursions begin with coach, which seats you in comfortable air-conditioned cars with access to an open-air car. Vista-dome class provides panoramic views under glass, food service, and a full-service bar. Riding in the refurbished *Sunshine Falls* parlor and bar car lets you enjoy unobstructed views out large windows. On the gourmet lunch and dinner trains, you can enjoy a three-course meal in a dining car or in the dome car.

WHEN TO GO: Trains begin running daily in mid-March and service expands during summer. Murder mystery trains run several times a year and other specials include an Octoberfest train and various holiday trains. Twilight is one of the best times to ride through the gorge.

GOOD TO KNOW: After looking up at the world's highest suspension bridge, 1,053 feet above the river, you can go up to Royal Gorge Bridge Park (admission required) and drive, walk, or tram across the gorge.

WORTH DOING: Rafting and kayak outfitters in the area offer half- and full-day trips for beginners and experienced paddlers alike. If you make it through Satan's Suckhole, watch out for the deceptively named Puppy Rapids.

DON'T MISS: On the popular Santa Express, children of all ages are encouraged to wear jammies and enjoy hot cocoa and a cookie on the way to the North Pole, which is decorated with more than 17,000 lights!

GETTING THERE: Cañon City is 115 miles from Denver and 45 minutes from Colorado Springs via Highway 115. Colorado Springs has the nearest airport.

CONNECTICUT

Connecticut Antique Machinery Association

The association features an operating three-foot-gauge railroad that is powered by a 1925 Baldwin locomotive that was used in the sugar cane fields of Hawaii. A variety of other locomotives and rolling stock fills out the collection. The site contains six other exhibits dedicated to antique industrial and agricultural machinery. It is open May through October.

LOCATION: 31 Kent-Cornwall Road (Route 7), Kent
PHONE: 860-927-0050
WEBSITE: ctamachinery.com
E-MAIL: form on website

Connecticut Trolley Museum

Founded in 1940, this museum offers a narrated three-mile, round-trip trolley ride. Its collection contains passenger and freight streetcars, interurban cars, elevated railway cars, service cars, and other rail equipment. A fire equipment museum and motor coach museum are also on site. The museum is open April through October with Winterfest taking place in November and December.

LOCATION: 58 North Road, East Windsor
PHONE: 860-627-6540
WEBSITE: ceraonline.org
E-MAIL: office@ceraweb.org

Danbury Railway Museum

This museum contains 70 pieces of equipment representing 11 different northeastern railroads and includes unique pieces such as a New Haven Railroad Mack FCD railbus. Vintage train rides in the yard include a spin around an operating turntable. The 1903 station features displays and a model layout of the Danbury yard. It is open year-round but closed on most holidays.

LOCATION: 120 White Street, Danbury
PHONE: 203-778-8337
WEBSITE: danbury.org/drm
E-MAIL: form on website

Shore Line Trolley Museum

The museum features a collection of 100 vintage transit vehicles. A three-mile round-trip trolley ride takes you along the area's scenic shore. Along the way, the trolley stops in the yard, where you can take a brief guided tour of the carbarn exhibits. You can also take a more comprehensive self-guided tour. The shop overlook allows you to view any restoration activities, and the station building contains additional exhibits. It is open May through October.

LOCATION: 17 River Street, East Haven
PHONE: 203-467-6927
WEBSITE: shorelinetrolley.com
E-MAIL: form on website

SoNo Switch Tower Museum

This 1896 New Haven Railroad switch tower has been restored, complete with an original armstrong 68-lever mechanical interlocking machine. Located next to the Northeast Corridor main line, the unique museum is open Saturdays and Sundays May through October.

LOCATION: 77 Washington Street, South Norwalk
PHONE: 203-246-6958
WEBSITE: westctnrhs.org/tower.htm
E-MAIL: info@westctnrhs.org

Connecticut Eastern Railroad Museum

LOCATION: 55 Bridge Street, Willimantic
PHONE: 860-456-9999
WEBSITE: cteastrrmuseum.org
E-MAIL: info@cteastrrmuseum.org

Robert LaMay

For anyone interested in seeing what takes place in a 1900s-era railroad village, this would be the place to visit. Located on the original site of the Columbia Junction freight yard and roundhouse, the Connecticut Eastern Railroad Museum is one of the few railroad museums to have a roundhouse complete with an operating standard gauge 60-foot armstrong turntable.

CHOICES: The museum features a variety of restored buildings including a station, section house, freight house, and crossing shanties. Numerous working projects occur every week throughout the museum's operating season. It houses several diesel locomotives, various railcars, and a steam locomotive. Tour guides are also on hand to show and explain the Ghost Train story and other tales of railroad history.

WHEN TO GO: The museum is open weekends from May into October. A variety of events take place during the season, such as music concerts, night photo shoots, and Metal Fest in May—a full day of blacksmithing events and demonstrations.

GOOD TO KNOW: With museum supervision, kids of all ages can ride on a replica 1850s pump car. You can also pretend that you are the engineer and sit in the engineer's seat of a New Haven Railroad FL9 passenger diesel locomotive.

WORTH DOING: Willimantic is situated in the "Last Green Valley," designated as Quinebaug and Shetucket Rivers Valley National Heritage Corridor. The valley contains seven state forests and five state parks. During Walktober, there are more than 100 guided walks and special events, including one at the Connecticut Eastern Railroad Museum.

DON'T MISS: Train rides are available if there is demand for them. The fare for the round trip from Columbia Junction to Bridge Street is $3.

GETTING THERE: Located about 30 miles east of Hartford in downtown Willimantic, the museum can be easily reached via numerous state roads such as Routes 6, 66, 32, 195, and 2. Once downtown, turn onto Bridge Street (Route 289 South), take a quick right, and follow the railroad tracks down a dirt road to the museum entrance.

Essex Steam Train & Riverboat

LOCATION: 1 Railroad Avenue, Essex
PHONE: 800-377-3987 or 860-767-0103
WEBSITE: essexsteamtrain.com
E-MAIL: valley.railroad@snet.net

Dave Crosby

The Essex Steam Train is unusual in offering a train ride that can be combined with a riverboat excursion, providing scenic views of the Connecticut River from both rail and water. The 12-mile rail round trip from Essex station to Deep River and Haddam takes about an hour while the rail-water package lasts 2.5 hours.

CHOICES: The Essex Steam Train is hauled by locomotive No. 40, which dates from 1920, or the far newer Chinese-built No. 3025, while the *Becky Thatcher*, a replica of a three-deck Mississippi-style riverboat, handles the water excursion. Beyond basic train and train-and-riverboat tours, the Valley Railroad Company offers a number of special events, including the annual Hot Steamed Jazz Festival and a circus train. On some weekends, a caboose is available for rides.

WHEN TO GO: The railroad operates mid-May through late October, with Day Out with Thomas weekends in spring and the Santa Special (afternoons) and North Pole Express (evenings) in November and December. Spring and fall are fine times to visit, with the leaves either a new green or brilliant autumn colors.

GOOD TO KNOW: Essex is a historic seaport village, with lots of white-clapboard New England charm. The charmingly Victorian Goodspeed Opera House in nearby East Haddam presents productions of classic musical comedies.

WORTH DOING: Nearby Gillette Castle is a whimsical faux-medieval mountaintop estate built of local fieldstone and completed in 1919 for actor and playwright William Gillette, most famous for his portrayal of Sherlock Holmes. Visit it on your own or as a train-ferry-hiking package offered by the railroad.

DON'T MISS: The diesel-hauled Essex Clipper Dinner Train operates seasonally and offers a four-course dinner. One of its two dining cars is a special treat: the heavyweight Pullman parlor car *Wallingford*, built in 1927 for the New York, New Haven & Hartford Railroad.

GETTING THERE: Essex is located on Route 9 just three miles from I-95. The nearest major airports are in New Haven and Hartford, roughly equidistant.

Naugatuck Railroad

LOCATION: 242 E. Main Street, Thomaston
PHONE: 860-283-7245
WEBSITE: rmne.org
E-MAIL: form on website

Scott Hartley

Today's Naugatuck Railroad runs over 19.6 miles of former New Haven Railroad, between Waterbury and Torrington, a line built by the original Naugatuck in 1849. The tracks follow the railroad's namesake river for the entire route. The Naugatuck Railroad, part of the Railroad Museum of New England, offers regularly scheduled train service over a nine-mile portion of its line, and periodic special excursions over other segments.

CHOICES: Departing the 1881 Thomaston station aboard 1920s heavyweight coaches built for Canadian National, you cross two trestles over the Naugatuck River, see century-old New England brass mills, and roll high across the face of giant Thomaston Dam. Operating locomotives include U23B 2203 (the last domestic U-Boat built by General Electric), EMD FL9 New Haven 2019 (the only FL9 still operating on original NH trackage), and Alco RS3 New Haven 529.

WHEN TO GO: Excursions run on Sundays and Tuesdays from Memorial Day through September, with Saturday departures added in October. The fall colors peak in early to mid-October, and this is the most popular time to ride the Naugatuck's trains. Northern Lights Limited and Santa Express trains run weekends late November through December, and wine-tasting trains run throughout the year.

GOOD TO KNOW: Built in 1881 by the original Naugatuck Railroad, the brick Thomaston station is being restored. The station features a display track of historic New England railroad rolling stock.

WORTH DOING: Thomaston offers a pleasant New England downtown with historic mills, a picturesque opera house, and restaurants. Nearby Litchfield has large 18th Century homes, shops, and restaurants. Waterbury's Mattatuck Museum shows visitors the history of Connecticut's brass industry.

DON'T MISS: Hank the Tank (Flagg Coal 0-4-0T) makes an annual visit to the Naugatuck, offering visitors a chance to ride behind live steam. Check with the railroad for the schedule.

GETTING THERE: Take I-84 to Waterbury and then Route 8 north to Exit 38.

DELAWARE

Wilmington & Western Railroad

LOCATION: 2201 Newport Gap Pike, Wilmington
PHONE: 302-998-1930
WEBSITE: wwrr.com
E-MAIL: form on website

Jim Wrinn

The Wilmington & Western is one of the premier tourist railroads on the East Coast. Attractive equipment, historic steam locomotives, and a scenic route through Delaware's Red Clay Valley make this line a must-see when visiting the mid-Atlantic.

CHOICES: The Wilmington & Western offers two basic trip options from Greenbank Station: a 90-minute round trip to the Mount Cuba picnic grove or a 2.5-hour round trip covering the entire 10-mile line to Hockessin. The train is comprised of vintage steel coaches with adjustable windows, and an open-air car is available during the warmer months. Power is provided by steam or diesel locomotives. A doodlebug also operates. A large variety of special events takes place and includes dinner trains, murder mysteries, train robberies, and geology trains.

WHEN TO GO: The W&W operates regular excursions beginning in March. Fall foliage and winter holidays see steam excursions nearly every weekend. Mid-October through early November is prime season for autumn leaves in the Red Clay Valley. December is Santa Claus Express time, with the focus on families and fun.

GOOD TO KNOW: Built by the American Locomotive Company in 1909 for the Mississippi Central, 4-4-0 American No. 98 is one of the few American Standard types operating.

WORTH DOING: Nearby attractions include a tall ship, Longwood Gardens, and Winterthur, a 1,000-acre estate featuring a 175-room house that showcases collections of antiques and Americana amidst meadows, woodlands, and an expansive garden.

DON'T MISS: On Pufferbelly Days, the railroad's two steam locomotives, 4-4-0 No. 98 and 0-6-0 No. 58, operate double-headed. On Civil War Skirmish Weekend, you can ride the train with the troops and then watch the battle.

GETTING THERE: Greenbank Station is about four miles southwest of downtown Wilmington on Route 41, close to I-95. Amtrak's Northeast Corridor provides service to downtown Wilmington, and Philadelphia International Airport is 35 miles away.

DISTRICT OF COLUMBIA

Smithsonian National Museum of American History

LOCATION: 14th Street and Constitution Avenue, Washington, D.C.
PHONE: 202-633-1000
WEBSITE: americanhistory.si.edu
E-MAIL: info@si.edu

National Museum of American History

The National Museum of American History features the landmark transportation exhibition America on the Move. Eighteen multimedia dioramas, each re-creating a specific time and place using artifacts, images, and sound, demonstrate how road and rail transportation shaped America, from before 1876 to 2000.

CHOICES: Must-see exhibits include the massive Southern Railway No. 1401, a 280-ton passenger locomotive built in 1926; *Jupiter*, a Baldwin-built narrow gauge 4-4-0; and a 19th century streetcar. The museum also displays *John Bull*, one of the oldest surviving steam locomotives in North America. This 1831 English-made locomotive is displayed on a vintage iron truss bridge that once served the Philadelphia and Reading Railroad.

WHEN TO GO: The museum is open every day of the year except Christmas Day. Spring sees the renowned cherry trees in bloom at the nearby Tidal Basin. The Smithsonian Folklife Festival, a huge outdoor exposition of living cultural heritage, takes place each year around Independence Day on the National Mall.

GOOD TO KNOW: The museum's west wing is currently being renovated and is scheduled to reopen in 2014. While some exhibits have moved or closed, the renovation does not affect the transportation displays.

WORTH DOING: Explore the National Mall, where you can visit the Washington Monument, Lincoln Memorial, Jefferson Memorial, and several war memorials.

DON'T MISS: Listen to the re-created conversation between the fireman and engineer of Southern No. 1401 as they discuss their upcoming run. Take a full-immersion multimedia journey around Chicago's famous loop as it was in 1959 aboard "L" car 6719.

GETTING THERE: Public transportation is the best option. The Metrorail subway offers convenient access to the museum from its Smithsonian and Federal Triangle stations. A DC Circulator bus loops around the museums on spring and summer weekends.

FLORIDA

Boca Express Train Museum

Guided tours take you through two restored 1947 Seaboard Air Line streamlined rail cars, both of which are listed on the National Register of Historic Places. The museum also includes a 1930 restored Florida East Coast depot, a 1940s Atlantic Coast Line caboose, and a Baldwin steam engine.

LOCATION: 747 S. Dixie Highway, Boca Raton
PHONE: 561-395-6766 ext. 101
WEBSITE: bocahistory.org
E-MAIL: tours@bocahistory.org

Central Florida Railroad Museum

Located in a former 1913 Tavares & Gulf Railroad station, the museum features a Clinchfield caboose and a 1938 Fairmont motor car. Exhibits focus on central Florida railroads. The museum is operated by the Winter Garden Heritage Foundation, which also operates the nearby Heritage Museum. That museum is housed in a 1918 Atlantic Coast Line depot and exhibits some railroad memorabilia, a Chessie caboose, and local historical items. Both museums are open daily.

LOCATION: 101 S. Boyd Street, Winter Garden
PHONE: 407-656-3244
WEBSITE: wghf.org
E-MAIL: museum@wghf.org

Flagler Museum

The home of Henry Flagler, who developed the Florida East Coast Railway, is now a museum of the Gilded Age. Docent-led tours are offered, or you can tour the 55-room Whitehall on your own. The Flagler Kenan Pavilion, designed in the style of a 19th century Beaux Arts railway palace, houses Henry Flagler's private railcar.

LOCATION: 1 Whitehall Way, Palm Beach
PHONE: 561-655-2833
WEBSITE: flaglermuseum.us
E-MAIL: form on website

Henry B. Plant Museum

You'll find the Henry B. Plant Museum on the University of Tampa campus. "Plant's Palace" was a hotel featuring Moorish architecture that was built as an exotic vacation resort for wintering Northerners. The building now contains exhibits on Plant and his network of Florida railroads. You can also view restored period rooms from America's Gilded Age. The museum is open Tuesdays through Sundays January through November and daily during December.

LOCATION: 401 W. Kennedy Boulevard, Tampa
PHONE: 813-254-1891
WEBSITE: plantmuseum.com
E-MAIL: form on website

Naples Depot Museum

Recently renovated, the museum is housed in a former Seaboard Air Line passenger station and listed on the National Register of Historic Places. It features restored railcars, interactive exhibits, and a model railroad. Miniature train rides are also offered.

LOCATION: 1051 Fifth Avenue South, Naples
PHONE: 239-262-6525
WEBSITE: colliermuseums.com
E-MAIL: colliermuseums@gmail.com

Southwest Florida Museum of History

Housed in the former Atlantic Coast Line Railroad depot, the museum displays a 1929 Pullman railcar. You can tour the *Esperanza* to get a glimpse of travel aboard a private car. The museum features exhibits from prehistoric times to modern day that showcase southwest Florida. It is open Tuesdays through Saturdays.

LOCATION: 2031 Jackson Street, Fort Myers
PHONE: 239-321-7430
WEBSITE: swflmuseumofhistory.com
E-MAIL: museuminfo@cityftmyers.com

Tampa Union Station

Tampa Union Station was opened in 1912 by the Atlantic Coast Line, Seaboard Air Line, and Tampa Northern railroads and is listed on the National Register of Historic Places. The Italian Renaissance Revival-style building was restored in 1998 and today serves Amtrak's *Silver Star* and connecting motor coaches. Displays in the ornate waiting room of the station chronicle the history of the station and the story of railroading on the west coast of Florida.

LOCATION: 601 N. Nebraska Avenue, Tampa
PHONE: 813-221-7600
WEBSITE: tampaunionstation.com
E-MAIL: tampaunionstation@gmail.com

Florida Railroad Museum

LOCATION: 12210 83rd Street East, Parrish
PHONE: 941-776-0906
WEBSITE: frrm.org
E-MAIL: form on website

Florida Railroad Museum

The Florida Railroad Museum operates diesel-powered trains on a 13-mile round trip in southwest Florida. Leisurely rides in air-conditioned and open-air coaches through farmland, piney woods, and palmetto flats give riders a glimpse of Florida before Disney and interstate highways.

CHOICES: Variety is the order for the day with the Florida Railroad Museum's equipment. Passenger equipment comes from a wide range of railroads including the Lackawanna, Union Pacific, and Louisville & Nashville. Regardless of the time of year, you'll want to opt for the air-conditioned rolling stock instead of open air—after all, air-conditioning was invented by Florida physician John Gorrie in 1851 for good reason! Get there well before train time to get a cool seat. Special events include a World War II reenactment, a train robbery, and Halloween and Christmas trains.

WHEN TO GO: The Florida Railroad Museum operates weekends year-round. Mid-December through Easter is Florida's high season. The Florida Railroad Museum is at its busiest then, but this season also boasts Florida's mildest weather, making it the perfect time to combine a ride on the railroad with a canoe trip or a picnic at nearby Little Manatee River State Park.

GOOD TO KNOW: The Florida Railroad Museum's locomotive rental program allows you to train in the operation of a locomotive and then take the controls for an hour.

WORTH DOING: Other area attractions include Manatee Village Historical Park, which displays a variety of historic buildings and a steam locomotive, the South Florida Museum that also includes an aquarium and planetarium, and the Gamble Plantation Historic State Park.

DON'T MISS: Packing a lunch for the museum's picnic area makes for an enjoyable break, where a Porter 0-6-0T steam locomotive is on display.

GETTING THERE: You have plenty of choices. Tampa International Airport and Sarasota Bradenton International Airport are fairly close by. Amtrak serves Tampa by train and Sarasota and Bradenton by dedicated connecting motor coach. By car, take I-75 for speed or Highway 301 to see more of the real Florida.

Gold Coast Railroad Museum

LOCATION: 12450 SW 152nd Street, Miami
PHONE: 888-608-7246 or 305-253-0063
WEBSITE: gcrm.org
E-MAIL: webmaster@gcrm.org

Gold Coast Railroad Museum

With its impressive collection of rolling stock and locomotives—featuring the *Ferdinand Magellan*, a Pullman office car used by Presidents Roosevelt, Truman, Eisenhower, and Reagan—and its historic location on the site of a World War II airship base, the Gold Coast Railroad Museum is a fascinating place to visit.

CHOICES: Interested in former Florida East Coast Railway or *California Zephyr* passenger equipment? You'll find it here, along with diesels and steam locomotives from other railroads. On weekends, the Gold Coast offers a 25-minute standard gauge train ride using a diesel-electric (either an EMD E9 or GP7) and either a former Florida East Coast stainless coach or a caboose. On weekdays, the Gold Coast runs a two-foot gauge children's steam train or an electric trolley. Guided "mini" tours, which include the *Ferdinand Magellan*, are available during the week.

WHEN TO GO: The Gold Coast Railroad Museum is open daily year-round, except for some holidays. The museum offers special events around holidays and days out with Thomas the Tank Engine.

GOOD TO KNOW: Currently, restoration of the *Ferdinand Magellan*'s interior is taking place. The museum is now home to Florida East Coast caboose No. 715, which is also slated for restoration. Florida East Coast Railway 4-6-2 steam locomotive No. 153, like the *Ferdinand Magellan*, is a National Historic Landmark. Used on "the railroad that died at sea," No. 153 pulled a rescue train that delivered evacuees safely to Miami just before a hurricane destroyed the Key West line in 1935.

WORTH DOING: Consider combining your trip to the Gold Coast with a visit to Zoo Miami, which is located next to the railroad museum.

DON'T MISS: The Gold Coast offers cab rides on its weekend diesel-hauled passenger trains for an additional fee. Make sure, however, you call ahead for reservations.

GETTING THERE: Miami is served by all major airlines, Amtrak, and major highways. The museum is located between Miami and Homestead, off the Florida Turnpike.

Seminole Gulf Railway

LOCATION: 2805 Colonial Boulevard, Fort Myers
PHONE: 800-736-4853 or 239-275-8487
WEBSITE: semgulf.com
E-MAIL: reservations@semgulf.com

Scott Hartley

Seminole Gulf is a regional railroad with about 118 miles of track that operates a murder mystery dinner train as well as providing freight service to Gulf communities in the Fort Myers area.

CHOICES: Throughout the year, the railroad offers a variety of themed murder mysteries aboard a dinner train. Along the 3.5-hour entertaining journey, the train takes you across the Caloosahatchee River over a railroad drawbridge. The views from this and other numerous bridges you cross are especially scenic, not that you'll be able to watch the scenery. You will be busy enjoying a five-course meal and trying to solve a mystery. If you do and are a super sleuth, you may even win a prize.

WHEN TO GO: The mystery dinner train operates Wednesday through Sunday evenings year-round, but of course, Florida is always best enjoyed in winter! Several specials occur around various holidays.

GOOD TO KNOW: The railroad operates on the tracks of the former Atlantic Coast Line and Seaboard Air Line, which joined in 1967 to become Seaboard Coast Line.

WORTH DOING: Before your dinner, you can walk along Fort Myers Beach or a beach on a nearby barrier island, such as Sanibel or Captiva, and go shelling. For more adventure, Everglades National Park is 90 minutes away. You can visit the park's Gulf Coast Visitor Center at Everglades City, where you can take a boat tour or rent a canoe. You can enter the heart of the park from the east, which is about a three-hour drive.

DON'T MISS: A Christmas rail-boat event combines a train trip, dinner, and a boat ride through Punta Gorda Isles' lighted holiday festivities.

GETTING THERE: The railway is located in suburban Fort Myers, which is on the western Florida coast 40 miles north of Naples. The depot is located 1.5 miles from Highway 41 and three miles from I-75.

Florida

69

Tavares, Eustis & Gulf Railroad

Florida

LOCATION: 100 E. Ruby Street, Tavares
PHONE: 352-742-7200
WEBSITE: orangeblossomcannonball.com
E-MAIL: info@orangeblossomcannonball.com

Tavares, Eustis & Gulf Railroad

Tavares, Eustis & Gulf Railroad operates in scenic Lake County, and the route follows the shore of Lake Dora, providing riders ample opportunity to view Florida wildlife up close. The trains generally operate southward out of town through the old citrus packing district towards Dora Canal, Ellsworth Junction, and Lake Jem, offering a glimpse at undeveloped rural Florida life, a welcome step back in time.

CHOICES: TE&G offers a variety of regular excursions along with seasonal specials and themed excursions. One-hour excursions turn at Ellsworth Junction while the more popular two-hour trips go all the way to Lake Jem, passing orange and grapefruit groves, complete with a runaround move. Popular seasonal trips are offered for Halloween and Christmas along with wine-tasting, pizza, and other specials.

WHEN TO GO: Typical operations for the trains are Saturday and Sunday year-round, but specials can be found on other days. The mildest and most enjoyable weather is during October into April, while the other months tend to offer the South's famous muggy heat. The cars are open-air and not climate-controlled.

GOOD TO KNOW: The trains are pulled by a vintage 1942 center cab locomotive named *Herbie* or the famous No. 2, a Baldwin 2-6-0 steam locomotive, which has starred in *True Grit, 3:10 to Yuma, There Will Be Blood,* and other films.

WORTH DOING: While in Lake County, there are numerous things to do off the train. At Wooton Park, you can attend numerous events that take place lakeside, go boating or kayaking, or take a seaplane tour. Food festivals are always a good time to visit. Downtown Tavares has numerous shops and eateries as does nearby Mount Dora, which hosts some of the area's most attended cultural and art-related events.

DON'T MISS: Photographers will want to take part in one of the railroad's photo trains that offer runbys the regular excursions don't.

GETTING THERE: TE&G's depot is conveniently located in downtown Tavares at Wooton Park, about an hour's drive from Orlando. From Orlando, the easiest and most scenic route is I-4 to Highway 46 west to Highway 441 north into Tavares. Wooton Park is behind the county court house. Ample free parking is available.

TECO Line Streetcar System

LOCATION: St. Pete Times Forum Drive, Tampa
PHONE: 813-254-4278
WEBSITE: tecolinestreetcar.org
E-MAIL: customerservice@gohart.org

Scott Hartley

Nostalgic-looking streetcars take passengers along a 2.7-mile route that connects downtown Tampa, Channelside, and the Ybor City entertainment district.

CHOICES: You can ride a streetcar to Whiting Station in the heart of downtown Tampa. You can also board anywhere along the line's other 10 stops. Get off, enjoy the neighborhood, and catch a later car. Five stops are located in Tampa's Channel District, four are in historic Ybor City, and another is downtown at the Dick Greco Plaza. The TECO fleet includes a restored original Birney streetcar, replicas of Birney safety streetcars, and an open-air streetcar. Fares are charged per person per trip, but one-day unlimited ride cards are also available. The streetcar system also offers guided group tours.

WHEN TO GO: Cars operate year-round. They run every 15 to 20 minutes from morning through the evening with extended hours on Saturdays.

GOOD TO KNOW: Tampa's streetcar line dates back to 1892 when it carried workers between downtown and the cigar factories on the city's west side. The line peaked in the 1920s with some 24 million riders and then closed in 1946.

WORTH DOING: In Ybor City, within walking distance of the streetcar line, you can visit a cigar maker and even see craftsmen roll fresh cigars by hand. The Florida Aquarium and the Ybor City Museum are accessible from the line.

DON'T MISS: Public art at some stations reflects historical and contemporary designs. In Ybor City, bronze chair sculptures duplicate the lectern chairs used by the readers in cigar factories at the turn of the century. Another bronze sculpture of Dick Greco (a four-term mayor of Tampa) was installed at Greco Plaza.

GETTING THERE: If starting in Ybor City, which is east of downtown Tampa, take I-4 and follow the signs to Ybor City. At the Dick Greco Plaza downtown, you can connect to trolleys, buses, and taxis.

GEORGIA

Georgia Museum of Agriculture and Historic Village

On the 95-acre site, you can tour 35 buildings from the state's past including a railroad depot, sawmill, and steam-powered woodworking shop. Costumed interpreters explain the lifestyle found in late 19th century. On Saturdays and during special events, you can ride aboard a narrow gauge steam train that takes you around the site. The Agriculture Center contains exhibits related to Georgia's farming history. The site is open Tuesday through Saturday year-round.

LOCATION: 1392 Whiddon Mill Road, Tifton
PHONE: 229-391-5200
WEBSITE: abac.edu/museum
E-MAIL: gboone@abac.edu

Okefenokee Heritage Center

This regional art and history museum displays Old Nine, a restored 1912 Baldwin 2-8-2 steam locomotive. The rail exhibit also includes a baggage car, REA Express car, passenger coach, caboose, and an early Waycross depot that describes regional rail history. Music fans may be interested in the exhibit of Waycross native Gram Parsons.

LOCATION: 1460 N. Augusta Avenue, Waycross
PHONE: 912-285-4260
WEBSITE: okefenokeeheritagecenter.com
E-MAIL: sbean@wayxcable.com

River Street Streetcar

Savannah's River Street Streetcar makes six stops along the historic riverfront between Montgomery Street and the Waving Girl Landing, where passengers can connect with the *Savannah Belles* ferry. Built in Melbourne, Australia, during the 1930s, the W5 class streetcar now runs on battery power and biodiesel. It operates Thursdays through Sundays.

LOCATION: River Street, Savannah
PHONE: 912-447-4026
WEBSITE: connectonthedot.com
E-MAIL: comments@connectonthedot.com

Stone Mountain Scenic Railroad

A 1940s locomotive with open-air cars takes you on a five-mile, 30-minute excursion around Stone Mountain. Narration offers a look at rail history and provides interesting facts about the mountain. The train can be boarded from the marketplace depot in the Crossroads area. The park has plenty of other fun events and attractions including a mini golf course themed around the Great Locomotive Chase. In December, the train ride becomes a Christmas sing-a-long.

LOCATION: Highway 78 East, Stone Mountain
PHONE: 800-401-2407 or 770-498-5690
WEBSITE: stonemountainpark.com
E-MAIL: form on website

Thronateeska Heritage Center

The Thronateeska Heritage Center contains several historic railroad structures including an original 1857 freight depot and Railway Express Agency building, and its history museum is located in the 1912 Union Depot. Its transportation annex displays a variety of railcars and Georgia Northern Railway steam locomotive No. 107. The complex also includes a planetarium and science center.

LOCATION: 100 W. Roosevelt Avenue, Albany
PHONE: 229-432-6955
WEBSITE: heritagecenter.org
E-MAIL: info@heritagecenter.org

Blue Ridge Scenic Railway

LOCATION: 241 Depot Street, Blue Ridge
PHONE: 877-413-8724 or 706-632-8724
WEBSITE: brscenic.com
E-MAIL: info@brscenic.com

Blue Ridge Scenic Railway, Tim Griffin

The Louisville & Nashville's original route from Knoxville to Atlanta covered some rugged territory, and today it makes for a scenic ride into the wilderness. Following the unspoiled Toccoa River, this 26-mile round trip takes riders between the depot at Blue Ridge and McCaysville near the Tennessee border.

CHOICES: Trains depart downtown Blue Ridge from the depot, which was constructed in 1906 and is listed on the National Register of Historical Places. You can ride in either a closed-window car or an open-air car. As the diesel-powered train climbs through the north Georgia mountains, commentary is piped into the cars, and a conductor may add his own perspective to the trip.

WHEN TO GO: Trains run March through December, and spring and fall are great seasons for travel in the Southeast. The region's lush vegetation has a tendency to create a tunnel effect. During spring and autumn, you have the chance to see into the forest as well as take in the scenery. Pumpkin pickin' and Santa trains offer family fun.

GOOD TO KNOW: This railroad started out as a narrow gauge line in the late 1880s with the tracks being three feet wide. Later investors changed it to standard gauge. The railway is the only mainline railroad excursion service based in Georgia.

WORTH DOING: The railroad offers a tubing trip package for the Toccoa River, which the railroad crisscrosses, or a rafting trip on the nearby Ocoee River. The Toccoa is a slow run, while the Ocoee is a wild whitewater ride. Both packages include return transportation to Blue Ridge.

DON'T MISS: During your layover, take the opportunity to walk around McCaysville, have lunch, and visit some of the town's antique shops.

GETTING THERE: Blue Ridge is about 90 miles north of Atlanta and about 80 miles from Chattanooga, Tenn. From Atlanta, take I-75 north to I-575, which turns into Highway 515, and continue on Highway 515 to Blue Ridge. The depot is on the left side of Depot Street.

Georgia State Railroad Museum

LOCATION: 655 Louisville Road, Savannah
PHONE: 912-651-6823
WEBSITE: chsgeorgia.org
E-MAIL: info@chsgeorgia.org

Georgia State Railroad Museum

Part of the multi-site Coastal Heritage Society museum complex, Georgia State Railroad Museum is a must-see for those interested in early American railroading technology. Located on the edge of Savannah's renowned historic district, the museum encompasses 13 structures from the original Central of Georgia shops site, several of which date back to the early 1850s.

CHOICES: The 1926 roundhouse contains a collection of Georgia steam locomotives, passenger cars, and freight cars, including the 1886 0-6-0 shop switcher No. 8 and a rare 1878 wooden business car. A self-guided tour provides information about the history and technology of the site. The operating turntable in the roundhouse is a must-see. Special events, including family happenings, take place throughout the year. On select days, the museum offers diesel- or steam-powered train rides.

WHEN TO GO: The museum is open year-round. Savannah's near-tropical climate offers a welcome relief from northern cold throughout the winter months.

GOOD TO KNOW: Georgia State Railroad Museum is built on the site of the Battle of Savannah, which was fought in 1779. It is the largest pre-Civil War era railroad complex of it's size still operating.

WORTH DOING: The Savannah Historic District, a National Historic Landmark, is one of America's premier urban historic neighborhoods. You'll find fine examples of buildings in Georgian, Greek Revival, and Gothic styles.

DON'T MISS: Expand your tour with a visit to the other sites in the complex. The Savannah History Museum is housed in the 1850s Central of Georgia passenger station and train shed one block north of the roundhouse. Old Fort Jackson, a brick fort built before the War of 1812, presents cannon-firing demonstrations. Battlefield Park commemorates a Revolutionary War battle fought in Savannah.

GETTING THERE: Amtrak's station is three miles away. A number of major airlines or their regional affiliates serve Savannah International Airport. Highways 16 and 17 lead to Martin Luther King, Jr. Boulevard, which takes you to the museum.

SAM Shortline

LOCATION: 2459 Highway 280 West, Cordele
PHONE: 877-427-2457 or 229-276-0755
WEBSITE: samshortline.com

SAM Shortline

The SAM Shortline offers a relaxing trip through the small towns of southwest Georgia. The train leaves from Georgia Veterans State Park, and the main objective is to reach Archery. Along the way, you travel through the towns of Leslie, Americus, and Plains, the home of President Jimmy Carter.

CHOICES: There are six different excursion trains, each one laying over in different towns along the route. If you would like to explore a location longer, you may be able to catch the train on its return trip. You can board at any of the depots along the route. SAM offers coach, premium, and lounge seating. Premium seating is in the *Americus* car and features tables and chairs. Lounge seating is in the *Samuel H. Hawkins* car, and it offers lounges, booths, tables, and an observation area.

WHEN TO GO: Trains run Fridays and Saturdays as well as on other select days February through December. Days out with Thomas take place in October, and numerous special excursions operate throughout the season.

GOOD TO KNOW: Why SAM? The original railroad was the Savannah, Americus & Montgomery Railroad built during the 1880s and headed by Col. Samuel Hugh Hawkins of Americus.

WORTH DOING: In Americus, you can visit Habitat for Humanity's Global Village, and if you want to make a longer trip, the Andersonville National Historic Site and National POW Museum is 11 miles northeast.

DON'T MISS: Many of the excursions, such as the Peanut Express, stop in Plains and Archery, where you can visit Jimmy Carter's childhood farm. In Plains, the Seaboard Coast Line depot was his campaign headquarters during the 1976 election. While you're there, make sure to buy a bag of peanuts.

GETTING THERE: Cordele is about 140 miles south of Atlanta. From I-75, take Exit 101 and go west on Highway 280 for 10 miles, turn left into the park, and then take the first right.

Southeastern Railway Museum

LOCATION: 3595 Buford Highway, Duluth
PHONE: 770-476-2013
WEBSITE: srmduluth.org
E-MAIL: admin@southeasternrailwaymuseum.org

Jim Wrinn

This museum showcases railroading in Georgia and the Southeast with exhibits and more than 90 pieces of rolling stock. Among the highlights are a business car used to help convince leaders to bring the 1996 Olympics to Atlanta, a private car once used by President Warren G. Harding, and one of the famous green and gold *Southern Crescent* passenger diesels. It also offers short train rides.

CHOICES: The 34-acre museum features a variety of buildings and displays. Building One, the main exhibit hall, contains Southern Railway E8 passenger diesel-electric No. 6901 and the 1911 Pullman private car *Superb*, which was used by President Harding and is on the National Register of Historic Places. The museum's collection includes passenger coaches, private cars, trolleys, baggage cars, freight cars, cabooses, and maintenance-of-way equipment. A diesel-powered train ride takes you around the museum's site aboard vintage cabooses.

WHEN TO GO: The museum is open Thursdays, Fridays, and Saturdays all year. In summer, it is also open on Mondays, Wednesdays, and some Sundays. Train rides are offered in season, and special days take place during the year including Caboose Days and days with Santa. Second Thursdays at the museum are geared towards preschool children and features a different piece of equipment each month.

GOOD TO KNOW: The museum has added a miniature train ride to the grounds.

WORTH DOING: From professional sports to botanical gardens and the zoo, take a few days and see all that the Atlanta area has to offer.

DON'T MISS: View famous excursion engines Savannah & Atlanta Pacific type No. 750 and Atlanta & West Point Pacific type No. 290, the latter well known for appearing in the movie *Fried Green Tomatoes*.

GETTING THERE: The museum is located in Duluth, a northeast suburb of Atlanta. It is just south of downtown Duluth. From Atlanta, take I-85 to Exit 104 and take Pleasant Hill Road to Buford Highway. Turn right on Buford Highway and then left onto Peachtree Road to the museum.

Southern Museum of Civil War and Locomotive History

LOCATION: 2829 Cherokee Street, Kennesaw
PHONE: 770-427-2117
WEBSITE: southernmuseum.org

Southern Museum of Civil War and Locomotive History

A museum of high-caliber exhibits and static displays, the Southern Museum of Civil War and Locomotive History displays the famed steam locomotive *General*. The *General*, a Western & Atlantic Railroad 4-4-0 built in 1855, was the star in one of the Civil War's greatest acts of intrigue—the Great Locomotive Chase. The museum, part of which is located in a former cotton gin, is a must-see attraction.

CHOICES: While the story of the Andrews Raid and the *General* is still the biggest offering at the museum, additional railroading and Civil War displays are featured. It also chronicles the story of Georgia locomotive manufacturer Glover Machine Works. The Glover Machine Works manufactured steam locomotives, locomotive parts, and other industrial products from 1902 until the 1930s. Patterns from the casting shop are artfully displayed, and extensive exhibits cover the story of the locomotive manufacturer. The facility also features special railroad exhibits and events.

WHEN TO GO: The museum is open daily year-round, except for major holidays, and the weather is generally mild. The Atlanta area has lots of modern railroad action, and other museums, such as the Atlanta History Center, help tell the story of the Civil War and railroading in Atlanta.

GOOD TO KNOW: The story of the Andrews Raid was thrilling and unique enough to attract the attention of the Walt Disney Company, which released the film *The Great Locomotive Chase* in 1956.

WORTH DOING: Take a walking tour of historic Kennesaw (once known as Big Shanty) after exiting the front door of the museum and view a 1908 Western & Atlantic Railroad depot, numerous 19th century residences, and an 1887 grocery store.

DON'T MISS: The Atlanta Cyclorama, located in Grant Park, houses the *Texas*, the Western & Atlantic Railroad locomotive used by Confederates to hunt down Andrews Raiders.

GETTING THERE: Kennesaw is located off I-75 and Highway 41, about a 45-minute drive from Hartsfield-Jackson Atlanta International Airport, the world's busiest. Amtrak's *Crescent* also serves the city twice daily.

HAWAII

Laupahoehoe Train Museum

The musem is located on the Big Island along the Hamakua Heritage Coast. It is housed in a station agent's home, which has been restored and furnished to its early 1900s appearance. The museum contains photos and artifacts of the Hilo Railroad and displays a standard gauge caboose, narrow gauge boxcar, and diesel switcher.

LOCATION: 36-2377 Mamalahoa Highway, Laupahoehoe
PHONE: 808-962-6300
WEBSITE: thetrainmuseum.com
E-MAIL: laupahoehoetrainmuseum@yahoo.com

Hawaiian Railway

LOCATION: 91-1001 Renton Road, Ewa
PHONE: 808-681-5461
WEBSITE: hawaiianrailway.com
E-MAIL: info@hawaiianrailway.com

Robert Pisani

The Hawaiian Railway is the only active railroad on the island of Oahu. It offers regularly scheduled 90-minute, fully narrated rides over 6.5 miles of track. Along the way, you'll pass a variety of interesting and historical sites, including Fort Barrette. The train stops at Kahe Point, so you can take in the extraordinary ocean views.

CHOICES: Regular excursions take place twice each Sunday afternoon. On the second Sunday of each month, parlor car No. 64 is added to the regular train of open cars, and reservations (and an additional fare) are necessary for riding in this beautifully restored car. Three side-rod diesel locomotives have been restored to operation, and several steam locomotives have been cosmetically restored. The railway also has a collection of railcars and other equipment.

WHEN TO GO: The railway's train yard is open year-round. A haunted Halloween train, complete with ghost stories, runs in October.

GOOD TO KNOW: Parlor car No. 64 is the luxurious parlor car that Benjamin Dillingham, founder of the Oahu Railway & Land Company, had built for his personal use in 1900. Restored by the Hawaiian Railway Society, No. 64 is worth the ride, and the fare for riding the car goes toward its upkeep.

WORTH DOING: No trip to Oahu would be complete without a heart-rending visit to Pearl Harbor. You can also wander over Oahu and other islands and literally discover pieces of Hawaii's railroading past, which included sugar plantation, military, and common carrier railways.

DON'T MISS: The railway, which is situated on what was part of the Oahu Railway & Land Company main line, is north of Pearl Harbor. The scenery is incredible. Wear comfortable shoes and wander through the train yard and then relax with lunch in the picnic area.

GETTING THERE: The railway is minutes from Honolulu by bus or car. If you drive, take H1 west and exit on 5A Ewa. Then take Highway 76 south for 2.5 miles, turn right at Renton Road, and continue for 1.5 miles to the entrance.

Kauai Plantation Railway

LOCATION: 3-2087 Kaumualii Highway, Lihue
PHONE: 808-245-7245
WEBSITE: kauaiplantationrailway.com
E-MAIL: train@hawaiilink.net

David Lustig

The Kauai Plantation Railway operates daily on a genuine Hawaiian plantation. Experience plantation life and learn about Kauai agriculture as the train travels through more than 100 acres of unspoiled Hawaii on a three-foot-gauge train. Passengers enjoy a 40-minute journey through fields of sugar cane, pineapple, banana, papaya, coffee, tropical flowers, and hardwood trees.

CHOICES: Train rides leave from a Hawaiian train depot, and you can ride in a reproduction of a railway car from the time of King Kalakaua or an open-sided excursion car. In addition, there is a ride-hike-lunch-orchard tour. Currently, motive power is a pair of small diesels, including a restored 1939 Whitcomb engine.

WHEN TO GO: The train operates daily, and any day is a beautiful day in Hawaii, and there are up to five runs a day. Hawaii is in the tropics, and that suggests suntan lotion, a hat, and comfortable clothing.

GOOD TO KNOW: The three-foot-gauge railway was the first railroad built on Kauai in almost 100 years. More than 2.5 miles of roadbed was constructed with rails hand-spiked onto 6,000 wooden ties. More than 50 varieties of fruits and vegetables can be found on the plantation, from avocado and bananas to rambutan and sugar cane. The plantation also features a restaurant and shops as well as a tasting room for Kōloa Rum, which is produced on the island with sugar cane.

WORTH DOING: Public luaus are scheduled on Tuesday and Friday evenings, and a special train can take you there.

DON'T MISS: On the tour package, after riding the train, you can hike in the rain forest and sample fresh fruit picked right off the tree. You also have the opportunity to feed goats, sheep, and pigs.

GETTING THERE: The Kauai Plantation is just off Route 50 (Kaumualii Highway) approximately one mile south of Lihue, which is the main city on Kauai. The railway is located at Kilohana Plantation next to Kauai Community College. Just look for the white picket fence.

Lahaina Kaanapali Railroad

LOCATION: 975 Limahana Place, Lahaina
PHONE: 808-661-0080
WEBSITE: sugarcanetrain.com
E-MAIL: form on website

David Lustig

The Sugar Cane Train travels between the historical whaling town of Lahaina to the lush Kaanapali Resort on the Hawaiian island of Maui. Narrow gauge steam engines transport visitors in open-air cars through the Kaanapali golf courses, along the ocean, and across a scenic railroad trestle.

CHOICES: You can board the Sugar Cane Train from either the Lahaina station or the Puukolii station. On the round trip, the conductor entertains you with narration about the history of the train and the sugar cane industry as well as with fun Hawaiian facts. Don't miss the beautiful views of the Pacific Ocean and of the neighboring islands, Molokai and Lanai, from the 325-foot curved wooden trestle.

WHEN TO GO: Steam trains operate daily, all year round. While the most popular time is summer, if you visit between December and April, you just might see a breaching humpback whale from the train. During this time, many whales are active off the west Maui coast.

GOOD TO KNOW: While few Hawaiian railroads remain today, for more than 100 years, they hauled sugar cane to the mills and transported workers. You can learn more about the industry at the Alexander & Baldwin Sugar Museum.

WORTH DOING: There are a variety of luaus offered on the island, and you should experience at least one of these unique Hawaiian activities. West Maui is a premier Hawaii tourist destination, featuring five-star hotels and exquisite dining and shopping experiences. You'll be able to take a glass-bottom boat cruise, snorkel, try assorted water sports, and even dive into a tank of sharks at the Maui Ocean Center.

DON'T MISS: By sitting in the same seat, you will be able to experience both an ocean view and a mountain view. The views alternate depending on the direction of the train.

GETTING THERE: Many large airlines offer direct flights to Maui from mainland West Coast cities. Once on Maui, both of the railroad's stations are located off Honoapiilani Highway (Highway 30), the coast's main, and only, highway.

IDAHO

Nampa Train Depot Museum

Built in 1903, the building served as the Oregon Short Line depot and was then used as offices for the Union Pacific. The building now houses artifacts relating to local history. Outside, a 1942 UP caboose is available for viewing. The museum is open year-round. Depotfest takes place in August.

LOCATION: 1200 Front Street, Nampa
PHONE: 208-467-7611
WEBSITE: canyoncountyhistory.com
E-MAIL: info@canyoncountyhistory.com

Northern Pacific Depot Railroad Museum

Listed on the National Register of Historic Places, this building served as a station until the 1980s. The elegant chateau-style depot was built at the turn of the 20th century from brick transported from China and concrete panels made from mine tailings. It now serves as a museum that features exhibits on railroading in the area's mining district. Depot Day takes place in May.

LOCATION: 219 Sixth Street, Wallace
PHONE: 208-752-0111
WEBSITE: wallace-id.com/business.html#tourist

Silverwood Central Railroad

What started out as a small transportation museum turned into a large theme park with roller coasters and water slides. Silverwood's steam train is pulled by a 1915 Porter narrow-gauge locomotive. The 30-minute ride through the park and surrounding woods includes surprise appearances by train robbers. The park is open May through October.

LOCATION: 27843 N. Highway 95, Athol
PHONE: 208-683-3400
WEBSITE: silverwoodthemepark.com
E-MAIL: info@silverwoodthemepark.com

Thunder Mountain Line Railroad

Idaho

LOCATION: 120 Mill Road, Horseshoe Bend
PHONE: 877-432-7245 or 208-331-1184
WEBSITE: thundermountainline.com
E-MAIL: debra@thundermountainline.com

Thunder Mountain Line Railroad

This is one of the most scenic trips in the northern part of the Rocky Mountains. The train parallels the Payette River for most of the journey through sagebrush-covered hills, fir trees, and mountain meadows. Often visible are fox, deer, elk, blue heron, osprey, and bald eagles. Much of the river is excellent for whitewater rafting, so you not only get entertainment from the scenery but from the rafters as well.

CHOICES: On this line, you have almost 50 choices for a train ride aboard open-air or coach cars. In addition to the Horseshoe Bend excursion, there are more than 40 special theme trains. The Horseshoe Bend route travels along an old wagon road on its three-hour round trip between Horseshoe Bend and Banks. Along the way, the train winds through a narrow canyon, passes through Boise National Forest, and offers a variety of scenic views. From October through December, special event trains run west from Horseshoe Bend to the town of Montour. Many of the special events are themed around the Wild West. Three levels of service are offered: standard, first class, and executive class.

WHEN TO GO: The countryside is rugged and beautiful to travel through in any season. Trains operate Friday through Sunday beginning in April and run through the end of the year.

GOOD TO KNOW: The history of this line goes back more than 100 years when a railroad was planned to transport gold prospectors. It was completed in 1914. Eventually, it supported the timber industry and carried vacationeers.

WORTH DOING: Experience the scenic Payette River and Boise National Forest up close. You can raft or kayak through Class IV rapids or just float along the river. The forest offers over 1,300 miles of hiking trails and more than 70 camping and picnic spots.

DON'T MISS: The Horseshoe Bend train stops in Banks, so you can view gold-mining and other exhibits at the station house and take a look at a stagecoach.

GETTING THERE: The Horseshoe Bend depot is located about 25 minutes north of Boise. Take Highway 55 from Boise to Horseshoe Bend and once there turn right on Mill Road. Look for the gray tank car.

ILLINOIS

Amboy Depot Museum

Built in 1876, this former Illinois Central division headquarters building has been restored, inside and out. It is now a museum that presents the history of Amboy and features artifacts of the Illinois Central Railroad. The museum also contains a freight house with additional artifacts, an 0-8-0 Baldwin steam engine, a wooden caboose, and a schoolhouse. It is open year-round. The Depot Days festival takes place in August.

LOCATION: 50 S. East Avenue, Amboy
PHONE: 815-857-4700
WEBSITE: amboydepotmuseum.org
E-MAIL: information@amboydepotmuseum.org

Galesburg Railroad Museum

The Galesburg Railroad Museum displays a Chicago, Burlington & Quincy Hudson steam locomotive, a Railway Post Office car, a 1930 caboose, a Pullman parlor car, and various pieces of rail equipment and artifacts. The museum is open April through September, and Railroad Days take place in June.

LOCATION: 211 S. Seminary Street, Galesburg
PHONE: 309-342-9400
WEBSITE: galesburgrailroadmuseum.org
E-MAIL: jcbcswn@yahoo.com

Great Western Railroad Depot Museum

This depot museum displays artifacts of the Chicago Great Western Railway. The depot serviced the nearby Winston Tunnel, the longest railroad tunnel in Illinois. The museum features a Milwaukee Road caboose, a working telegraph, and operating model railroads. It is open weekends May through October.

LOCATION: 111 E. Myrtle Street, Elizabeth
PHONE: 815-858-2343
WEBSITE: elizabethhistoricalsociety.com

Greenup Depot

The historic Greenup depot is a museum that displays artifacts of railroad and telegraph history. The preserved 1870 Vandalia Line depot also maintains a collection of audio, visual, and written materials related to these subjects. It is open year-round. Just west of the town is a 200-foot reconstructed covered bridge; Abraham Lincoln helped construct the original bridge.

LOCATION: 216 Cumberland Street, Greenup
PHONE: 217-923-9306
WEBSITE: cumberlandcountyhistoricalsociety.org
E-MAIL: historic@rr1.net

Historic Pullman Foundation

The Historic Pullman Foundation operates the Pullman Visitor Center, which features artifacts, photos and a video that informs visitors about George Pullman, the Pullman Company, and Pullman's 1880s model industrial town. You can take a self-guided tour of the historic area or a guided walking tour, which are offered the first Sunday of the month from May through October.

LOCATION: 11141 S. Cottage Grove Avenue, Chicago
PHONE: 773-785-8901
WEBSITE: pullmanil.org
E-MAIL: foundation@pullmanil.org

Kankakee Railroad Museum

Kankakee's restored train depot displays railroad memorabilia and a model train layout of Kankakee in the 1950s. Also on display are a 1947 Pullman coach, a caboose, and a trolley that ran in Kankakee from 1916 until 1932. The museum is open Friday through Sunday.

LOCATION: 197 S. East Avenue, Kankakee
PHONE: 815-929-9320
WEBSITE: kankakeerrmuseum.com

Trolley Car 36

Departing from downtown's Riverview Park, a 45-minute trolley ride transports you along Rockford's historic riverfront, with a 10-minute stopover at Sinnissippi Rose Garden and Eclipse Lagoon. Excursions on the trolley take place during the summer, and riverboat cruises are also available.

LOCATION: 324 N. Madison Street, Rockford
PHONE: 815-987-8894
WEBSITE: rockfordparkdistrict.org
E-MAIL: rpdmail@rockfordparkdistrict.org

Union Depot Railroad Museum

The railroad museum is housed in an 1888 depot building. It contains displays related to the Chicago, Burlington & Quincy, Illinois Central, and Milwaukee Road. You can tour a 1923 Mikado type 2-8-2 steam locomotive, a Milwaukee Road combine car, and a 1911 caboose. You can also ride on the Gandy Dancer Express, a motorized inspection car. It is open Wednesdays, Saturdays, and Sundays.

LOCATION: 783 Main Street, Mendota
PHONE: 815-539-3373
WEBSITE: mendotamuseums.org
E-MAIL: mmhsmuseum@yahoo.com

Wheels O' Time Museum

Started by two guys looking for a place to store some collector cars, the museum now includes planes, trains, tractors, trucks, and smaller artifacts. Displayed outdoors are a Rock Island steam locomotive, Milwaukee Road combine car, Plymouth switch engine, and caboose. The museum is open Wednesday through Sunday May through October.

LOCATION: 1710 W. Woodside Drive, Dunlap
PHONE: 309-243-9020
WEBSITE: wheelsotime.org
E-MAIL: wotmuseum@aol.com

Fox River Trolley Museum

LOCATION: 361 S. LaFox Street, South Elgin
PHONE: 847-697-4676
WEBSITE: foxtrolley.org
E-MAIL: info@foxtrolley.org

Fox River Trolley Museum

Tucked away in the western suburbs of Chicago is the Fox River Trolley Museum, where young and old can take a nostalgic trolley ride along the scenic Fox River.

CHOICES: The museum operates a four-mile round trip over the last remaining section of the original Aurora, Elgin & Fox River electric line that once linked Carpentersville, Elgin, Aurora, and Yorkville. The trolley ride travels from South Elgin to the Jon J. Duerr Forest Preserve just north of St Charles. A variety of trolleys run including Car 20, which could be the oldest operating interurban trolley in the country. It entered service in 1902. Also look for Car 304, which is one of the last cars to operate on the Aurora, Elgin & Fox River electric line back in 1935. The trolleys board at the Castlemuir depot. A caboose and occasionally some of the museum's other cars are on display. And when the carbarn doors are open, you can sneak a peek at the cars inside.

WHEN TO GO: The museum is open on weekends and summer holidays as well as for several special events. It is open on Sundays Mother's Day through early November and on Saturdays beginning the last Saturday in June through Labor Day weekend. Trolleys depart every 30 minutes. On October weekends, families can enjoy the Pumpkin Trolley or Halloween Haunted Ghost Story Train.

GOOD TO KNOW: Picnic tables are available around the depot, and in the Jon J. Duerr Forest Preserve, there are covered shelters with grills that can be reserved.

WORTH DOING: For a unique look at the trolleys in action, hike or bike along the Fox River Bike Trail, which parallels the trolley line and crosses the Fox River on a bridge built on old railway piers and abutments.

DON'T MISS: The Village of South Elgin celebrates Riverfest for four days in August with live entertainment, carnival rides, food, fireworks, a craft show, and a car show. In conjunction, the museum runs Trolleyfest with trolley rides and railcar displays.

GETTING THERE: The museum is 40 miles west of Chicago. From Chicago, take I-90 or Highway 20 west to Elgin. Exit on Highway 31 (State Street which becomes LaFox Street) and go south two miles to the museum.

Illinois Railway Museum

LOCATION: 7000 Olson Road, Union
PHONE: 800-244-7245 or 815-923-4000
WEBSITE: irm.org

Kathi Kube

Just 90 minutes northwest from downtown Chicago, and about half an hour from Union Pacific's Geneva Subdivision, lies the Illinois Railway Museum, which prides itself on running more diesel trains than other comparable museums. The museum also pays homage to its beginnings as an electric railway museum by operating streetcars and interurban cars daily.

CHOICES: As an operating museum, there are many trains to ride, including streetcars, interurbans, and other commuter cars pulled by vintage diesels. You can even ride a trolley or electric bus from one equipment barn to another. When you're not riding trains, explore the 80 acres of land and 400 pieces of equipment, including almost 90 freight cars, plus signals, tools, signage, and other artifacts. Six barns contain rail equipment, and another has bus equipment. Admission includes unlimited rides.

WHEN TO GO: The museum is open daily Memorial Day through Labor Day and weekends in April, September, and October. During July and August, remember that not all the cars and none of the barns are air-conditioned. The museum operates numerous special events including Terror on the Railroad, Happy Holiday Railway, Vintage Transport Extravaganza, and two Day Out with Thomas weekends.

GOOD TO KNOW: IRM's signature piece, the Chicago, Burlington & Quincy *Nebraska Zephyr*, runs on Diesel Days, Museum Showcase Weekend, and several other times.

WORTH DOING: Union is centrally located between Rockford and suburban Chicago. It also offers tourists Donley's Wild West Town with gunslinger shows, pony rides, and gold panning.

DON'T MISS: Diesel Days in July and Museum Showcase Weekend in September are great times to see a lot of equipment running. Typically, 14 vintage locomotives are put to work pulling freight and commuter trains on Diesel Days. On Museum Showcase Weekend, the staff operates less-frequently run equipment.

GETTING THERE: If driving from Chicago, take I-90 to Highway 20, the Marengo exit. Drive northwest about 4.5 miles to Union Road and then take Union Road north.

Monticello Railway Museum

LOCATION: 992 Iron Horse Place, Monticello
PHONE: 877-762-9011 or 217-762-9011
WEBSITE: mrym.org
E-MAIL: info@mrym.org

Jim Wrinn

In the midsection of Illinois, this museum offers one of the best collections of rolling stock and a good train ride to boot. All decked out in their original attire, two streamlined diesel locomotives of the 1950s, one from Canadian National and the other from the Wabash Railroad, are among the most popular locomotives.

CHOICES: Although the museum has several steam engines, it has one of the Midwest's premier diesel locomotive collections. The collection features a Milwaukee Road NW2 and a former Illinois Central RS3 as well as more than 80 pieces of rolling stock. You can board the eight-mile round trip over former Illinois Central and Illinois Terminal trackage from two historic depots, one at the museum and the other in downtown Monticello. At either location, you can make a layover for additional exploration and then catch a later return trip.

WHEN TO GO: The museum is open on weekends and holidays May through October. Special events, including Railroad Days in September, are scheduled throughout the year for train buffs and families alike.

GOOD TO KNOW: After a 15-year restoration process, Southern Railway steam engine No. 401 pulls excursions one weekend each month for the museum. On an average excursion day, No. 401 goes through about 300 gallons of oil and 5,000 gallons of water. The Baldwin engine was built in 1907.

WORTH DOING: Just a short drive away, on Allerton Road, is one of the Seven Wonders of Illinois. The Allerton Park and Retreat Center was once a private mansion. And you can now walk through its 14 miles of wooded trails and gardens, which contain 100 sculptures.

DON'T MISS: For a fee, you can operate a locomotive for 30 minutes under the supervision of a regular member of the train crew during spring and fall throttle times.

GETTING THERE: The museum is located between Champaign and Decatur, just off I-72. At Exit 166, take Market Street to Iron Horse Place and follow the frontage road to the end. The town of Monticello is just a few miles away via Highway 105.

Museum of Science and Industry

LOCATION: 57th Street and Lake Shore Drive, Chicago
PHONE: 773-684-1414
WEBSITE: msichicago.org
E-MAIL: contact@msichicago.org

Angela Pusztai-Pasternak

One of the Windy City's premier attractions, the Museum of Science and Industry provides an enjoyable, interactive, and educational experience for everyone. You can "ride" the famous *Pioneer Zephyr*, take a coal mine adventure, and view a railroad journey from Chicago to Seattle in miniature.

CHOICES: The museum has many railroad-themed exhibits, highlighted by the *Pioneer Zephyr*, which completed a record-setting 13-hour run from Denver to Chicago in 1934. You can tour the locomotive cab, and a tour guide takes you through an observation car, a baggage car, and several other cars. You'll also want to take the coal mine tour, where you can see coal loaded onto a train, and then board a work train.

WHEN TO GO: The museum is open daily with extended hours on select days. Special exhibits, including the coal mine and submarine, cost extra.

GOOD TO KNOW: There's a lot to see, so it's best to plan your day around the coal mine tour and the *Pioneer Zephyr* experience. You can bring your lunch or grab sandwiches at the museum's Brain Food Court. (The museum is not within walking distance of restaurants.) When exiting the food court, watch the Swiss Jolly Ball, where a metal ball rides a locomotive, while navigating around a pinball-type contraption.

WORTH DOING: The museum is home to the only German submarine in the United States, which is a popular tour. Also, take a look at silent film star Colleen Moore's Fairy Castle, a miniature dollhouse made in the 1930s using real gold and jewels.

DON'T MISS: The world's largest model railroad, called The Great Train Story, runs on 1,425 feet of track with 30 trains making their way through Midwest farm fields, around mountains, and over 28 bridges.

GETTING THERE: Take a train. Amtrak offers free rides to kids on the *Hiawatha* on summer weekends. Chicago's Metra Electric District and Indiana's South Shore Line trains stop two blocks from the museum's north entrance (the 57th Street Station).

Silver Creek & Stephenson Railroad

LOCATION: 2954 S. Walnut Road, Freeport
PHONE: 815-232-2306 or 815-235-2198
WEBSITE: thefreeportshow.com

Jim Wrinn

This railroad offers a four-mile ride behind a 1912 geared Heisler steam engine. Trains leave from a reproduction of the original Illinois Central depot in Elroy, and the building houses a large collection of railroad memorabilia.

CHOICES: A Heisler steam locomotive pulls several cabooses and an open-air car through farmlands and across Yellow Creek on a 30-foot-high cement and stone pier bridge. The Silver Creek depot houses the ticket office and railroad displays.

WHEN TO GO: The train ride operates on various weekends and holidays between Memorial Day and the end of October. The Train of Terror operates in October.

GOOD TO KNOW: Volunteers created this railroad on the abandoned right of way of the Chicago, Milwaukee, St. Paul & Pacific Railroad. Because rails and ties were removed prior to purchase, members had to haul rail in from as far away as Minnesota, and ties were salvaged from across Illinois. Members of the Stephenson County Antique Engine Club laid their first tracks in May 1985.

WORTH DOING: While in Freeport, visit the Silver Creek Museum. It contains 28 rooms of historical displays. It is open the same days as the railroad.

DON'T MISS: Give the 36-ton Heisler a close inspection. Unlike most steam locomotives, it is driven with a V-2 arrangement of the cylinders on either side of the boiler; they run a crankshaft that moves a gearbox and wheels. Fewer than 1,200 of these locomotives were built, and only a handful remain in operation today.

GETTING THERE: Freeport is about 20 miles west of Rockford on Highway 20, and the museum is on the corner of Walnut and Lamm Roads.

INDIANA

Carthage, Knightstown & Shirley Railroad

After departing from the old New York Central station, the CKS takes you on a 10-mile, 75-minute round trip from Knightstown to Carthage. When you pull back into the station, you can look over the railroad's assortment of antique equipment. The CKS offers special events, including train robberies, during its season. It operates Fridays, Saturdays, and Sundays May through October.

LOCATION: 112 W. Carey Street, Knightstown
PHONE: 765-345-5561
WEBSITE: cksrail.com
E-MAIL: cksrrinc@netzero.net

Depot Railroad Museum

A replica of Salem's former Monon depot, this depot was built by high school students. It features a Monon caboose, various artifacts, and a model railroad. The museum is open Tuesdays through Saturdays April through December and Saturdays only the rest of the year. The depot is part of the John Hay Center museum complex, which also contains a pioneer village and the Stevens Memorial Museum.

LOCATION: 206 S. College Avenue, Salem
PHONE: 812-883-1884
WEBSITE: salemdepot.com
E-MAIL: info@salemdepot.com

Linden Depot Museum

The Linden Depot Museum contains memorabilia from the two railroads it served, the Nickel Plate Road and the Monon Railroad. It displays a caboose from the NKP, several railcars, and other pieces of equipment. Built in 1907, it is listed on the National Register of Historic Places. It is open April through October.

LOCATION: 520 N. Main Street, Linden
PHONE: 765-339-7245
WEBSITE: lindendepot.com
E-MAIL: lindendepotmuseum@gmail.com

Madison Railroad Station

This restored 1895 Pennsylvania Railroad station is known for its unique octagon waiting room with stained glass windows. Exhibits describe the railroad station and Madison's railroad incline. You can visit an agent's office, try the functional telegraph key, and walk through a restored, wooden caboose.

LOCATION: 615 W. First Street, Madison
PHONE: 812-265-2335
WEBSITE: jchshc.net
E-MAIL: form on website

Monon Connection Museum

The museum features a completely furnished, full-size replica of an Illinois Central depot and outdoor displays. Exhibits include a large collection of dining car china, hundreds of hand-held lanterns, and restored brass steam locomotive bells and whistles. It is open Tuesday through Sunday. The Whistle Stop restaurant adjoins the museum.

LOCATION: 10012 N. Highway 421, Monon
PHONE: 219-253-4101
WEBSITE: mononconnection.com
E-MAIL: info@mononconnection.com

National New York Central Railroad Museum

You begin your journey through the history of the New York Central by entering through a 1915 passenger coach. In the main gallery, which is a 100-year-old freight house, hands-on exhibits let you construct track and operate a steam locomotive. Outside, the museum's collection of locomotives and rolling stock includes an NYC Mohawk 4-8-2 and a Pennsylvania Railroad GG1.

LOCATION: 721 S. Main Street, Elkhart
PHONE: 574-294-3001
WEBSITE: elkhartindiana.org
E-MAIL: info@nycrrmuseum.org

Princeton Depot Museum

The Princeton Depot Museum features artifacts of the railroads that served the area and displays a caboose. It is located in the restored Chicago & Eastern Illinois passenger depot, which was built in 1875. The museum shares the depot with the Gibson County Visitors Bureau and is open Monday through Friday.

LOCATION: 702 W. Broadway Street, Princeton
PHONE: 812-385-0999
WEBSITE: gibsoncountyin.org
E-MAIL: info@gibsoncountyin.org

Spirit of Jasper

Owned by the city, the *Spirit of Jasper* operates an excursion to French Lick as well as a dinner train. The excursion allows you to explore the Indiana Railway Museum, French Lick Springs Resort & Casino, and the West Baden Springs Hotel. Aboard the dinner train, you can partake in a meal provided by a local German restaurant. Fall foliage, Strassenfest, and other special excursions also run.

LOCATION: 201 Mill Street, Jasper
PHONE: 812-482-5959 or 812-482-9229
WEBSITE: spiritofjasper.com
E-MAIL: info@spiritofjasper.com

Wabash Valley Railroaders Museum

The museum features two interlocking towers with operating machines, a depot, a PRR caboose, and a viewing platform adjacent to CSXT main lines. Haley Tower was one of the last manned interlocking towers in the Midwest, and the 1910 Spring Hill Tower was the last lever interlocking machine on the Canadian Pacific. It is open weekends May through October.

LOCATION: 1316 Plum Street, Terre Haute
PHONE: 812-238-9958
WEBSITE: wvrrm.org

Fort Wayne Railroad Historical Society

LOCATION: 15808 Edgerton Road, New Haven
PHONE: 260-493-0765
WEBSITE: fortwaynerailroad.org
E-MAIL: contact@fwrhs.org

Dave Crosby

The Fort Wayne Railroad Historical Society operates one of the nation's largest coal-burning steam locomotives, Nickel Plate Road 2-8-4 No. 765, which runs on various tourist railways.

CHOICES: On weekends, you can tour the shop and check out the 400-ton No. 765, when it is not on tour, and other pieces of historic rail equipment. Make sure to talk with the volunteers who restore everything from baggage carts to locomotives. Excursions on Nickel Plate Road No. 765 take place on tourist railroads throughout the East and Midwest.

WHEN TO GO: During the society's annual open house, you can view No. 765 and ride aboard a vintage caboose, and Santa trains run in December.

GOOD TO KNOW: No. 765, a 1944 Berkshire type, is one of the most modern and powerful steam locomotives still capable of operation.

WORTH DOING: In September, take in the Johnny Appleseed Festival in honor of the folk hero, who is buried in Fort Wayne. It features, music, crafts, food, and apples, of course.

DON'T MISS: Don't miss No. 765. You can track where the locomotive is when it is in motion. Check the society's website for details.

GETTING THERE: The restoration shop is just east of Fort Wayne in the village of New Haven. From Fort Wayne, take I-469 to Exit 21. Turn right on Harper Road, then right on Ryan Road, and left on Edgerton Road.

Hesston Steam Museum

LOCATION: 1201 E. County Road 1000 North, La Porte
PHONE: 219-778-2783 or 219-872-5055
WEBSITE: hesston.org
E-MAIL: form on website

Jeff Terry

This museum runs steam trains of two narrow gauges, two-foot and three-foot, in a parklike setting. It also offers miniature live steam operations and other steam-powered attractions including a sawmill and a steam crane.

CHOICES: Ride a steam locomotive, in your choice of gauges, through the museum's 155-acre site. Each train travels over a different route. Wander through a unique collection of steam equipment. Be sure to look for an 1889 Scottish-built locomotive and a Czech 0-4-0 built in 1940. On special days, watch the 92-ton, steam-powered log crane feed logs to the steam-powered lumber mill.

WHEN TO GO: Trains run weekends and holidays Memorial Day through Labor Day and then on several Sundays in October, when you can enjoy apple cider made from an antique press. On Memorial Day weekend and over the July 4th holiday, additional steam equipment runs, the sawmill operates, and other activities take place. In fall, ride the ghost train if you dare, and in December, try the Candy Cane Express. Several other special days are planned during the season.

GOOD TO KNOW: Keep an eye out for a Kiddieland train ride. The museum operates two of the locomotives from the now-closed suburban Chicago amusement park. The locomotives are coal-powered steam engines.

WORTH DOING: You can visit the La Porte County Historical Society Museum, which contains 80,000 artifacts. Among them are more than 800 antique firearms and weapons. If you visit in July, you can attend the La Porte County Fair, which features Pioneerland and its collection of historic buildings that includes a log home, blacksmith shop, and barns.

DON'T MISS: The annual Hesston Steam & Power Show takes place over Labor Day weekend. Beside train rides, the event features the operation of antique farm equipment, tractors, and other machinery.

GETTING THERE: The museum is in northern Indiana near the Michigan border and is about a 90-minute drive from Chicago. It is easily accessible from either I-94 (Exit 1) or the Indiana toll road (Exit 49) on County Road 1000.

Hoosier Valley Railroad Museum

LOCATION: 507 Mulberry Street, North Judson
PHONE: 574-896-3950
WEBSITE: hoosiervalley.org
E-MAIL: questions@hoosiervalley.org

Don Nickel

North Judson hosted the Chesapeake & Ohio, Erie, Pennsylvania, and New York Central Railroads. The Hoosier Valley Railroad Museum recaptures the flavor of bygone eras with equipment and displays from the railroads that served not only North Judson but also northwestern Indiana. Excursions also run along portions of former C&O and Erie track.

CHOICES: The HVRM has expanded its operating schedule with the addition of newly restored equipment and new events. Passengers now have the opportunity to ride trains pulled by a rare GE 95-ton switcher in addition to an Erie Lackawanna S1. Seating for the scenic excursions is available aboard a restored Long Island coach, open-air cars, and a variety of cabooses. Excursions travel to either English Lake or La Crosse.

WHEN TO GO: The museum is open on Saturdays year-round. Regular excursions or special trains run Saturdays from May through October. A few additional special events take place in April and December. The numerous special train rides include Easter trains, picnic trains, fall harvest trains, Santa trains, and the Mint Festival Flyer, which operates in June. The museum operates on Central Standard Time.

GOOD TO KNOW: At the museum, you can view displays and photos in a replica C&O depot and view more than 30 pieces of rolling stock including a massive 2-8-4 steam locomotive.

WORTH DOING: The North Judson Erie Trail, which starts at the HVRM, is a nine-mile trail built along the former Erie Railroad right-of-way for walking or biking.

DON'T MISS: Until restoration work on Grasseli Tower is completed, and tours are available, you can take a peek at this historic interlocking tower that was built for the Indiana Harbor Belt in East Chicago.

GETTING THERE: North Judson is located on Highways 10 and 39 in northern Indiana. Signs on Highway 10 direct you to the museum site, or you can just follow the tracks to the museum grounds.

Indiana Railway Museum

LOCATION: 1 Monon Street, French Lick
PHONE: 800-748-7246 or 812-936-2405
WEBSITE: frenchlickscenicrailway.org
E-MAIL: infoirm@psci.net

Jim Wrinn

For many years, the Southern Railway and the Monon Railroad brought scores of vacationers to the mineral spring baths in the southern Indiana hill country. Today, the museum offers a 20-mile round trip that leaves from the historic 1907 depot that served both railroads and travels through beautiful forested country and the 2,200-foot Burton tunnel.

CHOICES: Located in a historic passenger depot, the museum operates the French Lick Scenic Railway. Two-hour excursions through the Hoosier National Forest travel along lakes and limestone cuts. The railway has added three new climate-controlled bi-level gallery cars (former Chicago & North Western/Metra) to its trains. The museum features an impressive collection of equipment that includes steam and diesel locomotives and more than 65 passenger and freight cars.

WHEN TO GO: The museum is open year-round. Trains begin operating in March with special trains running throughout the year including train robberies and the popular *Polar Express* in November and December. Trips in October feature beautiful fall colors of the scenic Hoosier National Forest.

GOOD TO KNOW: French Lick is on Eastern Standard Time, which is good to remember when visiting from the Central time zone. You are still able to soak in the sulfer-rich spring water with 25-minute baths at the spas of the French Lick Springs Hotel and the West Baden Springs Hotel.

WORTH DOING: Southern Indiana is home to a variety of caves ready for exploring, such as Squire Boone Caverns, Wyandotte Caves, and Marengo Cave.

DON'T MISS: Be sure to check out the former Louisville, New Albany & Corydon Railroad boxcar No. 14023 repainted as a Pluto water car that shipped Pluto mineral water that was bottled by the French Lick Springs Hotel.

GETTING THERE: French Lick is in southern Indiana, easily accessible from Bloomington (60 miles), Columbus (90 miles), and Indianapolis (110 miles). From Indianapolis or Bloomington, take Highway 37 to Highway 56. Take Highway 56 west to French Lick and the museum. From Columbus, take I-65 to Highway 56.

Indiana Transportation Museum

LOCATION: Forest Park Drive, Noblesville
PHONE: 317-773-6000 or 317-776-7887
WEBSITE: itm.org
E-MAIL: info@itm.org

Don Nickel

Located in Forest Park in Noblesville, the Indiana Transportation Museum offers visitors an excellent assortment of historic operating equipment, static displays, and various train rides.

CHOICES: Regular excursions on Saturdays and Sundays feature either vintage 1930s stainless steel passenger consist or a caboose train, depending on the length of the trip. The caboose trains are used on shorter rides. Other excursions include dinner trains, special events trains, and festival trains. Dinner trains take passengers to Tipton for fine dining or pizza options. Festival trains take you to the Tipton County Pork Festival, Arcadia May Festival, French Flea Market, and other fun fests. The month of August brings the Indiana State Fair, and ITM operates the FairTrain, which delivers passengers from Fishers to the fairgrounds.

WHEN TO GO: Indiana Transportation Museum's operating season begins in May, continues through October, and then resumes with holiday trains in December. During the operating season, the museum grounds are open on Saturday and Sunday except during FairTrain operation.

GOOD TO KNOW: Tickets purchased for any excursion provide entry to the museum grounds, allowing riders to enjoy the displays located at Noblesville.

WORTH DOING: Make an entire day of your trip to the museum. Forest Park offers a wide assortment of opportunities for family fun. These include an aquatic center, carousel, miniature golf, and a playground area. Picnic areas are also available.

DON'T MISS: By making advance arrangements, you can tour several exhibits with a museum docent including an 1898 Florida East Coast business car and Nickel Plate Road No. 1, a 1929 Pullman heavyweight business car.

GETTING THERE: The museum is located in Forest Park, which is just north of Highway 32 on Highway 19 in Noblesville. Just 20 miles north of Indianapolis, the museum is easily accessed from I-69 and Highway 31.

Whitewater Valley Railroad

LOCATION: 455 Market Street, Connersville
PHONE: 765-825-2054
WEBSITE: whitewatervalleyrr.org
E-MAIL: form on website

Whitewater Valley Railroad

This surprising 19-mile line travels from Connersville to Metamora with much of the trip near the Whitewater Canal. The scenic route features excellent views of area forests and farms.

CHOICES: The railroad offers standard, open-window coaches as well as caboose rides on its 32-mile, five-hour round trip. A two-hour layover gives you a chance to tour Metamora, a restored canal town.

WHEN TO GO: Regular excursion trains operate on Saturdays and Sundays from May through October. During the year, watch for special event trains, such as the one to Metamora Canal Days, the Wild West Train, a dinner train, and fall foliage trains. Other events are themed around holidays and children's activities.

GOOD TO KNOW: Look for New York Central transfer caboose No. 18278 and try to ride aboard this unique railcar.

WORTH DOING: Metamora is a popular getaway spot with plenty of art galleries, shops, and restaurants. Take time to explore the city's historic buildings. You can also watch its water-powered grist mill in action and take a boat ride along the canal. Enjoy Canal Days in October with a train ride, shopping, food, and arts and crafts.

DON'T MISS: Inspect the operating diesel built by the Lima Locomotive Works of Lima, Ohio. Believed to be the last of its kind in operation today, locomotive No. 25 was one of only 174 diesels built by this company, one of the most famous steam locomotive manufacturers of all time. The museum also owns three others from this builder.

GETTING THERE: Connersville is about 65 miles southeast of Indianapolis and is accessible from all directions. If coming from the north, take Highway 1 off I-70 into Connersville. The depot is on your left between Fourth and Fifth Streets.

IOWA

Marquette Depot Museum

Housed in a renovated Milwaukee Road depot, the museum contains Milwaukee Road exhibits and general railroad artifacts. A restored caboose is on display. The museum is open daily May through October, and the depot also contains a travel information center.

LOCATION: 216 Edgar Street, Marquette
PHONE: 563-873-1200
WEBSITE: mcgreg-marq.org
E-MAIL: form on website

Oelwein Railway Museum

This museum consists of a former Railway Express Agency building, Chicago Great Western yard office, and tower, with a display of locomotives, railcars, and artifacts. Climb the yard tower for a great view of the area. During Oelwein's annual Heritage Days weekend, you can ride on one of the museum's handcars.

LOCATION: 26 Second Avenue SW, Oelwein
PHONE: 319-283-1939
WEBSITE: cgwoelwein.com
E-MAIL: cgwo@mchsi.com

RailsWest Railroad Museum

This former Chicago, Rock Island & Pacific passenger depot was built in 1899. Open year-round, the museum displays a Chicago, Burlington & Quincy 4-6-0 locomotive, Union Pacific 4-8-4 (Northern) locomotive, Plymouth locomotive, and Rock Island caboose. While in Council Bluffs, be sure to visit the one-of-a-kind Squirrel Cage Jail with its three floors of revolving cells.

LOCATION: 16th Avenue and S. Main Street, Council Bluffs
PHONE: 712-323-5182
WEBSITE: thehistoricalsociety.org
E-MAIL: info@thehistoricalsociety.org

Boone & Scenic Valley Railroad

LOCATION: 225 10th Street, Boone
PHONE: 800-626-0319 or 515-432-4249
WEBSITE: scenic-valleyrr.com
E-MAIL: info@bsvrr.com

Jeff Terry

Iowa isn't known for rolling terrain, but this fascinating railroad provides a scenic ride with interesting landscape through the Des Moines River Valley. The railroad runs across two impressive bridges, with the 156-foot-tall Bass Point Creek High Bridge being the highlight of a 15-mile round trip. The railroad's dinner, dessert, and picnic trains run on a slightly longer route.

CHOICES: The railroad is one of the few in the country that offers steam-, diesel-, and electric-powered trains. You can ride a 1920s excursion in coach class or opt for the *Valley View* car, an open-air car that was formerly a C&NW transfer caboose. There is also limited seating in the train's caboose. Hop the restored 1915 Charles City & Western electric trolley for an interurban run through downtown Boone. Picnic trains travel the same route as the dinner or dessert trains, you just have to supply the lunch.

WHEN TO GO: Between Memorial Day and the end of October, excursion trains run daily, with steam locomotives on Saturdays. Dinner trains are scheduled on Fridays and Saturdays. Dessert trains run on Saturdays and picnic trains on Sundays. Trolleys operate on weekends. The museum is open Monday through Saturday.

GOOD TO KNOW: The James H. Andrew Railroad Museum & History Center is a new 9,000-square-foot facility that includes displays and memorabilia about railroading in Iowa.

WORTH DOING: The city of Boone celebrates its railroad heritage during Pufferbilly Days, an annual September event with train rides, a model train display, a parade, and a spike-driving contest.

DON'T MISS: On the dinner, dessert, and picnic trains, step outside on the *City of San Francisco*'s rear observation deck for a unique experience.

GETTING THERE: The railroad is in central Iowa, an hour's drive northwest of Des Moines. Take I-35 to Ames and travel west on Highway 30 to Boone. Go north on Story Street through the business district to 10th Street and then go west six blocks to the depot.

Midwest Central Railroad

LOCATION: 405 E. Threshers Road, Mount Pleasant
PHONE: 319-385-2912
WEBSITE: oldthreshers.org or mcrr.org
E-MAIL: info@oldthreshers.org

Jeff Terry

The Midwest Central Railroad was established when volunteers built a 1.25-mile loop of track around the Midwest Old Threshers Reunion site and acquired several steam locomotives and cars. Later, to bring visitors and exhibitors into the grounds, a counter-clockwise trolley loop line was built, dubbed the Midwest Electric Railway.

CHOICES: Both the railroad and the electric railway are in full operation during the Old Threshers Reunion. During the reunion, the trains haul approximately 35,000 to 40,000 passengers. In 2012, the railroad began operating Baldwin 2-6-2 locomotive No. 12, which was built for Hawaii's Kahului Railroad in 1929.

WHEN TO GO: The Midwest Old Threshers Reunion begins the Thursday before Labor Day and ends on Labor Day. In addition, both the railway and the electric line operate trips over haunted rails each October, and the railroad runs a train for the 4th of July as well as a North Pole Express.

GOOD TO KNOW: The Old Threshers Reunion is the largest of its kind in the United States. Farmers and tractor enthusiasts gather for fun and demonstrations of steam tractors, early gas tractors, and other period farm implements. There are tractor pulls, a steam-powered merry-go-round, and much more. It's like an old-fashioned state fair, but its emphasis is on living agricultural history.

WORTH DOING: If you're a camper, stay at the Old Threshers campground and take the trolley into the grounds and then ride the train. You can take in the whole show without the hassle of parking and enjoy the sights and sounds of steam as you camp.

DON'T MISS: On the grounds, two museums operate during the year. Open year-round, the Heritage Museum focuses on agriculture, and in summer, you can visit the Theatre Museum, which preserves artifacts from early repertoire theatre, and even take in a live performance.

GETTING THERE: Probably the best way to visit Mount Pleasant is by driving. Located in southeastern Iowa, Mount Pleasant is south of Iowa City on Highway 218. The city is also served daily by Amtrak trains 5 and 6, the *California Zephyr*.

Union Pacific Railroad Museum

LOCATION: 200 Pearl Street, Council Bluffs
PHONE: 712-329-8307
WEBSITE: uprrmuseum.org
E-MAIL: acape@up.com

Union Pacific Railroad

Few railroads have gone to the great lengths of the Union Pacific to preserve and document their past. The Union Pacific Railroad Museum houses one of the oldest corporation collections of any kind in the country. Visitors will not find lines of steam locomotives, diesels, or rolling stock. Rather, they will be inundated with a tasteful display of artifacts, photographs, and documents that trace the development of the UP and the role it played in American West.

CHOICES: The museum can be taken in whole or digested by specific eras depending on your interests. The Union Pacific's history is a history of the American West. The collection dates from the mid-1800s and features original manuscripts such as reports from survey teams searching for the best route for laying track. Surveying equipment, early rail equipment, and nonrail artifacts from outlaws and Native Americans fill the building.

WHEN TO GO: With the exception of a raging snowstorm, even winter is a good time to visit the museum. It is open Tuesdays through Saturdays. Exhibits are changed and special events occur periodically during the year.

GOOD TO KNOW: One of the museum's permanent exhibits is devoted to passenger service. It features cutaway coach, lounge, and dining cars as well as multimedia exhibits and thousands of artifacts.

WORTH DOING: Take time to tour both Council Bluffs and Omaha. Both are culturally rich cities with much to offer visitors. Council Bluffs has several casinos and is Iowa's leading gaming spot. The Henry Doorly Zoo in Omaha is a world-class zoo that appeals to adults as well as children.

DON'T MISS: The museum has a combination of static and interactive displays. The working locomotive simulator is educational as well as a lot of fun.

GETTING THERE: Omaha is an important regional airline hub with numerous flights from all directions daily, and Amtrak serves Omaha. Located on the east side of Council Bluffs, the museum is easily accessible for motorists from I-80 or I-29.

KANSAS

Atchison Rail Museum

The Atchison Rail Museum features an outdoor collection of railcars. On summer weekend, the cars are open for viewing and a miniature railroad operates. It is adjacent to a restored 1880 Santa Fe depot that now houses the county's historical society museum. In summer, trolleys leave from the depot on 45-minute, narrated historical tours.

LOCATION: 200 S. 10th Street, Atchison
PHONE: 913-367-2427
WEBSITE: atchisonkansas.net

Great Overland Station

The elegant and ornate former Union Pacific station is the setting for a museum, which features exhibits on the Union Pacific, Santa Fe, Kansas rail history, and Harvey Houses. It was designed by Gilbert Stanley Underwood, who also designed Omaha's Art Deco station. A rail park with a Santa Fe station and collection of railcars is being completed.

LOCATION: 701 N. Kansas Avenue, Topeka
PHONE: 785-232-5533
WEBSITE: greatoverlandstation.com
E-MAIL: contactus@greatoverlandstation.com

Great Plains Transportation Museum

The museum features an outdoor display of locomotives, cabooses, and cars, including Santa Fe steam locomotive No. 3768 and Santa Fe FP45 diesel No. 93. Indoor exhibits feature railroad signs, lanterns, tools, and other artifacts. It is open year-round on Saturdays and also on Sundays from April to October. On the museum's website, you can view some historical railroad documents.

LOCATION: 700 E. Douglas Avenue, Wichita
PHONE: 316-263-0944
WEBSITE: gptm.us
E-MAIL: info@gptm.us

Heart of the Heartlands

The museum complex includes a building of rail exhibits, two Missouri Pacific depots, and a collection of locomotives and railcars. The museum offers several short train excursions and motor car rides. The buildings are open the first and third weekends June through August, while the outdoor displays are available for viewing any time.

LOCATION: 6769 NW 20th Street, Scammon
PHONE: 620-396-8594
E-MAIL: heartlands@cox.net

Kansas Belle Dinner Train

The former Fremont Dinner Train has relocated to Baldwin City. It operates over the Midland Railway's route from Baldwin City to Ottawa. The dinner train is also pulled by Midland Railway's motive power. The dinner train has been in operation since 1988.

LOCATION: 1515 High Street, Baldwin City
PHONE: 800-942-7245
WEBSITE: dinnertrain.net
E-MAIL: office@dinnertrain.net

Abilene & Smoky Valley Railroad

LOCATION: 200 SE Fifth Street, Abilene
PHONE: 888-426-6687 or 785-263-1077
WEBSITE: asvrr.org
E-MAIL: asvrail@gmail.com

Patrick Hiatte

A 90-minute, 10-mile round trip takes you through the Smoky Hill River Valley from historic Abilene to Enterprise. Along the way, you'll cross the Smoky Hill River on an early steel truss bridge, see stone houses and barns built by German settlers, and enjoy America's agricultural heartland.

CHOICES: Ride behind a Santa Fe Pacific or an Alco S1. A restored Katy railroad coach, a pair of open-air (but shaded) gondola cars, and an ex-Union Pacific caboose are the regular consist. An extra fare will get you on board the caboose or in the cab of the steam or diesel locomotive. On some Saturdays, you can extend your trip on the Silver Flyer railbus, which meets the train in Enterprise and runs on rail to the German/Swedish community of Woodbine, where lunch is included.

WHEN TO GO: Trains run Wednesday through Sunday from June through August and on weekends in May, September, and October. The steam engine typically operates on Memorial Day, Independence Day, and Labor Day weekends and for the Central Kansas Fair the first weekend in August. Dinner trains catered by local restaurants run on select Saturday evenings.

GOOD TO KNOW: The Dwight D. Eisenhower Presidential Library and Museum site, including Ike's boyhood home, is across the tracks from the ASV depot.

WORTH DOING: Enjoy a cold bottle of sarsaparilla with a dinner of chicken fried in a cast-iron skillet in Old Abilene Town, which is just south of the depot. It features replica buildings, gunfights, and dancing girls. Other nearby attractions include a 100-year-old operating carousel and the Greyhound Hall of Fame (dogs not buses).

DON'T MISS: In addition to the ASV's restored Rock Island depot, the Santa Fe (now BNSF) combination depot and the Union Pacific depot and freight house are still standing. The UP depot is open to the public and houses the Abilene Visitor Center, where you can enjoy a sugar cookie made from Mamie Eisenhower's recipe.

GETTING THERE: Abilene is on I-70 about 150 miles west of Kansas City and about 90 miles north of Wichita. The ASV depot is about two miles south of I-70 off Highway 15 (Buckeye Avenue), just south of the Eisenhower complex.

Midland Railway

LOCATION: 1515 W. High Street, Baldwin City
PHONE: 913-721-1211 or 785-594-6982 (depot)
WEBSITE: midland-ry.org
E-MAIL: form on website

Ralcon Wagner

The Midland Railway offers 20-mile round trips in the pleasant Kansas countryside between Baldwin City and Ottawa. The Midland has a roster of first-generation diesels including an Alco RS3 in its original New York Central livery and an EMD NW2 in Midland Railway green. It uses several passenger coaches, cabooses, and a transfer caboose on its excursions.

CHOICES: Regular service includes one-hour excursions from Baldwin City to Norwood that cross two 200-foot trestles and two-hour trips to the end of the line at Ottawa Junction, where the line meets BNSF's Transcon. Midland also offers Thomas the Tank Engine, Halloween, Christmas, the Ice Cream Express, and other specials.

WHEN TO GO: The Midland operates primarily on weekends from June to October, with Thursday trains added for summer. The Midland also participates in various community festivals including the Maple Leaf Festival, which takes place the third weekend in October.

GOOD TO KNOW: The Kansas Belle Dinner Train operates over the Midland Railway's route from Baldwin City to Ottawa.

WORTH DOING: Journey south to Ottawa and visit the Old Depot Museum, housed in a restored 1888 Santa Fe depot or stroll down the Prairie Spirit Trail (the trailhead is behind the Old Depot Museum), a converted rail trail.

DON'T MISS: Look through the Midland's 1906 Baldwin City depot, which is on the National Register of Historic Places.

GETTING THERE: The closest Amtrak stops are in Lawrence and Kansas City, Mo., and the closest major airport is in Kansas City. Baldwin City is 45 miles southwest of Kansas City on Highway 56. The Midland depot is on High Street, just west of the town square.

Kansas

109

KENTUCKY

Historic Railpark & Train Museum

Bowling Green's restored Louisville & Nashville depot contains a rail museum featuring two floors of interactive exhibits. Visitors can explore a passenger train with a post office car, diner, sleeper, business car, and E8 locomotive. New exhibits include a 1945 Army hospital car and a "Jim Crow" passenger car. The site is open year-round, and its Festival of Trains takes place the first weekend in December.

LOCATION: 401 Kentucky Street, Bowling Green
PHONE: 270-745-7317
WEBSITE: historicrailpark.com
E-MAIL: info@historicrailpark.com

Paducah Railroad Museum

Operated by the Paducah Chapter of the National Railway Historical Society, the museum displays equipment and memorabilia from railroads including the three that served Paducah. It features replicas of a waiting room and freight office as well as section cars, tools, and an operating signaling system. A steam engine, caboose, and baggage car are displayed a block away.

LOCATION: 200 Washington Street, Paducah
PHONE: 270-908-6451
WEBSITE: paducahrr.org

Railway Museum of Greater Cincinnati

The museum collects, restores, and displays equipment that belonged to the seven railroads that served Cincinnati. The outdoor yard contains more than 70 cars and locomotives. It includes a large number of Pullman cars, several switchers, and Pennsylvania Railroad diesel locomotives. It is open Saturdays year-round.

LOCATION: 315 W. Southern Avenue, Covington
WEBSITE: cincirailmuseum.org
E-MAIL: questions@cincirailmuseum.org

Big South Fork Scenic Railway

LOCATION: 100 Henderson Street, Stearns
PHONE: 800-462-5664 or 606-376-5330
WEBSITE: bsfsry.com
E-MAIL: info@bsfsry.com

Big South Fork Scenic Railway

In the 20th century, short lines and branches brought forth coal for use nationwide, and one of the primary locations was Stearns, home of the Kentucky & Tennessee short line. The coal is gone now, but the K&T has been reborn as a scenic railroad.

CHOICES: The railway offers three-hour trips through the Daniel Boone National Forest and Big South Fork National River and Recreation Area on the former Kentucky & Tennessee Railway. The train follows mountain streams, passes through a tunnel, and crosses a bridge as it descends 600 feet to the floor of the river valley. The ride includes a layover at the restored mining camp of Blue Heron.

WHEN TO GO: The railroad runs regular excursions on a varied schedule from April through October. During November, excursions run to the Big South Fork gorge. Several special events take place during the season, and Halloween and Christmas trains also run. Spring is especially beautiful in this part of the Appalachians because of all the blooming plants that inhabit the mountains.

GOOD TO KNOW: The bridge over Roaring Paunch Creek is unique. It was constructed in 1937 from a used railroad bridge. The bridge girders needed to be offset because the line crossed the creek at an angle. The bridge's girders were offset in the opposite direction, so it was placed upside down, and the ties and track then added.

WORTH DOING: The McCreary County Museum, which is housed in the Stearns Coal and Lumber Company headquarters that was built in 1907, exhibits many facets of Appalachian life including the coal and lumber industries.

DON'T MISS: Take the walking tour of the Blue Heron Mine at the end of the run. Built in 1937, this mine and coal tipple operated until abandoned in 1962. The mine was restored with ghost structures (representations of where the actual buildings stood) and oral history exhibits by the National Park Service as part of the Big South Fork River and Recreation Area. You can also camp, hike, fish, and raft the river.

GETTING THERE: Stearns is 70 miles from Knoxville, Tenn., and 120 miles from Lexington. From Knoxville, take I-75 north to Exit 141. Take Route 63 west to the junction with Route 27. Take Route 27 north to Stearns. Turn left on Route 92 and travel west one mile to the depot.

Bluegrass Scenic Railroad

LOCATION: 175 Beasley Road, Versailles
PHONE: 800-755-2476 or 859-873-2476
WEBSITE: bgrm.org
E-MAIL: form on website

Bluegrass Scenic Railroad

The railroad offers 90-minute, 11-mile round-trip excursions over former Southern Railroad track through the heart of Kentucky's Bluegrass region.

CHOICES: The railroad's museum operates a diesel-powered train made up of vintage coaches from the 1920s and 1930s. A new passenger car offers premium service with plush reclining seats and air-conditioning (or heat). Many trips have a special theme, which include Civil War train robberies, haunted trains, and Santa specials. Locomotive cab rides are also available. You can view outdoor displays of railcars, equipment, and a rare watchman's shanty. Inside, museum exhibits showcase artifacts from Kentucky's railroad history.

WHEN TO GO: The grounds of the museum are open every day, so you can inspect or photograph equipment when you like. The indoor displays are open on Saturdays and Sundays from mid-May through October, and excursions also operate on those Saturdays and Sundays.

GOOD TO KNOW: While in Bluegrass Country, you can tour its noted horse farms and bourbon distilleries.

WORTH DOING: Minutes away from the museum are several other local attractions that include the Aviation Museum of Kentucky and the Wildside Winery and Vineyard. If you like smaller trains, visit the Nostalgia Station Toy Museum in downtown Versailles. It is housed in a restored 100-year-old Louisville & Nashville Railroad depot and contains numerous antique toy trains.

DON'T MISS: The museum has a large collection of locomotives and rolling stock in various stages of restoration. Interesting cars include U.S. Army boxcars, a Seaboard safety training car, and a Louisville & Nashville bay window caboose.

GETTING THERE: From Versailles, proceed south and west on Highway 62 for approximately 1.5 miles. Turn right onto Beasley Road into Woodford County Park. The museum is on the left after you cross the tracks.

Kentucky Railway Museum

LOCATION: 136 S. Main Street, New Haven
PHONE: 800-272-0152 or 502-549-5470
WEBSITE: kyrail.org
E-MAIL: info@kyrail.org

Kentucky Railway Museum

Housed in a replica of the original New Haven station, the Kentucky Railway Museum has more than 50,000 items in its collection and more than 120 locomotives and pieces of rolling stock. The museum also operates excursions on 17 miles of former Louisville & Nashville track.

CHOICES: The museum's excursion trains take you on a 22-mile, 90-minute round trip through the scenic and historic Rolling Fork River Valley between New Haven and Boston. The museum operates a steam locomotive, ex-L&N 4-6-2 No. 152, on various steam weekends during the year—but the locomotive is down indefinitely for maintenance. Diesel operating power includes ex-Monon BL2 No. 32 and ex-AT&SF CF7 No. 2546. You can ride in open-air or air-conditioned coaches.

WHEN TO GO: The museum is open year-round, and excursions take place April through December. Trains run on weekends throughout the season with several Tuesday and Friday runs added during summer. Spring and fall scenery is nice, with temperatures in the 70s and low 80s.

GOOD TO KNOW: Steam engine No. 152 was built in 1905, is listed on the National Register of Historic Places, and was designated the official steam locomotive of the Commonwealth of Kentucky.

WORTH DOING: Abraham Lincoln was born nearby, and historical sites to visit include his birthplace, boyhood home, and the Lincoln Museum. Mammoth Cave National Park, Fort Knox, the Patton Museum of Cavalry and Armor, and My Old Kentucky Home State Park are also close by.

DON'T MISS: The museum offers special excursions that include dinner trains, murder mystery trains, locomotive cab rides, train holdups, Santa trains, and days out with Thomas the Tank Engine.

GETTING THERE: The museum is about 45 miles from Louisville and 65 miles from Lexington. If driving from Louisville, take I-65 south to Exit 105, Route 61 to Boston, and then Route 52 to New Haven. From Lexington, take Highway 60 west to the Martha Layne Collins Parkway. Take the parkway to Exit 21 and then Route 31E to New Haven.

My Old Kentucky Dinner Train

LOCATION: 602 N. Third Street, Bardstown
PHONE: 866-801-3463 or 502-348-7500
WEBSITE: kydinnertrain.com
E-MAIL: info@kydinnertrain.com

R. J. Corman

My Old Kentucky Dinner Train operates in 1940s dining cars on 16 miles of former Louisville & Nashville track between Bardstown and Limestone Springs. The passenger waiting room is located in Bardstown's former limestone freight house, which dates from 1860 and is on the National Register of Historic Places.

CHOICES: The train offers both lunch and dinner trips, as well as murder mystery, Halloween, North Pole, and other special event trains. It offers 2.5-hour lunch excursions on Saturdays. Other lunch and dinner excursions run Tuesday through Sunday on a varied schedule. Trains are pulled by two ex-Southern FP7s. The Budd-built lightweight cars are of AT&SF, C&O, and PRR ancestry, including the former C&O No. 1921 that operated on President Dwight Eisenhower's funeral train. Two restored depots, Deatsville and Limestone Springs, can be seen on the line.

WHEN TO GO: The train operates year-round, and the scenery is especially nice in spring and fall, with temperatures in the 70s and low 80s. Tobacco is grown from June through August and can be viewed along the route.

GOOD TO KNOW: Founded in 1780, Bardstown is Kentucky's second-oldest city and features a mix of old and new inns, restaurants, and shops. Several local distilleries give tours, and the Kentucky Railway Museum is 15 minutes away.

WORTH DOING: The area is rich in history and includes Abraham Lincoln's birthplace and his boyhood home. The Civil War Museum at Old Bardstown Village is dedicated to the war's western theater. The village also contains 11 historic log cabins. The Women of the Civil War Museum and several other museums are also nearby.

DON'T MISS: The train passes through part of the Bernheim Forest, a private 14,000-acre nature preserve, a habitat for a variety of trees, vegetation, and wildlife. While in the forest, the train passes slowly over the 310-foot-long, 60-foot-high Jackson Hollow timber trestle built for predecessor Bardstown & Louisville Railroad in 1860.

GETTING THERE: Bardstown is about 40 miles south of Louisville and 55 miles southwest of Lexington. When driving from Louisville, take I-65 south to Exit 112 and then Route 245 east. From Lexington, take Route 60 west and then the Martha Layne Collins Parkway.

LOUISIANA

DeQuincy Railroad Museum

Home to the DeQuincy Railroad Museum, the former Kansas City Southern depot is an outstanding example of Mission Revival architecture and is on the National Register of Historic Places. It displays a 1913 Alco steam locomotive, a caboose, and a passenger coach as well as artifacts and memorabilia. It is open Tuesdays through Saturdays. The annual Louisiana Railroad Days Festival is held here in April.

LOCATION: 400 Lake Charles Avenue, DeQuincy
PHONE: 337-786-2823
WEBSITE: dequincyrailroadmuseum.com
E-MAIL: form on website

Southern Forest Heritage Museum

At this museum, a guided tour takes you around a 57-acre historic sawmill complex, where you'll see a roundhouse and other industrial structures, three early logging locomotives, two McGiffert loaders, a Clyde skidder, and other steam equipment. Railbus rides on original Red River & Gulf Railroad track are available. An exhibit also highlights the history of the railroad.

LOCATION: 77 Long Leaf Road, Long Leaf
PHONE: 318-748-8404
WEBSITE: forestheritagemuseum.org
E-MAIL: sfhmwebadmin@cox.net

New Orleans Streetcars

LOCATION: Carrolton Avenue, Claiborne Avenue, Canal Street, New Orleans
PHONE: 504-248-3900
WEBSITE: norta.com
E-MAIL: comments@norta.com

David Lustig

Streetcars are a great way to see New Orleans, and if you have the desire, you can ride several different streetcar lines, operated today by the city's transit agency. While all of them make it simple to get around the Big Easy, each has its own character and charm that truly offers a fascinating view of this diverse city.

CHOICES: The St. Charles Line features the oldest continuously operating street railway system in the world. It passes antebellum mansions, historic monuments, universities and other sights. The Canal Street Line, which has two branches, takes passengers from the French Market through the central business district to City Park Avenue and an area of historic cemeteries. The Riverfront Line travels the downtown area along the Mississippi River. The new Loyola Corridor Streetcar Line runs down Loyola from New Orleans Union Passenger Terminal to Canal Street and has three other stops: Julia Street, Poydras Street, and Tulane.

WHEN TO GO: All lines run every day of the year. As with most coastal cities, expect humidity and high temperatures in summer; this is especially noticeable on the St. Charles Line as its historic Perley Thomas cars lack air-conditioning.

GOOD TO KNOW: Despite fewer amenities, fans of history and interurbans alike will enjoy the trip along St. Charles Avenue. The line was built in 1835, and since it's on the National Register of Historic Places, the cars must remain as they were in back in 1923.

WORTH DOING: It's hard to think of New Orleans and not associate Mardi Gras with it. The parties and parades actually begin the weekend before, and as the city's population explodes during this time, consider that when making travel plans.

DON'T MISS: Sure, there's the French Quarter, but outside this half-square-mile box, you'll find a Mississippi River cruise aboard an authentic steamboat, the National World War II Museum, the Audubon Nature Institute, plus music festivals and restaurants featuring notable indigenous cuisine.

GETTING THERE: Thanks to the line's sprawling routes, there are many places to catch a New Orleans streetcar. One of the best is via the new Canal Street Line connection at the New Orleans Union Passenger Terminal.

MAINE

Belfast & Moosehead Lake Railway

Excursion trains depart from City Point Railroad Museum in Belfast, run to Waldo, and return. You can enjoy the 70-minute trip aboard a coach, an open-air car, or a caboose. Special fall and pizza trains also operate. For a unique perspective, and some exercise, try pedaling a rail bike along the tracks for four miles from Thorndike to Knox.

LOCATION: 13 Oak Hill Road, Belfast
PHONE: 207-722-3899
WEBSITE: brookspreservation.org
E-MAIL: information@brookspreservation.org

Boothbay Railway Village

Powered by one of three operating engines, a two-foot-gauge steam train takes you around a re-created historic village with several stations and an engine house. Exhibits show the history of Maine's narrow gauge railroads, and various pieces of rolling stock and equipment are on display, as are more than 50 antique or classic automobiles and other vehicles.

LOCATION: 586 Wiscasset Road, Boothbay
PHONE: 207-633-4727
WEBSITE: railwayvillage.org
E-MAIL: staff@railwayvillage.org

City Point Central Railroad Museum

The museum is located in a station house that was moved from Corinna. Among its exhibits is a large collection of photographs of the Belfast & Moosehead Lake Railroad. On display are a variety of railcars and cabooses as well as Belfast & Moosehead Lake Railroad engine No. 51, an A-4 gang car, and a section house. It is open April through October.

LOCATION: 13 Oak Hill Road, Belfast
PHONE: 207-323-4402
WEBSITE: belfastmaine.com/museums
E-MAIL: cpcrailroad@yahoo.com

Cole Land Transportation Museum

The museum houses 200 antique land transportation vehicles and 2,000 photographs of life in early Maine. Its railroad collection includes one of the first Bangor & Aroostook diesels, a Canadian Pacific section shack, a Maine Central caboose, and a relocated station.

LOCATION: 405 Perry Road, Bangor
PHONE: 207-990-3600
WEBSITE: colemuseum.org
E-MAIL: mail@colemuseum.org

Oakfield Railroad Museum

Exhibits in the restored Oakfield station include hundreds of photographs dating to the beginning of the Bangor & Aroostook Railroad in 1891, vintage signs, signal lanterns, railroad maps, and telegraph equipment. A restored caboose, handcar, and motor car are also displayed. It is open summer on Saturday and Sunday afternoons.

LOCATION: 40 Station Street, Oakfield
PHONE: 207-757-8575
WEBSITE: oakfieldmuseum.org
E-MAIL: collierarthur7@gmail.com

Sandy River & Rangeley Lakes Railroad

Trains operate on select weekends from June through October. Included with the train ride is a walking tour of the museum and a visit to the replica roundhouse. The train is pulled by a replica of Forney locomotive No. 4. A ghost train runs in October.

LOCATION: 128 Bridge Street, Phillips
PHONE: 207-778-3621
WEBSITE: srrl-rr.org

Downeast Scenic Railroad

LOCATION: 32 High Street, Ellsworth
PHONE: 866-449-7245
WEBSITE: downeastscenicrail.org
E-MAIL: info@downeastscenicrail.org

Downeast Scenic Railroad

The Downeast Scenic Railroad offers a 90-minute round-trip excursion that travels along the former Calais Branch of the Maine Central Railroad from Ellsworth to Ellsworth Falls and then to Washington Junction and back. Along this stretch of the Calais Branch Line, you'll see Little Rocky Pond, Green Lake, marshes, and glacial deposits including massive boulders. You may even see ospreys, eagles, and deer.

CHOICES: The train is pulled by a vintage diesel locomotive. Seating options include restored passenger coaches from the 1910s, an open-air car made from a log car, and a caboose. You can reserve tickets, but specific seats are not assigned, so arrive early to pick out your seat. The open-air car has picnic tables for dining al fresco, and well-behaved dogs are allowed on this car.

WHEN TO GO: The railroad runs excursions on weekends starting Memorial Day weekend. That weekend, service begins with one trip each day. From the end of June into October, two trips are offered.

GOOD TO KNOW: At Washington Junction Yard, the recently rehabilitated wye turns the train for the return trip to Ellsworth.

WORTH DOING: The coast is less than an hour away, where you can visit Mount Desert Island and Acadia National Park. Activities in the area include hiking, kayaking, and whale watching. Also, while in the area, be sure to indulge in fresh lobster and other seafood and homemade blueberry pie in many of the numerous restaurants.

DON'T MISS: At Washington Junction Yard, the staging area for the railroad, you'll be able to see vintage maintenance-of-way equipment and diesel locomotives.

GETTING THERE: Ellsworth is 24 miles east of Bangor. From there, take Highway 1A straight into Ellsworth, where it becomes High Street. The boarding location is behind Cadillac Mountain Sports, which you can reach by taking stairs from Cadillac Mountain Sports or via the Maine Community Foundation parking lot.

Maine Eastern Railroad

LOCATION: 4 Union Street, Rockland
PHONE: 866-637-2457
WEBSITE: maineeasternrailroad.com
E-MAIL: info@maineeasternrailroad.com

Alex Mayes

The Maine Eastern offers scenic coastline views from big-windowed, stainless steel coaches pulled by former New Haven Railroad FL9 locomotives. The railroad operates on a 57-mile branch line between Brunswick and Rockland. Along the line, there are 33 bridges and more than 100 curves.

CHOICES: The Maine Eastern's season runs spring through fall. Beginning in late June, a full schedule of daily trains runs between Rockland and Brunswick with additional trains added in October. You can also stop at other stations along the way. All trains include air-conditioned coaches and a cafe dining car. Extra fare parlor accommodations are also offered.

WHEN TO GO: Ride to Rockland to attend the North Atlantic Blues Festival or the Maine Windjammer Parade in July, or enjoy the Maine Lobster Festival in August. There are numerous special events in the fall during the color season, and the train is a great way to avoid the traffic jams on Route 1.

GOOD TO KNOW: Maine Eastern offers an array of travel packages to suit every taste, including train and sail options, stop-offs to explore the quaint towns of Bath and Wiscasset, lighthouse tours, and multi-day offerings. Trips on sailing vessels and even working lobster boats can be arranged.

WORTH DOING: There is plenty to do in the mid-coast area, including whale-watching trips, antique shops, museums, and historic sites. Well-known Acadia National Park is further up the coast, and ferries from Rockland carry visitors to several offshore islands. Scenic beaches, quaint villages, and fabulous views are everywhere.

DON'T MISS: Nearby attractions include the Owl's Head Transportation Museum, the Wiscasset, Waterville & Farmington Railway Museum, and Boothbay Railway Village.

GETTING THERE: Brunswick is just off I-295, about half an hour north of Portland and 2.5 hours from Boston, while Rockland is another 90 minutes north. Traffic on Route 1 between Brunswick and Rockland is heavy and slow-moving, especially on summer and fall weekends.

Maine Narrow Gauge Railroad & Museum

LOCATION: 58 Fore Street, Portland
PHONE: 207-828-0814
WEBSITE: mainenarrowgauge.org
E-MAIL: info@mainenarrowgauge.org

Maine Narrow Gauge Railroad

The Maine Narrow Gauge Railroad runs along the Eastern Promenade fronting Casco Bay. Excursions offer spectacular views of ferries, sailboats, cruise ships, lobster boats, and freighters as well as the many islands that dot the bay. The museum helps preserve Maine's two-foot gauge railways.

CHOICES: The railroad operates diesel and steam locomotives with historic open-window coaches and open-sided excursion cars. Tour the museum and see several beautifully restored passenger coaches, including *Rangeley*, the only two-foot gauge parlor car ever built. Also on display is a railbus used on the Sandy River and Bridgton & Harrison Railroads.

WHEN TO GO: The Museum is open daily May through October, with diesel-powered trains running on weekdays and steam power used on most weekends. Various special events, including a *Polar Express* train, take place throughout the year.

GOOD TO KNOW: Most of the railroad's equipment once operated on two of Maine's famed two-footers: the Sandy River & Rangeley Lakes and the Bridgton & Harrison. Steam engine No. 4 from the Monson is in service, and Bridgton & Harrison No. 7 is under overhaul and is expected to return to service in 2013.

WORTH DOING: The Portland waterfront is a busy area for tourists, and there are many other attractions in the area, including excellent seafood restaurants and shops constructed in Federal-style architecture.

DON'T MISS: Ride on the water side of the train for the best views. A walking and bike path follows the line for its entire length, which makes taking action photos easy.

GETTING THERE: Portland International Airport is nearby, and Boston's Logan Airport is about two hours south. Amtrak's *Downeaster* runs daily between Boston's North Station and Portland. I-95 passes just west of the city.

Seashore Trolley Museum

LOCATION: 195 Log Cabin Road, Kennebunkport
PHONE: 207-967-2712
WEBSITE: trolleymuseum.org
E-MAIL: form on website

Karl Zimmermann

Founded in 1939, the Seashore Trolley Museum is touted as the oldest, largest electric railway museum in the world. Its international collection includes more than 250 transit vehicles, mostly streetcars, and virtually every major United States city that operated trolleys is represented. Much of this equipment is under cover in three exhibit car barns.

CHOICES: Included in the museum admission is a streetcar ride over the two miles of rebuilt trackage. This ride, a treat for all the senses, is the best way to relive the trolley and interurban experience. If just riding isn't enough, you can take advantage of the Be a Motorman program and actually operate a trolley. In the visitor center, you can view an exhibit chronicling the way trolleys changed life in Maine and their relevance to the contemporary world.

WHEN TO GO: The museum is open seven days a week from Memorial Day through Columbus Day and weekends in May and for the balance of October. There are a number of special events, including sunset ice cream rides on certain summer weekends and pumpkin patch trolleys on September weekends.

GOOD TO KNOW: On Transit Weekend in October, the museum brings out rapid transit cars, buses, and trackless trolleys that do not usually operate.

WORTH DOING: Kennebunkport and adjacent Kennebunk are resort towns with Atlantic beaches and old-world New England charm. There are antique shops, galleries, restaurants (lobsters a specialty), and opportunities for whale watching and other sea-related activities.

DON'T MISS: The restoration shop is open to the public. From elevated walkways, you can watch the painstaking work on the cars going forward.

GETTING THERE: The museum is located just a few miles from I-95 (the Maine Turnpike) off Exit 25. Amtrak's Boston-Rockland *Downeaster* stops in Saco, about eight miles away, where taxis are available. The nearest major airport is in Portland, 25 miles distant.

Wiscasset, Waterville & Farmington Railway

LOCATION: 97 Cross Road, Alna
PHONE: 207-882-4193
WEBSITE: wwfry.org
E-MAIL: info@wwfry.org

Steve Hussar

The WW&F is a faithful re-creation of a segment of the original Wiscasset, Waterville & Farmington, which shut down in 1933 after a wreck. The museum has relaid 2.5 miles of track on the original grade.

CHOICES: Steam- and diesel-powered trains operate on the route north from Sheepscot station, passing the flag stop at Alna Center. A ride on "the little train that time forgot" takes riders back to the days when the railroad carried milk and cream, potatoes, lumber, mail, and people from inland villages to the seaport of Wiscasset. After your ride, visit the railway's shop, where volunteers maintain and rebuild rolling stock using traditional skills and techniques. A Model T Ford railcar also operates over the rails.

WHEN TO GO: The museum is open every Saturday year-round, as well as on Sundays beginning Memorial Day weekend through mid-October. Trains run April through December. September and October are the best months to visit, after the summer crowds have diminished and the insects are dormant.

GOOD TO KNOW: In 2013, the museum expects to put engine No. 9, an 1891 Portland Co. product, in service, following a major overhaul. Maine was famous for its two-foot gauge railways, a thrifty New England response to the expense of building and maintaining a railroad, and No. 9, which last ran in 1933 on the WW&F, operated on three of Maine's five two-footers.

WORTH DOING: The mid-coast region of Maine features plenty of attractions, lodging choices, and restaurants. Be sure to sample the bounty of the sea, especially lobsters, clams, and fish.

DON'T MISS: Visit the museum during the spring and fall work sessions. At these events, volunteers gather at Sheepscot to lay track, work on equipment, and build and maintain structures at the museum. You are welcome to join in if you wish.

GETTING THERE: The museum itself is on a rural road just off Route 218 about four miles from Wiscasset and Route 1.

MARYLAND

Bowie Railroad Museum

This museum consists of a renovated freight station, switch tower, waiting shed, and caboose. The station and tower contain photos and artifacts. The museum is open Tuesday through Sunday. The Old Town Bowie Welcome Center and Interactive Children's Museum is next to the railroad museum.

LOCATION: 8614 Chestnut Avenue, Bowie
PHONE: 301-809-3089
WEBSITE: cityofbowie.org
E-MAIL: pwilliams@cityofbowie.org

Chesapeake Beach Railway Museum

From 1900 until 1935, the Chesapeake Beach Railway carried passengers to the Chesapeake Beach resort in cars such as the *Dolores*, which is on display. Housed in the original station, the museum exhibits photographs and artifacts of the railroad and the resort. It is open daily April through October and on weekends in March and November. Special events also take place throughout the year.

LOCATION: 4155 Mears Avenue, Chesapeake Beach
PHONE: 410-257-3892
WEBSITE: cbrm.org
E-MAIL: cbrailway@co.cal.md.us

Ellicott City Station

Located on the B&O Railroad's historic Old Main Line, Ellicott City Station could be the oldest surviving railroad station in the country. The main depot building was completed in 1831, and the freight house was built in 1855. The museum displays a replica of the first horse-drawn passenger railcar, the *Pioneer*, and a 1927 caboose. Joint admission with the B&O Railroad Museum in Baltimore is available.

LOCATION: 2711 Maryland Avenue, Ellicott City
PHONE: 410-461-1945
WEBSITE: borail.org/ellicott-city-station.aspx
E-MAIL: sitemanager@borail.org

Gaithersburg Community Museum

The museum features permanent and rotating exhibits in a restored 1884 B&O freight house. A new addition to the museum is a former B&O Budd Rail Diesel Car. Also on display are a 1918 Buffalo Creek & Gauley steam locomotive and a C&O bay window caboose. You can also visit the adjacent History Park and restored station, which is now a MARC station. The museum is open Thursday through Saturday.

LOCATION: 9 S. Summit Avenue, Gaithersburg
PHONE: 301-258-6160
WEBSITE: gaithersburgmd.gov/museum
E-MAIL: parksrec@gaithersburgmd.gov

Hagerstown Roundhouse Museum

Located near the roundhouse site in a historic building, the museum presents local rail history through artifacts, photos, and model train layouts. A Baldwin diesel, two Western Maryland cabooses, and a Hagerstown & Frederick trolley are on display. It is open Friday through Sunday.

LOCATION: 300 S. Burhans Boulevard, Hagerstown
PHONE: 301-739-4665
WEBSITE: roundhouse.org
E-MAIL: form on website

B&O Railroad Museum

LOCATION: 901 W. Pratt Street, Baltimore
PHONE: 410-752-2490
WEBSITE: borail.org
E-MAIL: info@borail.org

Alexander Mitchell IV

With nearly 200 locomotives and railcars and hundreds of thousands of smaller artifacts, the B&O Railroad Museum contains one of the largest and most diverse collections of railroad history in a unique, 40-acre setting.

CHOICES: The museum occupies several vintage buildings, including a fully covered roundhouse and turntable built in 1884. The domed roundhouse is a distinctive feature of Baltimore's skyline. The museum houses the largest collection of 19th century locomotives in North America. Later steamers and diesels are well represented, and passenger cars and freight cars round out the collection. Locomotive No. 545, the *A.J. Cromwell*, built in 1888 and named for its designer, the B&O's chief mechanical officer, is again on display after being repaired from the damage it suffered when the museum's roof collapsed in 2003.

WHEN TO GO: Through December 2015, the museum is featuring numerous displays and events focused on the 150th anniversary of the Civil War and its connections to American railroading. The museum is open year-round, with special events scheduled throughout. Train rides are offered Wednesday through Sunday April through December and weekends in January.

GOOD TO KNOW: Allow at least a half day for a full tour of the museum and include a 20-minute train ride along the first commercial mile of railroad track laid in America.

WORTH DOING: The museum is in a residential neighborhood just west of downtown and the city's major stadiums. Baltimore has a host of other attractions, including the Baltimore Streetcar Museum, Civil War Museum (in the President Street Station), National Aquarium, Irish Railroad Workers Museum, Fort McHenry, and the nearby Edgar Allan Poe House, which is now managed by the B&O Railroad Museum.

DON'T MISS: Combined admission to the nearby Ellicott City Railroad Museum, the oldest railroad station in America, and Mount Clare Museum House, a colonial Georgian plantation house, is also available.

GETTING THERE: Baltimore is served by many airlines, Amtrak, and mass transit, and the museum is only a few minutes off I-95 by car.

Baltimore Streetcar Museum

LOCATION: 1901 Falls Road, Baltimore
PHONE: 410-547-0264
WEBSITE: baltimorestreetcar.org
E-MAIL: form on website

Alexander Mitchell IV

Since 1968, the Baltimore Streetcar Museum has operated its distinctive and unique collection of streetcars and other transit equipment. You can relive a piece of Baltimore's history by hopping on one of the city's original streetcars for a one-mile ride.

CHOICES: The museum's streetcar ride takes you along the former right-of-way of the Maryland & Pennsylvania in the Jones Falls Valley and passes a historic freight house and roundhouse before turning on a loop for the return trip. On a guided tour of the car house, you can view 13 historic Baltimore streetcars, ranging from a horse car to the last PCC that ran in Baltimore. You'll also see three Philadelphia streetcars (one a snowsweeper), a replica Baltimore PCC (originally a San Diego car), several buses, and trackless trolleys.

WHEN TO GO: The museum is open on Sunday afternoons year-round and also on Saturday afternoons June through October. If visiting Baltimore in summer, it can be excessively hot and muggy. Special events, such as Santa's Streetcar, take place during the year.

GOOD TO KNOW: Admission to the museum also includes unlimited streetcar rides and guided car house tours. A family admission plan is also available.

WORTH DOING: Baltimore is full of interesting things to see including the picturesque Inner Harbor, National Aquarium, and the USS *Constellation*. The historic Mount Vernon neighborhood, with the Walters Art Museum, Meyerhoff Symphony Hall, eclectic shops and restaurants, is a short distance to the south.

DON'T MISS: In the visitor center, you can view historical displays as well as a short video about the trolleys and streetcars that ran in Baltimore from 1859 to 1963.

GETTING THERE: The museum is just west of Charles Street (one way north) and Maryland Avenue (one way south) off North Avenue. Baltimore has plenty of transportation alternatives. It is a short walk from Amtrak's Penn Station. The MTA Light Rail—spiritual successor to the streetcars—also serves Penn Station with connections to downtown and Baltimore/Washington International Airport.

National Capital Trolley Museum

LOCATION: 1313 Bonifant Road, Colesville
PHONE: 301-384-6088
WEBSITE: dctrolley.org

National Capital Trolley Museum

Inspired by streetcar buildings of the past, the National Capital Trolley Museum has a striking new look. The new visitor center provides an educational and entertaining look at the history of the region's streetcar systems, complete with an authentic trolley ride.

CHOICES: The museum is divided in three halls. In the Main Hall, you'll learn about the history of local streetcar systems, watch several silent films starring streetcars and actor Harold Lloyd, and see a model electric railway. Conduit Hall contains exhibits that explain how streetcars were powered. In Streetcar Hall, you get a close-up look at a variety of trolleys in the museum's collection, some that have not been on recent display. Unlimited trolley rides are included with admission.

WHEN TO GO: The museum is open weekends year-round as well as on select Thursdays and Fridays April through November. In summer, the museum offers special programs for children that include activities such as storytelling and crafts.

GOOD TO KNOW: One of the more interesting items at the museum is not a streetcar. It is a switch tower that allowed attendants to route street cars by setting switches and signaling motormen near Union Station.

WORTH DOING: Downtown Washington, with its wealth of cultural and historic attractions, is just 14 miles away.

DON'T MISS: Among the museum's streetcar collection, look for Blackpool Transit System No. 606, an unusual open car that ran on Blackpool's promenade in the UK.

GETTING THERE: The museum is located in Northwest Branch Park, about a 20-minute drive from the Capital Beltway. Bonifant Road is 5.5 miles north of I-495. Glenmont is the closest Washington Metrorail subway station. From there, Montgomery County Ride-On Bus No. 26 leaves for the museum at 30-minute intervals on Saturdays and Sundays.

Walkersville Southern Railroad

LOCATION: 34 W. Pennsylvania Avenue, Walkersville
PHONE: 877-363-9777 or 301-898-0899
WEBSITE: wsrr.org
E-MAIL: admin@wsrr.org

Alexander Mitchell IV

The Walkersville Southern Railroad takes you on a pleasant eight-mile, 70-minute round trip through woods and farmland, past a restored century-old lime kiln, and across the Monocacy River.

CHOICES: Trains depart from the original Pennsylvania Railroad station pulled by one of the railroad's collection of switchers, which includes a 1939 Davenport gas-mechanical, a rare 1942 EMD Model 40 four-wheel diesel, a GE 45-tonner, and a 1942 Plymouth gas-mechanical. Look for a PRR GE 44-tonner to begin operating in 2013. Passengers may ride in former Long Island Rail Road coaches, a covered open-air car, or a caboose. Parks and picnic stands are located at both ends of the line.

WHEN TO GO: From May through October, there are two departures on Saturdays. In October, there are additional trips on Sundays. Dinner trains run on some holidays and on two Saturdays every month May through October. Trains that combine some mystery with dinner run on select dates. Special events are scheduled throughout the year and include robberies by Jesse James and ghost trains. For kids, there are bunny trains, teddy bear picnics, and Santa trains. Steam trains may also run several weekends.

GOOD TO KNOW: The railroad has recently restored to service an additional three miles of track north of Walkersville, which is usually for dinner trains.

WORTH DOING: For Civil War buffs, Gettysburg and Harpers Ferry are about an hour away. The railroad also conducts a Civil War reenactment.

DON'T MISS: The railroad's museum occupies a former ice plant and features rail artifacts from the line and a model railroad.

GETTING THERE: The railroad is 50 miles from Baltimore or Washington, D.C. From Baltimore, take I-70 west to Exit 53B near Frederick. Follow Route 15 north for six miles and then turn right onto Biggs Ford Road. Travel about two miles and look for a grain elevator, which is adjacent to the station.

Western Maryland Scenic Railroad

LOCATION: 13 Canal Street, Cumberland
PHONE: 800-872-4650 or 301-759-4400
WEBSITE: wmsr.com
E-MAIL: form on website

Dave Crosby

Of all the Appalachian freight railroads, the Western Maryland was one of the most beloved because of its excellent steam power. Today, the trip out of Cumberland on the roadbed of the main line, with a short detour the last few miles onto a branch into Frostburg, is one of the best parts of the Western Maryland.

CHOICES: Traveling through the mountains of western Maryland, this 32-mile round trip take takes you from Cumberland's restored Western Maryland Railway station to an 1891 Cumberland & Pennsylvania depot in Frostburg. You'll ride aboard restored coaches pulled by a 1916 Baldwin steam locomotive or a vintage diesel engine. Regular excursions offer coach, club, and first-class seating. First-class seating is available on Saturdays and some Sundays. It includes reserved seating in a dining or café car with lunch and dessert. The railroad also offers murder mystery, Christmas, and other special trains.

WHEN TO GO: Trains run May through December. October, during the height of the color season, is especially beautiful, and reservations are required for fall excursions.

GOOD TO KNOW: When the train arrives in Frostburg, you have a 90-minute layover. Be sure to find a good spot to watch the locomotive change directions on the turntable. You will also have time to walk down Main Street for shopping or dining.

WORTH DOING: The Western Maryland station houses the Chesapeake & Ohio Canal National Historical Park's Cumberland Visitor Center, where you can learn more about the C&O Canal.

DON'T MISS: Stick to the right side of the train. Leaving Cumberland, the train passes through the Narrows, a gap in the mountain that also allows the highway and parallel CSX (the former B&O) an escape to the west. Just beyond is famous Helmstetter's Curve, a sharp turn in the railroad tracks. From here on, views remain mostly on the right side as the train makes its way higher into the mountains.

GETTING THERE: When driving, Cumberland is about 2.5 hours from Baltimore, Washington, or Pittsburgh. From either direction, the Western Maryland station is easily reached from Exit 43C off I-68 in downtown Cumberland.

MASSACHUSETTS

Berkshire Scenic Railway Museum

The museum's restored 1903 New Haven Railroad passenger station contains extensive historical displays. Housed in an old coach on the museum grounds, the Gilded Age exhibit displays the history of this era in Berkshire County. It features many pieces of rolling stock including vintage diesel locomotives and a New Haven caboose. You can take a guided tour through the rail yard on a short train ride. At this time, the museum is unable to offer its 90-minute excursions as the railroad owning the track Berkshire Scenic travels over has not renewed the easement for use of the track.

LOCATION: 10 Willow Creek Road, Lenox
PHONE: 413-637-2210
WEBSITE: berkshirescenicrailroad.org
E-MAIL: form on website

Chatham Railroad Museum

This restored country depot is situated on its original site. Museum exhibits feature hundreds of railroad artifacts from the Chatham Railroad Company and other railroads, including a restored 1910 New York Central caboose and telegraph instruments. It is open Tuesdays through Saturdays.

LOCATION: 153 Depot Road, Chatham
PHONE: 508-945-5199
WEBSITE: town.chatham.ma.us
E-MAIL: form on website

Edaville USA

This is a family fun park with a two-mile train ride through a 1,300-acre cranberry plantation. There is a variety of amusement rides and an indoor play area. Special events include National Cranberry Festival, Christmas Festival of Lights, and others.

LOCATION: 5 Pine Street, Carver
PHONE: 877-332-8455 or 508-866-8190
WEBSITE: edaville.com
E-MAIL: info@edaville.com

Lowell National Historical Park

The park includes a variety of structures related to industry, 5.6 miles of canals, and restored mill buildings. It displays a Boston & Maine 0-6-0 Manchester locomotive built in 1910, a combine car, and several open-air trolleys. Trolley tours as well as several boat tours are available. You can also take in the National Streetcar Museum, which is across from the park's visitor center.

LOCATION: 246 Market Street, Lowell
PHONE: 978-970-5000
WEBSITE: nps.gov/lowe
E-MAIL: form on website

Old Colony & Fall River Railroad Museum

The museum is located in four railroad cars, including a renovated Pennsylvania Railroad coach, and it features artifacts of New England railroads such as Penn Central, Conrail, Amtrak, and the New Haven. You can visit its haunted rail yard in October.

LOCATION: 2 Water Street, Fall River
PHONE: 508-674-9340
WEBSITE: ocandfrrailroadmuseum.com
E-MAIL: info@ocandfrrailroadmuseum.com

Shelburne Falls Trolley Museum

The museum features a 15-minute ride on restored trolley car No. 10, which was built in 1896. For an added fee, and with a little instruction, you can become an instant motorman and run No. 10 yourself. Pump car rides are also available. The museum displays railroad and trolley artifacts, a steam locomotive, and a caboose. It is open late May through October.

LOCATION: 14 Depot Street, Shelburne Falls
PHONE: 413-625-9443
WEBSITE: sftm.org
E-MAIL: trolley@sftm.org

Cape Cod Central Railroad

LOCATION: 252 Main Street, Hyannis
PHONE: 888-797-7245 or 508-771-3800
WEBSITE: capetrain.com
E-MAIL: form on website

Cape Cod Central Railroad

The Cape Cod Central Railroad operates diesel-powered scenic excursions and dinner trains, which also include lunch and brunch outings. It runs from Hyannis over 23 miles of the former Old Colony Railroad that became part of the New York, New Haven & Hartford. Along the way, you'll pass cranberry bogs, forests, and marshes.

CHOICES: For evening dining, passengers can select either the Elegant Dinner Train, involving multiple courses served with all the flourishes, or the Family Supper Train, which offers less formal service, a shorter ride, lower fares, a magic show, and special children's meals. The popular Murder Mystery Train, a variation on the Elegant Dinner Train, runs on occasional evenings. The Gourmet Wine Train is another variation. Boarding is also possible at Sandwich and West Barnstable (Sundays).

WHEN TO GO: Trains run from late May through October in various combinations and with varying frequencies. Some special event trains run in November and December, including the *Polar Express*, which operates from both Buzzards Bay and Hyannis. Sea breezes mean that Hyannis typically remains temperate throughout the railroad's operating season but visiting outside of summer may minimize crowds.

GOOD TO KNOW: Hyannis is quintessential Cape Cod, with all the sun, sand, salt—and tourists. Whale watching, beaching, fishing, golfing, and biking are among the available outdoor activities. The John F. Kennedy Hyannis Museum is located in town. There are many lodging choices and a wide variety of fine restaurants.

WORTH DOING: The railroad offers a package with Hy-Line Cruises that includes a one-hour boat tour of Hyannis harbor and the Kennedy compound. The boat is a little gem: Maine-style coastal steamer *Prudence* (the real McCoy, though now dieselized, built in 1911).

DON'T MISS: The Elegant Dinner Train offers one decided advantage—in addition to the cuisine—over the other meal trains (and scenic excursions as well). While the other trains are all two hours in length and run briefly along the Cape Cod Canal, only the three-hour Elegant Dinner Train crosses it on a lift bridge into the town of Buzzards Bay. This bridge features outstanding aesthetics and was the longest of its kind when completed in 1935.

GETTING THERE: Hyannis is located on the Atlantic Ocean at the elbow of Cape Cod. Barnstable Municipal Airport hosts commercial flights from Boston and New York.

MICHIGAN

Clinton Northern Railway Center

Housed in a historic Grand Trunk depot, the museum's artifacts include tools, signs, and station agent items. A 1902 Barney & Smith sleeper car, a 1903 post office-baggage car, a 1926 Ann Arbor maintenance-of-way crew car, and a 1927 wooden caboose are also on display.

LOCATION: 107 E. Railroad Street, St. Johns
PHONE: 989-224-6134 or 502-214-0479
WEBSITE: clintonnorthernrailway.org
E-MAIL: mccampbell60@gmail.com

Coopersville & Marne Railway

Powered by an EMD SW9 diesel locomotive, this railway's 14-mile, 75-minute excursion travels through farmland and over an open-deck girder bridge. At Marne, you can watch the engine uncouple, run along a passing siding, and couple to the other end. Excursions run Wednesdays and Saturdays May through October (and Saturdays in other months), and theme trains run as well.

LOCATION: 311 Danforth Street, Coopersville
PHONE: 616-997-7000
WEBSITE: coopersvilleandmarne.org

Durand Union Station

This 100-year-old depot museum was the second busiest depot in Michigan, and its lower level has been restored to its former glory with terrazzo floors and oak trim. Still functioning as a depot, the building also houses the Michigan Railroad History Museum. The museum contains changing exhibits on state and local railroading.

LOCATION: 200 Railroad Street, Durand
PHONE: 989-288-3561
WEBSITE: durandstation.org
E-MAIL: dusi@durandstation.org

Flushing Area Museum

The museum's collection includes permanent displays of railroad artifacts as well as local historical exhibits. It is housed in the Flushing depot, which was built in 1888 and provided passenger service until 1971. The building was restored to its former appearance by the Flushing Area Historical Society.

LOCATION: 431 W. Main Street, Flushing
PHONE: 810-487-0814
WEBSITE: flushinghistorical.org
E-MAIL: fahs@att.net

Houghton County Historical Museum

The museum includes the restored Mineral Range depot, which contains a collection of Copper County railroad artifacts, and other historic buildings. The museum operates the Lake Linden & Torch Lake Railroad. A narrow gauge 0-4-0 Porter steam locomotive or a diesel engine takes you on a half-mile ride. The museum is open June through September.

LOCATION: 53102 Highway M-26, Lake Linden
PHONE: 906-296-4121
WEBSITE: houghtonhistory.org
E-MAIL: president@houghtonhistory.org

Michigan Transit Museum

The Michigan Transit Museum is housed in a depot restored to its 1900 appearance and includes railroading exhibits from that time. The transit museum displays several locomotives and railcars. It also offers a 30-minute, round-trip train ride that departs from Joy Park. Located near the Selfridge Military Air Museum, the transit museum is open weekends year-round, and trains run Sundays June through October.

LOCATION: 200 Grand Avenue, Mount Clemens
PHONE: 586-463-1863
WEBSITE: michigantransitmuseum.org
E-MAIL: information@michigantransitmuseum.org

Old Road Dinner Train

The train provides dining and entertainment from two locations, Blissfield and Charlotte. The murder mystery dinner trains provide a five-course dinner as you participate in a comical, interactive mystery show. A family pizza train runs occasionally.

LOCATION: 301 E. Adrian Street, Blissfield
PHONE: 888-467-2451
WEBSITE: murdermysterytrain.com
E-MAIL: form on website

Saginaw Railway Museum

Located in a restored 1907 Pere Marquette Railway depot, this museum displays an RS1 locomotive, several cabooses, a combine coach, and various boxcars. It includes an 1898 armstrong interlocking tower as well as a variety of smaller artifacts. It is open select Saturdays May until November.

LOCATION: 900 Maple Street, Saginaw
PHONE: 989-790-7994
WEBSITE: saginawrailwaymuseum.org
E-MAIL: info@saginawrailwaymuseum.org

Southern Michigan Railroad

The railroad offers passenger excursions, including a variety of themed rides, between Clinton and Tecumseh. Along each 45-minute leg of the round trip, the train crosses River Raisin twice. The railroad also operates a museum that is open on Saturdays during the regular season, mid-May through September.

LOCATION: 320 S. Division Street, Clinton
PHONE: 517-456-7677 or 517-423-7230
WEBSITE: southernmichiganrailroad.com
E-MAIL: smrs49236@yahoo.com

SS City of Milwaukee

The SS *City of Milwaukee*, a national historic landmark, is the last surviving traditional Great Lakes railroad car ferry. Built in 1931, the *City of Milwaukee* served the Grand Trunk Western and Ann Arbor Railroads. The car deck houses five Ann Arbor boxcars that serve as exhibit spaces and a theater. The Coast Guard cutter *Acacia* is docked on site, and tours of both ships are offered.

LOCATION: 99 Arthur Street, Manistee
PHONE: 231-723-3587
WEBSITE: carferry.com
E-MAIL: form on website

Tri-Cities Historical Museum

The Tri-Cities Historical Museum operates out of two buildings including a former Grand Trunk Western depot that was built in 1870. Located on the banks of the Grand River, the Depot Museum of Transportation contains exhibits related to railroad, maritime, and other forms of transportation. On display is a Pere Marquette Railway steam locomotive.

LOCATION: 1 North Harbor Drive, Grand Haven
PHONE: 616-842-0700
WEBSITE: tri-citiesmuseum.org
E-MAIL: kpott@tri-citiesmuseum.org

Greenfield Village at the Henry Ford

LOCATION: 20900 Oakwood Boulevard, Dearborn
PHONE: 800-835-5237 or 313-982-6001
WEBSITE: thehenryford.org
E-MAIL: form on website

Jeff Terry

The Henry Ford claims to be America's greatest history attraction, and even though it's in the capital of—and shrine to—the automobile, railroads are well represented here. The centerpiece for this is the Detroit, Toledo & Milwaukee roundhouse, a reconstruction of the original in Marshall, Mich., believed to be one of only seven 19th century roundhouses remaining. A steam railroad encircles the historic 90-acre village.

CHOICES: You can ride the train around the village in open-air cars on a 30-minute narrated trip. Departing from the 1859 Smiths Creek depot, the train also makes stops at strategic locations throughout the village. The roundhouse includes hands-on railroading displays and a 1902 Atlantic engine. A mezzanine provides an excellent vantage point from where you can see work going on. Also, be sure to go inside the Henry Ford museum to view railroad cars and locomotives, including an Allegheny type, one of the largest steam locomotives ever built.

WHEN TO GO: Greenfield Village is open daily mid-April until early November. In mid-November, it is open Friday through Sunday, and in December, it is open select evenings for Holiday Nights. It is closed the remainder of the year.

GOOD TO KNOW: Railroad Junction, where the roundhouse and depot are located, is one of seven different historic districts in Greenfield Village. In Henry Ford's Model T District, you can tour a replica of Ford's first factory and ride in a Model T.

WORTH DOING: On December nights, celebrate the holidays in Greenfield Village. The Holiday Nights event features entertainment, carriage and Model T rides, Santa and reindeer, ice skating, and fireworks.

DON'T MISS: Get to the roundhouse early in the day to help the crew turn the steam engine on the turntable. It's so well balanced that two people can do it, but it's more fun when you get to push a giant engine around.

GETTING THERE: Just west of Detroit, the Henry Ford is located in Dearborn on the corner of Village Road and Oakwood Boulevard, just west of the Southfield Freeway and south of Michigan Avenue (Highway 12). There is easy access from I-94 or I-75. You may also ride an Amtrak train that stops at the museum.

Huckleberry Railroad

LOCATION: 6140 Bray Road, Flint
PHONE: 800-648-7275 or 810-736-7100
WEBSITE: geneseecountyparks.org
E-MAIL: parkswebteam@gcparks.org

Jeff Terry

The Huckleberry Railroad is part of a historical village that is operated by Genesee County Parks in Flint. The narrow gauge railroad is built on an abandoned Pere Marquette Railway right-of-way. An eight-mile, 40-minute ride carries passengers through neighborhoods, by a lake, and into wooded areas.

CHOICES: Ride in one of the railroad's historic coaches or cabooses pulled by a Baldwin 4-6-0 or a Baldwin 2-8-2.

WHEN TO GO: Trains run Memorial Day weekend through Labor Day, with special events held throughout the year, including days out with Thomas the Tank Engine. During the railroad's railfan weekend, usually held in August, you can see all the trains, get good photos, and talk with the train crews.

GOOD TO KNOW: The Huckleberry Railroad was named because it ran so slow that a person could jump off the train, pick some huckleberries, and jump back on the train without breaking a sweat.

WORTH DOING: Take a stroll through Crossroads Village, which has 34 historic structures on 51 acres. Costumed interpreters welcome you to the homes, mills, and shops that date back to the 1800s. Special events are scheduled throughout the summer, and you can take a ride on a paddle-wheel riverboat.

DON'T MISS: Take a close look at Rio Grande 2-8-2 No. 464, which is one of a rare class of narrow gauge Mikado type steam locomotives on the Colorado railroad. Built in 1903 and restored in 2005, it was nicknamed *Mudhen* because it waddled like a chicken as it went down the tracks.

GETTING THERE: The railroad is located just north of Flint, about an hour from Detroit. From Detroit, take I-75 to I-475. Follow I-475 north to Saginaw Street (Exit 13). Take Saginaw Street north to Stanley Road, turn east on Stanley Road, and then turn south on Bray Road to the village and railroad.

Little River Railroad

LOCATION: 29 W. Park Avenue, Coldwater
PHONE: 260-316-0529 or 574-215-0751
WEBSITE: littleriverrailroad.com
E-MAIL: customerservice@littleriverrailroad.com

Jeff Terry

Whoever said bigger is better never visited the Little River Railroad. This railroad is home to one of the smallest standard gauge steam locomotives of its type ever built. No. 110 is a 57-ton Pacific that has all the charm of a ballerina, and the railroad offers 90-minute trips behind it from Coldwater to nearby Quincy.

CHOICES: Ride in a coach or open-air car. During the 30-minute layover in Quincy, be sure to exit the train and watch as the locomotive is switched to the other end of the train. At times, a second locomotive, 0-4-0T No. 1, is in service. The railroad offers a variety of special events throughout the year including fall color trains, haunted trains, Christmas trains, and Easter trains.

WHEN TO GO: Trains run weekends Memorial Day through September. On Labor Day weekend, Little River runs both of its engines as well as a motor car and pump car.

GOOD TO KNOW: Engine No. 110 started out on the Little River Railroad in east Tennessee. An Indiana family, the Blooms, rescued her and rebuilt it for excursion work in the 1970s, and members of that same family continue this tradition of preservation.

WORTH DOING: The area features many antique shops and preserved buildings. In Coldwater, take in a film at the Capri Drive-in, one of the last of its kind.

DON'T MISS: Take time to look over the exhibits in the Coldwater depot, an 1883 Lake Shore & Michigan Southern depot.

GETTING THERE: Coldwater is in south-central Michigan. Take I-69 to Exit 13 for Coldwater. Follow Highway 12 west, turn left onto Division Street, and then turn right onto Park Avenue to the depot.

Steam Railroading Institute

LOCATION: 405 S. Washington Street, Owosso
PHONE: 989-725-9464
WEBSITE: michigansteamtrain.com
E-MAIL: dlshorter@mstrp.com

Jim Wrinn

The Steam Railroading Institute is all about preserving steam locomotives, and there is always restoration work going on. The institute displays equipment and offers some all-day train rides.

CHOICES: Both steam- and diesel-powered excursions are offered, and after its restoration, Pere Marquette 2-8-4 No. 1225 should be back in operation during the 2013 season. The seven-acre site includes a roundhouse, a turntable, and a variety of railcars. It also features an operational miniature train. Look around the visitor center, which is housed in a renovated freight warehouse that was also a creamery. It now contains exhibits, artifacts, and a model train layout.

WHEN TO GO: The rolling stock collection can be seen all year, and special events are scheduled as well. In November and December, the North Pole Express is the big event as a diesel locomotive takes visitors on a 24-mile round trip to the North Pole, where kids can enjoy hot cocoa, activities, and visiting Santa. Reserve early, as this event sells out fast.

GOOD TO KNOW: No. 1225 was the model and sound effects source for the steam train in the poplar movie, *The Polar Express*.

WORTH DOING: If you like to watch things go fast, the Owosso Speedway offers short track racing on Saturday, Saturday, Saturday.

DON'T MISS: The Michigan Railroad History Museum is housed in historic Durand Union Station, 20 minutes away in Durand.

GETTING THERE: Owosso is about 30 miles northeast of Lansing and 30 miles west of Flint. From Flint, take Highway 21 west to Owosso. From Lansing, take I-69 to Highway 52 north to Owosso. In Owosso, the Steam Railroading Institute is on south Washington Street.

MINNESOTA

The Depot

Visitors have several options in exploring this restored 1915 train depot, which is listed on the National Register of Historic Places. You can experience the depot's architecture, waiting rooms, freight room, and exhibits on your own or with a guide. Group tours, with or without lunch, are also available. It is open Memorial Day weekend through August.

LOCATION: 100 Aldrich Avenue SW, Wadena
PHONE: 218-632-5999
WEBSITE: thedepotwadena.org
E-MAIL: thedepotwadena@gmail.com

Depot Museum

Located in the 1907 headquarters of the Duluth & Iron Range Railroad, this museum highlights the timber industry, iron mining, and the railroad. On display is a Mallet steam locomotive and a Baldwin 3-Spot. The Lake County Historical Society operates this museum and three others including an 1896 tugboat. The museums are open daily Memorial Day weekend through mid-October.

LOCATION: 520 South Avenue, Two Harbors
PHONE: 218-834-4898
WEBSITE: lakecountyhistoricalsociety.org
E-MAIL: lakehist@lakenet.com

End-O-Line Railroad Park & Museum

End-O-Line Railroad Park includes a 1901 manually operated turntable, a rebuilt engine house, an original four-room depot, a water tower, an 1899 section foreman's house, a Grand Trunk Western caboose, and two steam locomotives. Open Memorial Day to Labor Day, the site also includes other buildings of historical interest.

LOCATION: 440 N. Mill Street, Currie
PHONE: 507-763-3708
WEBSITE: endoline.com
E-MAIL: endoline@co.murray.mn.us

Iron Horse Railroad Park

Housed in an 1895 St. Paul & Duluth station, the park's museum contains changing rail exhibits. Also on display are more than 20 historic railcars. A homebuilt, yellow-and-black motor car and a steam engine provide train rides around the park's grounds.

LOCATION: 24880 Morgan Avenue, Chisago City
PHONE: 651-357-3394
WEBSITE: ironhorsecentral.com
E-MAIL: thompson@ironhorsecentral.com

Kandiyohi County Historical Museum

The museum complex consists of several buildings including a one-room schoolhouse and the former Kandiyohi railroad station depot, which is the entrance to the main museum. Great Northern No. 2523, a Baldwin P-2 class steam locomotive, is also on display. It is open Memorial Day through Labor Day.

LOCATION: 610 NE Highway 71, Willmar
PHONE: 320-235-1881
WEBSITE: kandiyohicountyhistory.com
E-MAIL: kandhist@msn.com

Minnehaha Depot

Located in Minnehaha Park, the tiny depot's architecture features delicate gingerbread details. Built in 1875, the building replaced an earlier Milwaukee Road depot on the first line into the Twin Cities from Chicago. Managed by the Minnesota Transportation Museum, the depot is open Sundays Memorial Day weekend through Labor Day.

LOCATION: Highway 55 and Minnehaha Parkway, Minneapolis
PHONE: 651-228-0263
WEBSITE: mtmuseum.org
E-MAIL: contact@mtmuseum.org

Minnesota Discovery Center

The center offers a 2.5-mile trolley ride to a re-created mining community. The 40-minute trip, aboard a 1928 Melbourne trolley, offers views of the Pillsbury mine. Preserving Iron Range history, the center includes a museum, hall of geology, and mini golf course. It is open year-round, with trolleys operating late May into October.

LOCATION: 1005 Discovery Drive, Chisholm
PHONE: 800 372 6437 or 218 254-7959
WEBSITE: mndiscoverycenter.com
E-MAIL: info@mndiscoverycenter.com

Minnesota Museum of Mining

The museum tells the story of iron ore mining in the state. Along with mining equipment and vehicles, a 1907 Alco steam locomotive is on display with ore cars and a caboose. Inside, you'll find a re-created mining town, a building-filling train layout, and a simulated underground mine. It is open Memorial Day to Labor Day, and picnicking is encouraged.

LOCATION: 701 West Lake Street, Chisholm
PHONE: 218-254-5543
WEBSITE: mnmuseumofmining.org
E-MAIL: form on website

Minnesota Streetcar Museum

This museum operates two different streetcar lines from May into fall, with a variety of special events. Located southwest of downtown Minneapolis, the Como-Harriet Line runs between Lake Harriet and Lake Calhoun. The Excelsior Line is about 15 miles west of downtown Minneapolis. The museum exhibits electric streetcars, railcars, and a steamboat.

LOCATION: 2330 W. 42nd Street, Minneapolis
PHONE: 952-922-1096
WEBSITE: trolleyride.org
E-MAIL: mnscmuseum@gmail.com

Jackson Street Roundhouse

LOCATION: 193 E. Pennsylvania Avenue, St. Paul
PHONE: 651-228-0263
WEBSITE: mtmuseum.org
E-MAIL: contact@mtmuseum.org

Steve Glischinski

The former Great Northern Jackson Street Roundhouse was built in 1907 to service passenger locomotives. Closed in 1959, the roundhouse was converted to nonrailroad use and the tracks were removed. The Minnesota Transportation Museum purchased it in 1985 and reinstalled the turntable, which you can see in operation.

CHOICES: Visitors can roam through the roundhouse and the outdoor grounds, participate in interactive exhibits, and on Saturdays take a short caboose ride pulled by a switch engine or possibly by the *Hustle Muscle*, a 20-cylinder, 3,600-horsepower, turbocharged SD45 locomotive. Tours of the roundhouse where equipment restoration takes place are also available. A variety of freight and passenger cars are displayed outside, and several boxcars have been neatly repainted in their original color schemes.

WHEN TO GO: The museum is open Wednesdays and Saturdays year-round. Summer or early fall are the best times to visit since it can be chilly inside the roundhouse in the winter and downright cold outside.

GOOD TO KNOW: Walk inside the cab of Dan Patch Lines No. 100, built in 1913 by General Electric, and you've walked into history. One of the first locomotives to use an internal combustion engine, it is the granddaddy of today's diesel locomotives.

WORTH DOING: After taking in the roundhouse, you can visit the St. Paul home of James J. Hill, the Great Northern's founder. Completed in 1891, the 36,000-square-foot mansion was the largest and most expensive home in Minnesota at the time. The Minnesota Historical Society conducts 75-minute guided tours.

DON'T MISS: Take a ride on the miniature *Rock Island Rocket*, a perfect 1/6 replica of the *Twin Star Rocket*. The train was built in 1947 by Larry Sauter, a high school industrial arts teacher, in his spare time. The museum adds a few feet of special narrow gauge track for the train every year, and the kids will love the quick acceleration!

GETTING THERE: The Twin Cities of Minneapolis and St. Paul have Amtrak, airline, and bus service. The roundhouse is located north of the Minnesota State Capitol. Take the Pennsylvania Avenue exit off I-35E and drive west two blocks to the roundhouse.

Lake Superior & Mississippi Railroad

LOCATION: 7100 Grand Avenue, Duluth
PHONE: 218-624-7549
WEBSITE: lsmrr.org
E-MAIL: info@lsmrr.org

Jeff Terry

Here's a laid-back operation that is a great complement to the marshlands near Duluth. A 90-minute ride on this railroad is a great way to relax and enjoy nature along the St. Louis River estuary, Spirit Lake, and Mud Lake. Keep your eyes on the marshes for egrets!

CHOICES: While taking in the scenery and wildlife when riding in a restored, open-window coach, you can listen to narration of the area's rich history. The coaches, built in 1912, operated between the Iron Range and Duluth. For a truly outdoor experience, ride the Safari Car, a converted flatcar. Power is provided by a General Electric industrial switcher built in 1946.

WHEN TO GO: Excursions operate on Saturdays and Sundays, beginning in June and running into October.

GOOD TO KNOW: The railroad takes its name from the first line built between the Twin Cities and Duluth, and it uses some of that line's original track.

WORTH DOING: Duluth and the Lake Superior area offer much to do. There are historic ships to see (SS *William A. Irvin*, SS *Meteor*), museums to tour, and parks to explore.

DON'T MISS: For a Duluth doubleheader, visit the nearby Lake Superior Railroad Museum, where you can catch a train ride to Two Harbors.

GETTING THERE: Duluth is on Lake Superior, about 150 miles from the Twin Cities. In Duluth, go south on I-35, take Exit 251B onto Grand Avenue. The boarding location is across from the Lake Superior Zoo.

Lake Superior Railroad Museum

LOCATION: 506 W. Michigan Street, Duluth
PHONE: 218-727-8025 (museum) or 218-722-1273 (train)
WEBSITE: lsrm.org
E-MAIL: form on website

Jim Wrinn

This is a combination of a great railroad museum and a great train ride. The Lake Superior Railroad Museum is located in a historic depot in downtown Duluth. Its extensive rolling stock collection rests in the train shed, and just outside, excursion trains ply the route to Two Harbors, with outstanding views along the way.

CHOICES: The Lake Superior Railroad Museum has a large collection of steam, diesel, and electric locomotives as well as passenger coaches, freight cars, and cabooses. Much of the equipment was used on Minnesota railroads, including the first locomotive operated in the state. The museum also operates the North Shore Scenic Railroad, which conducts two regular excursions. A six-hour round trip takes you through the countryside into Two Harbors. A shorter (90-minute) excursion runs along the shores of Lake Superior to Lester River. Also operating are an elegant dinner train, a pizza train, and a variety of specials.

WHEN TO GO: The museum is open year-round, with extended summer hours. Regular excursions are offered late May through mid-October. Soo Line 4-6-2 steam locomotive No. 2719 operates on select weekends in August and September on trips to Two Harbors.

GOOD TO KNOW: Take a close look at the *William Crooks*, the first locomotive operated in Minnesota. Built in 1861, it is one of a handful of engines remaining from the Civil War era.

WORTH DOING: The Duluth depot (St. Louis County Heritage and Arts Center) is also home to the Duluth Art Institute, St. Louis County Historical Society museum, and several arts groups.

DON'T MISS: Watch the massive Duluth, Missabe & Iron Range Railroad Yellowstone type locomotive come to life. Clever museum folks have set it up so that every 30 minutes an electric motor sets the drivers in motion, rotating the running gear, and operates lights and sounds.

GETTING THERE: Situated on Lake Superior, Duluth is 150 miles from the Twin Cities. To reach the museum, take Exit 256 off I-35 and follow Michigan Street to the depot.

Milwaukee Road 261

LOCATION: 401 Harrison Street, Minneapolis
PHONE: 651-765-9812
WEBSITE: 261.com
E-MAIL: form on website

Steve Glischinski

Railroading Heritage of Midwest America and its operating arm, The Friends of the 261, operate mainline excursion trips around the Midwest. Until former Milwaukee Road steam locomotive No. 261 returns to service, which should be in 2013, diesel-powered excursions are being operated. The group also operates its historic passenger cars on Amtrak trains, most frequently on the *Empire Builder* between the Twin Cities and Chicago. These trips are usually open to the public.

CHOICES: Friends of the 261 offers several options for passengers. All trips include coach, first-class, and premium-class services. Premium class includes hors d'oeuvres and gourmet meals prepared onboard and a ride in one of two former Milwaukee Road *Hiawatha* cars: Skytop lounge observation *Cedar Rapids* or full-length Super Dome No. 53. First class includes an upscale meal plan with hors d'oeuvres and a ride in parlor or lounge cars. Both first and premium class include complimentary beverages.

WHEN TO GO: Generally the Friends operate trips beginning in May and running as late as October. One of the most popular and scenic routes is along the Mississippi River between Minneapolis and Winona, especially in early autumn when the leaves begin to change.

GOOD TO KNOW: For a complete Milwaukee Road experience, stay in one of the two hotels at the former Milwaukee Road Minneapolis passenger depot, built in 1898 and beautifully restored. Rail memorabilia and photographs can be found throughout the building.

WORTH DOING: Trains usually leave from the 261 shop facility in northeast Minneapolis. Head down to the shop in Minneapolis the evening before a trip just to take in the sights and sounds.

DON'T MISS: Get a close look at Skytop lounge observation car *Cedar Rapids*. Built by the Milwaukee Road in 1948, with their large glass area, the Skytops were unlike any other rail passenger car. The *Cedar Rapids* is the only Skytop still in operation.

GETTING THERE: Minneapolis-St. Paul has Amtrak, airline, light rail transit, and bus service. A short walk from the Metro Transit bus stop at Central Avenue and Broadway will get you to the shop, or you can take a taxi. Ample parking is available at the shop on excursion days.

MISSISSIPPI

Canton Train Museum

Canton's depot served Illinois Central freight and passenger trains such as the *Green Diamond, Panama Limited,* and *City of New Orleans*. Built in 1890, the depot has been restored as a museum that showcases the rail history of Canton and the surrounding area. While in town, you can also visit several movie museums, which are dedicated to films such as *O Brother, Where Art Thou,* that were filmed in Canton.

LOCATION: 108 Depot Drive, Canton
PHONE: 601-859-4733
WEBSITE: cantontourism.com/trains.html
E-MAIL: trains@canton-mississippi.com

McComb Railroad Museum

Housed in an Illinois Central passenger terminal, the museum contains almost 1,500 artifacts related to railroading in southwest Mississippi. Outside, you can view a restored Illinois Central steam locomotive, aluminum refrigerator car, and caboose. The museum is open Mondays through Fridays.

LOCATION: 108 N. Railroad Boulevard, McComb
PHONE: 601-684-2291
WEBSITE: mcrrmuseum.com
E-MAIL: trainmaster@mcrrmuseum.com

MISSOURI

Belton, Grandview & Kansas City Railroad

At this laid-back railroad, you can walk around the yard, look at displayed equipment, and talk to the crew before boarding a five-mile excursion. The 45-minute round trip runs south from Belton. Rides in the locomotive with the engineer are also available.

LOCATION: 502 E. Walnut Street, Belton
PHONE: 816-331-0630
WEBSITE: beltonrailroad.org
E-MAIL: info@beltonrailroad.org

Chicago & Alton Railroad Depot

Built in 1879, the two-story Chicago & Alton depot features a restored four-room stationmaster's residence on the second floor. The first floor contains a waiting room, baggage room, and stationmaster's room. The depot contains hundreds of C&A artifacts. It is open April through October, and guided tours are available.

LOCATION: 318 W. Pacific Avenue, Independence
PHONE: 816-325-7955
WEBSITE: chicagoalton1879depot.org
E-MAIL: info@chicagoalton1879depot.org

Columbia Star Dinner Train

This gourmet dinner train offers year-round trips on weekends with dinner service on Saturdays and brunch on Sundays. Rolling through the Missouri countryside, diners can enjoy a relaxing four-course dinner aboard two articulated 1938 Pullman cars pulled by a 1950s locomotive. The meals are prepared in the train's kitchen car.

LOCATION: 6501 N. Brown Station Road, Columbia
PHONE: 877-236-8511 or 573-474-2223
WEBSITE: dinnertrain.com
E-MAIL: form on website

KC Rail Experience

Located in historic Union Station, the KC Rail Experience features a vintage railcar, a diesel engine, artifacts, and a locomotive simulator. Admission is included with a ticket to Science City, an interactive science center. You can also view trains of all sizes, from a model railroad exhibit to actual operating trains that you can see from a footbridge over the tracks.

LOCATION: 30 W. Pershing Road, Kansas City
PHONE: 877-724-2489 or 816-460-2020
WEBSITE: unionstation.org
E-MAIL: visitor@unionstation.org

Railroad Historical Museum

Located in Grant Beach Park, this train museum is an actual train. A locomotive, baggage car, commuter car, and caboose contain artifacts from the St. Louis-San Francisco and other railroads. After touring the museum, you can enjoy the park's pool, playground, and picnic area. It is open Saturdays May through October.

LOCATION: 1300 N. Grant Street, Springfield
PHONE: 417-865-6829
WEBSITE: rrhistoricalmuseum.zoomshare.com
E-MAIL: rrhistoricalmuseum@zoomshare.com

St. Louis Iron Mountain & Southern Railway

From May through December, this railway offers a large variety of trips including sightseeing excursions, murder mysteries, train robberies, and holiday-themed rides. Trains are pulled by Pennsylvania Railroad No. 5898, a 1950 E unit.

LOCATION: Highway 61 at Highway 25, Jackson
PHONE: 800-455-7245 or 573-243-1688
WEBSITE: slimrr.com
E-MAIL: slimrr1@gmail.com

Branson Scenic Railway

LOCATION: 206 E. Main Street, Branson
PHONE: 800-287-2462 or 417-334-6110
WEBSITE: bransontrain.com
E-MAIL: form on website

Patrick Hiatte

Enjoy a 40-mile round trip through the Ozarks on the former Missouri Pacific Railroad White River Line, which was built more than a century ago. View historic towns and town sites as you pass through tunnels and over high bridges along the banks of the White River and its tributaries.

CHOICES: The train may run north or south from Branson, depending on freight traffic on the host Missouri & North Arkansas Railroad. There is open seating on the two vintage dome cars, 60-seat deluxe coach, and lounge car that comprise the regular train. In addition, a dinner train, serving a candlelit, four-course meal, operates on Saturday evenings June through October. Beginning in late November, the *Polar Express* begins its holiday run.

WHEN TO GO: The Ozarks are scenic any time of the year, but especially in the fall, when the oaks and other hardwoods turn red, yellow, and orange in a display that rivals any fall foliage in the country. BSR operates four trains a day in October when the colors are usually at their peak, as well as during June and July. At least two trains a day operate from June through mid-December.

GOOD TO KNOW: Seating is open and boarding is by group based on ticket number—the sooner you buy your ticket, the more likely you are to get a seat in a dome.

WORTH DOING: Branson offers more than 100 shows, including Elvis and Beatles tributes, music and comedy headliners, and dozens of country music shows. For a quiet (and free) getaway, walk the boardwalk along the shore of Lake Taneycomo and enjoy the fire and water fountain show at Branson Landing.

DON'T MISS: At Silver Dollar City theme park, you can ride the RiverBlast, PowderKeg, giant swing, or the Frisco Silver Dollar steam train, named for the Frisco Railway, which had its operating headquarters just up the road in Springfield.

GETTING THERE: Branson is in southwest Missouri about 45 miles south of Springfield on Highway 65. Although most visitors drive to Branson, there's also scheduled air service to the Branson and Springfield airports. The depot is downtown on Main Street (Highway 76).

Museum of Transportation

LOCATION: 3015 Barrett Station Road, St Louis
PHONE: 314-965-6212
WEBSITE: museumoftransport.org

Dave Crosby

If you want to be surrounded by trains, this is the place. A visit here brings you in touch with more than 70 locomotives of steam, diesel, and electric power. You'll see scores of railcars and even one of the first railroad tunnels west of the Mississippi. The 150-acre site also houses airplanes, cars, and riverboats.

CHOICES: The museum features a new visitor center, 10 other buildings, and almost 200 pieces of rail equipment. Its collection has more than 30 steam locomotives, and stairs let you climb into the cabs of many of them. Many rare and unusual items grace the site, including the world's largest tank car, an Aerotrain, and even a cast-iron turntable.

WHEN TO GO: The museum is open year-round. It is open daily during its summer schedule, which begins in May and runs through Labor Day. During the rest of the year, the museum is open Thursday through Sunday.

GOOD TO KNOW: In the visitor center, you can board the miniature train that runs through the site. You can also view the 1889 Reading Black Diamond inspection locomotive, which is the only surviving example of an American steam inspection locomotive.

WORTH DOING: Of course, if you haven't already done so, enjoy the view from the top of Gateway Arch. You can also take a riverboat cruise, play some ragtime at Scott Joplin's home, enjoy the Missouri Botanical Garden, or view the mosaics at Cathedral Basilica.

DON'T MISS: Climb into the cab of the Union Pacific Big Boy No. 4006 and see what it felt like to be the engineer on one of the world's largest steam locomotives. And climb aboard Santa Fe No. 5011 and ring the engine's bell.

GETTING THERE: The museum is about 12 miles west of downtown St. Louis. When driving from I-270, either north or south, exit at Dougherty Ferry Road (Exit 8), go west about one mile to Barrett Station Road, and turn left. The museum is on the right.

MONTANA

Alder Gulch Short Line

This narrow gauge railroad connects the former gold-mining towns of Virginia City and Nevada City. The line winds along Alder Creek, where you can view the remains of gold-mining operations, dredge tailings, and a variety of wildlife. Be sure to explore the historic buildings and displays in Nevada City. The railroad's 1910 Baldwin locomotive is on display, while a gas-powered engine pulls the train.

LOCATION: Wallace Street, Virginia City
PHONE: 406-843-5247
WEBSITE: virginiacitymt.com

Charlie Russell Chew-Choo Dinner Train

This dinner train takes you on a 3.5-hour excursion over the old Chicago, Milwaukee, St. Paul & Pacific Railroad line. The ride crosses three historic trestles, passes through a 2,000-foot tunnel, and travels through the land that inspired artist Charles Russell. Along the way, you'll enjoy a catered prime rib dinner. Just keep your eyes open for masked bandits! North Pole runs take place in November and December. The train boards in Ware, a 40-minute drive from Lewiston.

LOCATION: 408 NE Main Street, Lewistown
PHONE: 866-912-3980 or 406-555-5436
WEBSITE: montanacharlierussellchewchoo.com
E-MAIL: lewchamb@midrivers.com

Historical Museum at Fort Missoula

Located in Fort Missoula, the Historical Museum includes a variety of structures that depict the area's history. One is the Drummond depot, which was constructed by the Chicago, Milwaukee, St. Paul & Pacific Railroad in 1910. Be sure to visit historic streetcar No. 50, a 100-year-old streetcar that was the last streetcar to run in Missoula. No. 50 has been restored and is now housed in a new carbarn.

LOCATION: South Avenue, Missoula
PHONE: 406-728-3476
WEBSITE: fortmissoulamuseum.org
E-MAIL: ftmslamuseum@montana.com

Upper Musselshell Museum

This museum is located in two historic buildings. The Marshall Building contains a large collection of models related to the Milwaukee Road and other railroads. It also displays a replica skeleton of an avaceratops dinosaur whose remains were found nearby. The Times Building contains 13 heritage rooms that are decorated by families who settled in the area. Also in town is a restored depot, Milwaukee Road ES-3 boxcab electric locomotive No. E57B, and several other pieces of equipment.

LOCATION: 11 and 36 S. Central Avenue, Harlowton
PHONE: 406-632-5519
WEBSITE: harlowtonmuseum.org
E-MAIL: museum@mtintouch.net

NEBRASKA

Cody Park Railroad Museum

The Cody Park Railroad Museum displays one of the two remaining Challenger class locomotives. Also displayed are a UP diesel engine, baggage car, mail car, and caboose. The restored Hershey depot contains Union Pacific items, telegraph equipment, and other exhibits. It is open May through September. Rail Fest takes place in September.

LOCATION: 1400 N. Jeffers Street, North Platte
PHONE: 308-532-4729
WEBSITE: visitnorthplatte.com/CodyParkRailroadMuseum.html
E-MAIL: info@visitnorthplatte.com

Durham Museum

Built in 1931, Omaha's Union Station is a beautiful example of Art Deco style. This historic railroad station now houses both permanent and temporary historical exhibits. Rail displays include an 1890s steam locomotive, a streetcar, a caboose, and several passenger cars. Be sure to have a malt, ice cream soda, or phosphate at the restored soda fountain as travelers did in 1931.

LOCATION: 801 S. 10th Street, Omaha
PHONE: 402-444-5071
WEBSITE: durhammuseum.org
E-MAIL: info@durhammuseum.org

Golden Spike Tower

Golden Spike Tower is an observation tower that overlooks the world's largest railroad yard. The visitor center includes artifacts of the Union Pacific. In September, you can attend Rail Fest and take a tour of the yard as well as enjoy food, music, and other activities.

LOCATION: 1249 N. Homestead Road, North Platte
PHONE: 308-532-9920
WEBSITE: goldenspiketower.com
E-MAIL: inforequest@goldenspiketower.com

Rock Island Depot Railroad Museum

The museum is located in one of the state's only remaining Rock Island depots. Built in 1914, the brick building also housed the railroad's Western Division Headquarters. The collection features Rock Island artifacts and a restored baggage room, lobby, and ticket office. The site also includes restored gardens. Rock Island Rail Days take place in June.

LOCATION: 910 Second Street, Fairbury
PHONE: 402-729-5131
WEBSITE: fairbury.com
E-MAIL: fairburyridepot@alltel.net

Stuhr Museum of the Prairie Pioneer

This interactive museum takes you back to an 1890s railroad town with more than 60 restored buildings. During the summer, townspeople dressed in period clothing demonstrate daily life on the Plains. A 1901 steam locomotive, a 1912 caboose, an 1871 coach, and other railcars are on display.

LOCATION: 3133 W. Highway 34, Grand Island
PHONE: 308-385-5316
WEBSITE: stuhrmuseum.org
E-MAIL: info@sturhmuseum.org

Trails & Rails Museum

The Rails portion of the museum includes an 1898 Union Pacific depot. The depot houses transportation exhibits, and its waiting room and ticket office have been restored. On display are a 2-8-0 Baldwin steam engine, a UP flatcar, a caboose, and other equipment. Open year-round, the museum contains other historic buildings including the distinctive Freighters Hotel.

LOCATION: 710 W. 11th Street, Kearney
PHONE: 308-234-3041
WEBSITE: bchs.us
E-MAIL: bchs.us@hotmail.com

NEVADA

Nevada Northern Railway Museum

LOCATION: 1100 Avenue A, East Ely
PHONE: 866-407-8326 or 775-289-2085
WEBSITE: nevadanorthernrailway.net
E-MAIL: info@nnry.com

Dave Crosby

The Nevada Northern is often hailed as the best-preserved standard gauge railroad in the country. The operating railway museum is headquartered on a 56-acre complex with 66 historic buildings, set amid the vastness of the Great Basin. The Nevada Northern was completed in 1906 to haul copper from area mines and smelters to the outside world. Most cars and locomotives have been on the railroad since the first day of their service lives, and they're maintained in the company's own shops.

CHOICES: The Nevada Northern offers something for everyone and operates excursions on two routes. The Keystone route goes through a 1907 tunnel on the way to Ruth, and the train can be either diesel- or steam-powered. The McGill Junction route runs diesel-powered rides through desert country to Adverse. The railroad also operates a variety of special and seasonal trains, including barbecue trains, geology trains, and a Halloween ghost train that features stories from the region's colorful past.

WHEN TO GO: The railroad operates from April through January. Summer is busy, with trains running daily. Temperatures are usually in the 80s.

GOOD TO KNOW: The Nevada Northern offers several unique lodging packages. You can spend a night in a local hotel and ride on the ghost train or the *Polar Express*. If you want an up-close look at the railway, you can stay overnight in a caboose or a bunkhouse.

WORTH DOING: Visit Great Basin National Park, which is 60 miles from Ely. In this diverse environment, you can see 13,000-foot mountains and 5,000-year-old bristlecone pines and explore Lehman Caves.

DON'T MISS: At the railway, you can view steam locomotives, wooden passenger cars, a steam-powered rotary plow, and a steam-powered wrecking crane. Structures include the original depot, engine house, freight shed, coaling tower, and water tower. Diesels include everything from an SD9 to a Baldwin VO1000 and a trio of Alco RS-model road switchers.

GETTING THERE: Ely is in east-central Nevada at the junction of Highways 6, 50, and 93.

Nevada Southern Railway

LOCATION: 600 Yucca Street, Boulder City
PHONE: 702-486-5933
WEBSITE: nevadasouthern.com
E-MAIL: volutneer@nevadasouthern.com

Dave Crosby

The railway offers a train ride with a historical twist. This was part of the construction railroad from Las Vegas to Hoover Dam, with tracks having been laid in 1931. It's a nice ride in the desert and a break from the hustle of Las Vegas.

CHOICES: Along the 45-minute round trip, you get an up-close look at desert plant life, especially when riding in the train's open-air car. The other cars are air-conditioned, restored Pullman coaches dating back to 1911. A generator car behind the locomotive supplies power to the coaches. Operated by the Nevada State Railroad Museum, the railway's outdoor interpretive area displays a variety of equipment, including steam locomotive No. 264 and its unique Vanderbilt tender.

WHEN TO GO: The railway operates on weekends. Summer in Nevada can be hot, with temperatures hitting triple digits. Santa, train robbery, and other special trains run.

GOOD TO KNOW: You'll save money in Boulder City. It is one of only two communities in Nevada where gambling is prohibited in the city limits, although two casinos operate nearby.

WORTH DOING: Take a trip to nearby Boulder Dam and tour this technological wonder. Boating on Lake Mead is a popular activity any time of the year.

DON'T MISS: Ride a train pulled by a historic diesel. One of the locomotives used, UP No. 844, is one of the last GP30 diesel locomotives—an early 1960s diesel that replaced the first generation of diesel locomotives that had themselves replaced steam power.

GETTING THERE: Boulder City is a 30-minute drive from Las Vegas and McCarran International Airport. It is an easy drive from Las Vegas along Highway 93 into Boulder City. Once there, turn left on Yucca Street to the museum and railway.

Nevada State Railroad Museum

LOCATION: 2180 S. Carson Street, Carson City
PHONE: 775-687-6953
WEBSITE: nevadaculture.org
E-MAIL: gfackerman@nevadaculture.org

Dave Crosby

Few states can claim as rich a railroading heritage as Nevada, and this museum does an admirable job of interpreting it. The first transcontinental railroad, the state's many mining railroads, and the historic Virginia & Truckee—which ran right past the museum property—are all represented here. The museum boasts a particularly fine collection of 19th century rolling stock, much of which originally came from the V&T and was used in dozens of Hollywood films and television shows.

CHOICES: The museum operates steam train and motor car rides throughout the season. Star of the museum's collection is *Inyo*, a wood-burning 4-4-0 built for the V&T in 1875. When *Inyo* isn't operating, it's on display along with other beautifully restored pre-1915 freight and passenger equipment.

WHEN TO GO: The museum is open Fridays through Mondays. Train rides take place weekends from May until September, with added fall and Christmas runs. Midsummer highs are usually in the 80s, with little chance of precipitation.

GOOD TO KNOW: Carson City's downtown area is very walkable. The state capitol grounds and surrounding neighborhoods of historic homes are particularly pleasant. A wide variety of hotels, motels, and restaurants can be found nearby.

WORTH DOING: For those whose interests run toward scholarly pursuits, the museum has impressive static displays exploring such topics as the Central Pacific Railroad in Nevada railroading and the evolution of V&T motive power. Lectures by leading rail historians are offered, and the museum also hosts an annual symposium on Nevada railroad history.

DON'T MISS: Ride aboard a national historic landmark. McKeen motor car No. 22 recently received this designation and operates several times each year, including Nevada Day in October. The self-propelled railcar was built for the Virginia & Truckee in 1910 and before being restored saw time as a restaurant and as a retail store.

GETTING THERE: The museum is on Highway 395 (Carson Street) on the south side of Carson City. Carson City is within a day's drive of most major cities on the West Coast.

Virginia & Truckee Railroad

LOCATION: 370 F Street, Virginia City
PHONE: 775-847-0380
WEBSITE: virginiatruckee.com
E-MAIL: info@virginiatruckee.com

Dave Crosby

The famous Comstock Lode yielded more than $400 million of silver and gold during a roughly 30-year period beginning in 1859—and it led to the creation of both Virginia City and the Virginia & Truckee Railroad. The city saw up to 45 arrivals and departures a day. Today's V&T operates a 35-minute, five-mile round trip from Virginia City to Gold Hill.

CHOICES: You can ride the historic route from Virginia City to Gold Hill and back, with spectacular views of rugged mountain scenery and mine ruins. This is a short trip. For those with the desire for a trip over a longer route, choose the Sisters in History run over the rebuilt track from just outside Carson City into Virginia City. The railroad powers its trains with either a 1916 Baldwin 2-8-0 steam locomotive from the Longview, Portland & Northern or a General Electric 80-ton diesel. Passenger cars include a restored 1914 Pullman coach and a 1907 private car.

WHEN TO GO: V&T operates daily from late May to the end of October, when it runs its haunted Halloween train that is not only fun but offers spectacular stargazing on V&T's mountain right-of-way, far from city lights. Civil War, candy cane, and other specials also run. Temperatures are comfortable throughout the operating season, with average highs topping out in the low 80s during July and August.

GOOD TO KNOW: Virginia City boasts a variety of restaurants, hotels, and B&Bs that recall the town's frontier heritage, and many are within walking distance of the V&T station.

WORTH DOING: The historic Virginia City walking tour provides a good sense of the Comstock mining boom. It includes historic mansions, churches, the Piper Opera House, and the *Territorial Enterprise* newspaper, where young Mark Twain worked as a reporter.

DON'T MISS: The Nevada State Railroad Museum in nearby Carson City displays more than 30 pieces of equipment that operated on the V&T.

GETTING THERE: Virginia City is on Highway 341, 25 miles south of Reno and 15 miles north of Carson City.

NEW HAMPSHIRE

Ashland Railroad Station Museum

The museum was built by the Boston, Concord & Montreal Railroad as a station around 1869. It is one of the state's best preserved examples of a 19th century passenger station. The museum contains rail artifacts and photo displays. Occasionally, an excursion train stops at the museum. It is open Saturdays during July and August.

LOCATION: 69 Depot Street, Ashland
PHONE: 603-968-7716
WEBSITE: oldashlandnh.org

Gorham Historical Society Museum

The 1907 former Grand Trunk Railroad station houses a museum that exhibits rail and local historical items. It displays a 1911 Baldwin steam locomotive, a 1949 F7 diesel locomotive, and several boxcars. Operated by the Gorham Historical Society, the museum is open Memorial Day weekend through mid-October.

LOCATION: 25 Railroad Street, Gorham
PHONE: 603-466-5338
WEBSITE: gorhamnewhampshire.com/railroadmuseum.html
E-MAIL: gorhamhistoricalsociety@gmail.com

Potter Place Railroad Station

The wooden Potter Place station, which was built in 1874, features striking Victorian Stick-style architectural elements. Listed on the National Register of Historic Places, the station includes a preserved station master's office and exhibits on local history. This historical site also includes a Central Vermont caboose and freight house, both from the early 1900s, as well as a general store and schoolhouse.

LOCATION: 105 Depot Street, Andover
WEBSITE: andoverhistory.org
E-MAIL: pres@andoverhistory.org

Sandown Depot Museum

The museum is located in the restored Sandown railroad depot that was built in 1873. It contains a stationmaster's room with a working telegraph key and a waiting room with a pot-bellied stove. The museum also features two Flanger cars. It is open weekends May through October.

LOCATION: 1 Depot Road, Sandown
PHONE: 603-887-6100
WEBSITE: sandown.us/historical_society/museum_main.htm

Silver Lake Railroad

Situated just south of North Conway, the Silver Lake Railway offers a 55-minute round trip through this scenic area. From the open-air cars, passengers can see a variety of scenery, from mountains to swamps, as well as an occasional moose. The railroad's museum displays a range of vintage equipment and buildings, including a restored 1941 diner, which you can use for picnics. It is open Memorial Day weekend into October. Train rides are by donation.

LOCATION: 1381 Village Road, Madison
WEBSITE: silverlakerailroad.com
E-MAIL: silverlakerr@yahoo.com

Cafe Lafayette Dinner Train

LOCATION: 3 Crossing at River Place, Route 112, North Woodstock
PHONE: 800-699-3501 or 603-745-3500
WEBSITE: nhdinnertrain.com

Cafe Lafayette Dinner Train

The Cafe Lafayette Dinner Train provides a top fine-dining experience while traveling through the lush forest and open fields of the Pemigewasset River Valley, which is surrounded by mountains that bear witness to New Hampshire's nickname—the Granite State.

CHOICES: The 20-mile round trip follows an ex-Boston & Maine right-of-way that once ran into nearby Lincoln. As the scenery rolls by, diners enjoy a five-course meal. Entree selections change on a regular basis, with orders taken onboard and then prepared to order. Menu items often highlight local ingredients, including blueberries and maple syrup, in season, and salad greens and herbs are grown in the train's adjacent garden.

WHEN TO GO: Café Lafayette operates seasonally, late May through October. Runs occur on Saturdays and Sundays in May and June, then Tuesdays, Thursdays, Saturdays, and Sundays late June to late October, with an expanded daily schedule based on demand from late August to late October. The fall foliage season, mid-September to the end of October, is an especially scenic time to visit. Book early as demand at this time of year is high.

GOOD TO KNOW: Café Lafayette began operation in 1989, making it America's longest continuously operating dinner train under the same name and in the same location, where the train is parked on its own siding.

WORTH DOING: There is much to do in the area as the nearby Hobo Railroad operates a number of excursions, as does the Conway Scenic Railroad, which is 40 miles east. Hiking and other recreational activities are found in the White Mountain National Forest and along the Appalachian Trail.

DON'T MISS: Enjoy dining under the dome of the *Granite Eagle*. This 1952 Pullman-built car ran on the Missouri-Pacific's *Texas Eagle* and then on the Illinois Central's popular *City of New Orleans*.

GETTING THERE: The Cafe Lafayette Dinner Train is located just west of I-93 at Exit 32 on Route 112.

New Hampshire

Conway Scenic Railroad

LOCATION: 38 Norcross Circle, North Conway
PHONE: 800-232-5251 or 603-356-5251
WEBSITE: conwayscenic.com
E-MAIL: info@conwayscenic.com

Scott Hartley

Here is a New England excursion train ride bursting with great scenery and Yankee character. The setting is in the Mount Washington Valley in the charming village of North Conway. With three different trips to choose from, this railroad offers a bounty of great journeys.

CHOICES: Two Valley Train excursions are offered: a 55-minute, 11-mile round trip to Conway and a longer 21-mile round trip to Bartlett. The Notch Train carries passengers from North Conway into the rugged Crawford Notch, as the first trains did more than 130 years ago. Passengers may choose from coach or first-class service. Valley Train passengers have lunch and dinner options aboard the *Chocorua*, and lunch service on the Notch Train aboard the *Hattie Evans*, which had been used on the Norfolk & Western's *Powhatan Arrow* and *Pocahontas*. Steam engines operate excursions and special trains on a limited basis.

WHEN TO GO: Valley Trains operate excursions April through December and the Notch Train runs June through October. Nothing is better than an autumn train ride in New England, but special trains operate throughout the year. For a change of scenery, try riding a steam train in snow-covered woods during December.

GOOD TO KNOW: Stick to the right side of the Notch Train as it ascends Crawford Notch and crosses the Frankenstein Trestle (named for artist Godfrey Frankenstein, not because it's a monster trestle) and Willey Brook Bridge for excellent views of bluffs, ravines, and streams. The later in fall you travel, the fewer colors you'll see, but the better the vistas are from the train.

WORTH DOING: The surrounding Mount Washington Valley and White Mountain National Forest offer four seasons of recreational activities, attractions, and spectacular scenery.

DON'T MISS: Well, you can't miss the Victorian station in North Conway. Take some time to appreciate this structure that's been at work as a railroad depot since 1874.

GETTING THERE: The Conway Scenic Railroad is less than a three-hour drive from Boston. From Boston, take I-95 to Route 16, which runs to North Conway.

Hobo & Winnipesaukee Scenic Railroads

LOCATION: 64 Railroad Street, Lincoln (Hobo)
LOCATION: 154 Main Street, Meredith (Winnipesaukee)
PHONE: 603-745-2135 (Hobo) or 603-279-5253 (Winnipesaukee)
WEBSITE: hoborr.com
E-MAIL: info@hoborr.com

Hobo Railroad, George Kenson

Boston & Maine's 72-mile White Mountain Branch from the state capital of Concord north to Lincoln long served paper mills and other forestry companies, but the railroad abandoned this route as those businesses shut down. Fortunately, the entire line has survived, and two tourist train operations on the northern 54 miles keep portions busy for visitors throughout the year.

CHOICES: The Hobo Railroad offers 15-mile round trips on the north end of the branch to the many tourists who visit the White Mountain region. Trains out of Lincoln follow the scenic Pemigewasset River south, crossing numerous trestles and passing such locations as Grandma's Crossing and Swimming Hole Bridge, before changing directions at the Jack O'Lantern Resort near Thornton. Farther south, on the shores of its namesake lake, the Winnipesaukee Scenic Railroad offers trains out of Meredith and Weirs Beach to and from Lakeport, always in view of New Hampshire's largest lake. Trains include open-window coaches and cabooses.

WHEN TO GO: Both railroads operate weekends from May through mid-June, and daily through the summer. The daily operations continue through the fall foliage season on the Hobo, while the Winnipesaukee reverts to a weekend schedule. Santa Claus and *Polar Express* trains run during late November and December.

GOOD TO KNOW: Lake Winnipesaukee is a major summer vacation destination, and the White Mountains also attract large crowds in summer and early October for fall foliage.

WORTH DOING: To see more of Lake Winnipesaukee, daytime and dinner cruises are available from Weirs Beach and other towns. You can explore the quaint shops, antique stores, and historic buildings of Meredith. There is much to do in the White Mountains, from hiking and kayaking to viewing covered bridges, waterfalls, and wildlife.

DON'T MISS: Try a hobo picnic lunch, complete with a souvenir bindle stick.

GETTING THERE: For the Hobo, take I-93 to Exit 32. For the Winnipesaukee, take I-93 to Exit 23. The drive through the center of New Hampshire is beautiful year-round.

Mount Washington Cog Railway

LOCATION: 3168 Base Station Road, Bretton Woods
PHONE: 800-922-8825 or 603-278-5404
WEBSITE: thecog.com

Karl Zimmermann

England may have invented the railroad, but the United States invented the mountain-climbing cog railroad. The first such successful cog—a standard railroad with flanged wheels but with the addition of a gear engaging a toothed "rack" rail in the center of the tracks—was the Mount Washington Cog Railway, which opened in 1869 and has been in operation ever since. The trip takes you to the top of 6,288-foot Mount Washington, infamous for its bad weather but famous for its vistas.

CHOICES: Sit back and enjoy the views during the trip to the summit and back. On a clear day, you can see four states, Canada, and the Atlantic Ocean. The trains operate on a steep track that resembles a ladder plunked down on the mountainside. The diesel-powered run up the mountain now allows visitors a full hour at the summit.

WHEN TO GO: Excursion trains operate late April through early December, and reservations are recommended. In fall, the White Mountains are always spectacular. Early in the season, trains operate only on weekends. From the beginning of June until the end of the season, service is daily. From November until closing, trains run only halfway to the summit.

GOOD TO KNOW: Though most trips are now powered by the railroad's biodiesel-powered engines, from mid-June through October, one trip a day, usually the first, is operated with a coal-burning steam locomotive.

WORTH DOING: Explore the mountains. Mount Washington State Park is at the summit and contains hiking trails, an observatory, a visitor center, and the stone Tip Top House—a hotel built in 1853 and restored as a museum. The surrounding White Mountain National Forest offers a variety of recreational activities.

DON'T MISS: View the railway's original cog engine, *Old Peppersass*, which is on display at Marshfield Base Station. The railway's museum is also located there.

GETTING THERE: The Cog Railway is a pleasant drive from Boston, Hartford, New York, or Montreal. It is 90 miles from Portland off Route 302. In Bretton Woods, follow Base Road for six miles to the railway.

White Mountain Central Railroad

LOCATION: 110 Daniel Webster Highway, Lincoln
PHONE: 603-745-8913
WEBSITE: whitemountaincentralrr.com
E-MAIL: info@clarkstradingpost.com

Scott Hartley

The White Mountain Central Railroad is part of the popular family-owned Clark's Trading Post amusement park deep in New Hampshire's White Mountains. The railroad offers 30-minute excursions across the Pemigewasset River over a 1904 Howe truss railroad covered bridge that was moved from the Barre & Chelsea Railroad in Vermont.

CHOICES: Once a center for the logging and paper industries, the region now caters to tourists and skiers. Five decades ago, the Clark family added a 1.25-mile railroad to their small amusement park and acquired an impressive collection of geared steam locomotives. Admission includes the train ride as well as other activities. During Railroad Days, all steam engines operate, while the daily steam ride is usually powered by a Climax locomotive. A 1943 diesel switcher also operates. The park includes a variety of museums, displays, and attractions.

WHEN TO GO: Operations are daily beginning in mid-June through the end of August and on weekends in late May, early June, September, and October. The best fall foliage usually occurs in early October, which is also the peak tourist season. Special excursions and displays occur on Railroad Days, which is scheduled in September.

GOOD TO KNOW: Lodging, including motels and B&Bs, and restaurants can be found in Lincoln and the surrounding communities. Rates will be the highest during fall, so reservations should be made far in advance for this season.

WORTH DOING: The White Mountain National Forest is worth visiting any time of year for camping, hiking, history, and scenic drives.

DON'T MISS: The star attractions of the park's operating locomotive fleet are a Beebe River Railroad two-truck Climax, a Baldwin 2-4-2T, a Porter 0-4-0T, and the only known Reo railbus. Other geared locomotives include an International Shoe two-truck Heisler and a Woodstock Lumber Shay.

GETTING THERE: If driving on I-93, take Exit 33, and go south one mile on Route 3 (Daniel Webster Highway). In fall, driving along the Kangamangus Highway from Conway offers exceptional views and plentiful wildlife.

NEW JERSEY

Maywood Station Museum

This station has been restored, inside and out, to preserve its Victorian style. The station museum features local history and railroad artifacts. Also on display are a restored caboose that contains additional exhibits and a New York, Susquehanna & Western Alco S2 diesel locomotive. It is open on a limited schedule.

LOCATION: 269 Maywood Avenue, Maywood
WEBSITE: maywoodstation.com
E-MAIL: info@maywoodstation.com

Black River & Western Railroad

LOCATION: 105 John Ringo Road, Ringoes
PHONE: 908-782-6622
WEBSITE: flemingtontrain.org
E-MAIL: info@flemingtontrain.org

Karl Zimmermann

The Black River & Western, which also hauls freight, hosts hour-long passenger excursions (operated by the nonprofit Black River Railroad Historical Trust) over a short segment of the former Pennsylvania Railroad's Flemington Branch between Flemington and Ringoes.

CHOICES: While all trains recently had been diesel-powered, steam engine No. 60 is now back in service and will operate on some trains. In addition to standard weekend excursions, various family-friendly special trains and events are offered throughout the year. These include an Easter Bunny Express, caboose hops, Santa Express, North Pole Express, and others. You can board the trains for round trips from either station. Occasionally two-hour round-trips are offered over the entire BR&W to Three Bridges.

WHEN TO GO: The Black River & Western operates on weekends from Memorial Day through Labor Day, and in October for the fall foliage season, when excursions run from Flemington to a corn maze and pumpkin patch.

GOOD TO KNOW: Flemington is a mixture of quaint and commercial, with 60 percent of its buildings on the National Register of Historic Places. At Ringoes, a new museum car houses a display of railroad artifacts and a model railroad.

WORTH DOING: Northlandz, an extraordinary model railroad rich in spectacle, is located in Flemington. With eight actual miles of track, dozens of trains moving at once, and 35-foot-tall model mountains, it's acres of whimsical fun. It also features a collection of 200 dolls.

DON'T MISS: Just across the Delaware River in Pennsylvania is the New Hope & Ivyland Railroad, which makes it easy to ride two excursion trains in the same day. Almost as close is the Delaware River Railroad in Phillipsburg, N.J.

GETTING THERE: Flemington is roughly 35 miles from Philadelphia and 50 miles from New York City. Ringoes is about 15 miles farther from each city. Both Ringoes and Flemington are located just off Route 202. The Flemington station is on Stangl Road.

Delaware River Railroad

LOCATION: 100 Elizabeth Street, Phillipsburg
PHONE: 877-872-4674 or 908-454-4433
WEBSITE: 877trainride.com
E-MAIL: ccotty@fastwww.com

Dave Crosby

Ride along the scenic Delaware River in western New Jersey from Phillipsburg to Carpentersville aboard one of only two operating steam locomotives in the state.

CHOICES: The Delaware River Railroad operates several themed trains in addition to the standard excursions along the Delaware River. Activities include Great Pumpkin, Corn Maze, and Mine Train specials, which are fun for the whole family as are the seasonal holiday rides, while the Warren County Wine Train offers more adult fare on its trip to two local wineries. Holiday excursions operate in November and December with diesel power.

WHEN TO GO: Beginning in May, regular excursions operate on Saturdays and Sundays through October. Autumn provides particularly breathtaking views of the changing leaves along the Delaware River.

GOOD TO KNOW: The Delaware River Railroad is operated by the New York Susquehanna & Western Technical and Historical Society, which also operates the Maywood Station Museum.

WORTH DOING: Across the river, nearby Easton, Pa., features a historic downtown with activities the whole family can enjoy such as visiting the Crayola Museum and the National Canal Museum.

DON'T MISS: Having been served by five different railroads, Phillipsburg is rich in railroad history. Be sure to visit the nearby Phillipsburg Union Station, a museum containing artifacts, maps, and photos of New Jersey railroad history. A short distance away, the Phillipsburg Railroad Historians offer a miniature train ride several times during summer.

GETTING THERE: Situated on the Delaware River, Phillipsburg is located along the New Jersey–Pennsylvania border. It is easily reached by automobile via Route 22 or I-78. The station is just off Main Street in Phillipsburg.

New Jersey Museum of Transportation

LOCATION: 4265 Route 524, Farmingdale
PHONE: 732-938-5524
WEBSITE: njmt.org
E-MAIL: office@njmt.org

New Jersey Museum of Transportation

The museum is home to many rare pieces of equipment, and it offers a short ride on a narrow gauge train on the grounds of Allaire State Park.

CHOICES: Besides looking at the equipment on display, you have the opportunity to tour the museum's shops and see the progress on various restoration projects. The train travels through the scenic state park, which is home to the Manasquan River.

WHEN TO GO: The vintage locomotives run weekends April through June and September through December. In July and August, diesel locomotives run daily. During the Railroader's Weekend Celebration in mid-September, all the equipment in running shape operates. The Christmas Express, which started more than 30 years ago, begins running in late November and continues into December.

GOOD TO KNOW: Founded by one of the oldest all-volunteer railroad preservation groups, the museum began as the Pine Creek Railroad in 1952, using rail salvaged from sand pits.

WORTH DOING: In the park, you can explore Allaire Village, a historic 19th century ironmaking town. The park also contains hiking and biking trails.

DON'T MISS: Look for the Ely-Thomas Lumber Company Shay locomotive. While not operable at present, it is one of the smallest Shays left in existence.

GETTING THERE: The museum is located in Allaire State Park, not far from the ocean. It is easily accessible from the Garden State Parkway or I-195 off Exit 31B. Signs show the way to the park.

Whippany Railway Museum

LOCATION: 1 Railroad Plaza, Whippany
PHONE: 973-887-8177
WEBSITE: whippanyrailwaymuseum.net
E-MAIL: info@whippanyrailwaymuseum.net

Whippany Railway Museum, Steve Hepler

The Whippany Railway Museum, which is housed in a restored 1904 freight house, displays a large selection of historic locomotives and rolling stock. Much of the collection focuses on New Jersey railroading. Look for steam locomotive No. 4039 (former U.S. Army 0-6-0 No. 4039 and ex-Virginia Blue Ridge Railway No. 5) to be back in service after its restoration.

CHOICES: The Whippany Railway Museum also operates several themed and special event excursions throughout the year including caboose rides and Easter, pumpkin, and Santa Claus trains. The museum's collection features a 100-year-old Baldwin 2-8-0 steam locomotive, a CNJ observation car, a D&H caboose, a railbus, and several vintage diesels including an RS1 and two GE 70-tonners. Among the structures on the grounds are a Morristown & Erie Railroad passenger station made of fieldstone and a wooden water tank. Interior exhibits are changed each year to highlight a different railroad.

WHEN TO GO: The Whippany Railway Museum is open Sundays April through October. Special excursions run on select dates throughout the year.

GOOD TO KNOW: The museum grounds are adjacent to the Morristown & Erie Railroad, an active freight hauler. The museum was originally founded as the Morris County Central Railroad Museum in 1967 to complement the Morris County Central's steam excursion line. Several pieces of former Morris County Central have been acquired by the museum.

WORTH DOING: The town of Whippany plays host to a number of outdoor recreational activities such as the Patriots Path hiking and biking trail.

DON'T MISS: Ride the 1927 Jersey Coast club car which has been magnificently restored and features a *Blue Comet* paint scheme.

GETTING THERE: Whippany is in northeast New Jersey, about 20 miles from Newark. It easily reached via I-80, I-78, or I-287. The museum is located at the intersection of Routes 10 and 511 (Whippany Road) in Whippany.

NEW MEXICO

Belen Harvey House Museum

Adjacent to the BNSF Division yard, the museum contains exhibits on Harvey Houses and the Santa Fe Railroad. Listed on the National Register of Historic Places, the Southwestern-style structure is one of state's few surviving Fred Harvey eating establishments. The museum is open Tuesday through Sunday.

LOCATION: 104 N. First Street, Belen
PHONE: 505-861-0581
WEBSITE: belenharveyhouse.com

Las Cruces Railroad Museum

The museum is housed in a 1910 AT&SF depot with a Mission Revival look. Its photographs, artifacts, and displays highlight the depot itself, railroad workers, and communication. It also features a model railroad train room. The museum offers a variety of lectures and programs, including Railroad Days in May. It is open Thursday through Saturday.

LOCATION: 351 N. Mesilla Street, Las Cruces
PHONE: 575-647-4480
WEBSITE: las-cruces.org
E-MAIL: gcourts@las-cruces.org

Cumbres & Toltec Scenic Railroad

LOCATION: 500 Terrace Avenue, Chama
PHONE: 888-286-2737 or 575-756-2151
WEBSITE: cumbrestoltec.com
E-MAIL: info@cumbrestoltec.com

Cumbres & Toltec Scenic Railroad

If you have ever craved going back in time to the 1920s to see what railroading was like, here's your chance. The Cumbres & Toltec operates 64 miles of track through the San Juan Mountains. Steam locomotives still labor up steep grades, cross 100-foot-tall trestles, and hug narrow shelves above yawning gorges. For more than 125 years, passengers have ridden over Cumbres Pass, and the line crosses the border between Colorado and New Mexico 11 times.

CHOICES: The railroad offers a choice of excursions, and you can leave from either Chama or Antonito, Colo. From either station, there is a round trip to Osier, Colo., where a hot meal is provided. To see the scenic area in two different ways, you can ride the train one way and return by motor coach. The ride from Chama to Antonito shows you steam locomotives at work as the 2-8-2 Mikado type engines original to this line dig in and go upgrade for several miles. Ride an open-window coach or a first-class car, and as your train moves along, be sure and walk back to the open gondola car. It's a great view and a lot of fun.

WHEN TO GO: Excursion trains operate daily from the end of May until mid-October. Wild West trains and other special events take place during the season. On some weekends, sunset trains will operate from Chama to the new pavilion at Cumbres.

GOOD TO KNOW: The Friends of the Cumbres & Toltec Scenic Railroad have installed two webcams that allow you to virtually visit the railroad's Chama yard. You can access them at www.coloradonewmexicosteamtrain.org.

WORTH DOING: The nearby Rio Grande National Forest contains the headwaters of the Rio Grande River and features the moonlike landscape of the Wheeler Geologic Area and a variety of other natural wonders.

DON'T MISS: Walk the Chama shop complex and yard, where you'll see the coaling tower, water tank, back shop, and all sorts of clutter that is natural to a railroad yard.

GETTING THERE: The railroad is located between Santa Fe and Colorado Springs. To reach Chama from Santa Fe, take Highway 285 to Highway 84. Highway 285 also takes you to Antonito.

Santa Fe Southern Railway

LOCATION: 430-A W. Manhattan Street, Santa Fe
PHONE: 505-989-8600
WEBSITE: sfsr.com
E-MAIL: depot@sfsr.com

David Lustig

One of the most famous railroad names of all is the Atchison, Topeka & Santa Fe Railway, usually known simply as the Santa Fe. This railway offers the chance to ride through the desert from Santa Fe along a historic spur to the junction city of Lamy.

CHOICES: Even if it wasn't a beautiful trip through the desert, the Santa Fe Southern offers something special: a chance to ride a working freight train. The railroad's scenic day train is a four-hour round trip aboard a real working mixed train. Along with vintage coaches, the train will most likely pull boxcars between Santa Fe and Lamy. Other excursions run as well. You have the choice of riding in coaches or vintage AT&SF *Super Chief* cars.

WHEN TO GO: The excursion trains operate year-round. There are numerous special events scheduled throughout the year, especially around holidays, as well as barbecue dinners and evening desert runs.

GOOD TO KNOW: If you would like to see one of the last surviving Harvey Houses, you can visit La Fonda Hotel located in Santa Fe's historic plaza.

WORTH DOING: The Lamy depot, built in 1880, has been renovated to match the style of the depot in Santa Fe.

DON'T MISS: Santa Fe is well known for its Southwest culture and art galleries, which number more than 200. Be sure and visit the Georgia O'Keeffe Museum.

GETTING THERE: Santa Fe is 60 miles northeast of Albuquerque on I-25 and Highway 285. In Santa Fe, the station is on Manhattan Street where it meets Guadalupe Street.

NEW YORK

Alco Heritage Museum

This new museum features items manufactured by American Locomotive Co. Among the items on display are a Boston & Maine RS3, an M-47 Patton tank, and a 1909 Black Beast automobile. It plans on outfitting a locomotive cab as a simulator. Located near the Alco plant site, the museum is open Saturdays and Sundays.

LOCATION: 1910 Maxon Road, Schnectady
PHONE: 518-557-2673
WEBSITE: ahts.org
E-MAIL: form on website

Brooks Alco Railroad Display

Located at the Chautauqua County Fairgrounds, this display features an Alco-Brooks 0-6-0 locomotive built in 1916, a Delaware & Hudson wood-sided boxcar, a wooden New York Central caboose, and other railroad artifacts.

LOCATION: 1089 Central Avenue, Dunkirk
PHONE: 716-366-3797
WEBSITE: dunkirkhistoricalmuseum.org
E-MAIL: contact@dunkirkhistoricalmuseum.org

Central Square Station Museum

The museum has various pieces of rail equipment on outdoor display including two 0-4-0 steam locomotives, a 1929 Brill car, a circus car, a streetcar, and a GE diesel switcher. Indoor exhibits are housed in an early 20th century depot. It is open Sundays May through October.

LOCATION: 132 Railroad Street, Central Square
WEBSITE: cnynrhs.org/CentralSq.html
E-MAIL: csquare@cnynrhs.org

Cooperstown & Charlotte Valley Railroad

While track repairs are being made, regular excursion and special trains are currently operating between Milford Depot and Cooperstown Dreams Park. (Check website for updates.) In the restored 1869 Milford depot, you can view an array of railroad displays.

LOCATION: 136 E. Main Street, Milford
PHONE: 607-432-2429 or 607-286-7805
WEBSITE: lrhs.com
E-MAIL: wendy@lrhs.com

Empire State Railway Museum

Through photos, films, and artifacts, the museum highlights the history of railroads that served the Catskills. The museum, located in a restored 1899 Ulster & Delaware Railroad station, is also restoring several railway cars and a 1910 2-8-0 locomotive. It is open weekends and holidays from Memorial Day through October.

LOCATION: 70 Lower High Street, Phoenicia
PHONE: 845-688-7501
WEBSITE: esrm.com
E-MAIL: ovondrak@yahoo.com

Hyde Park Railroad Station

Built in 1914, the Hyde Park Railroad Station is listed on the National Register of Historic Places. You can tour the restored station, which was designed by the same architects who designed Grand Central Station, and view displays on the area's railroading history. It is open weekends and holidays during summer and on Monday evenings year-round.

LOCATION: 34 River Road, Hyde Park
PHONE: 845-229-2338
WEBSITE: hydeparkstation.com
E-MAIL: milotsukroff@netscape.net

Martisco Station Museum

This restored 1870 New York Central station contains two floors of local railroad artifacts. On the first floor of this Victorian-style brick structure, you'll enter a replica of a small-town railroad station. Items are displayed outside as well. It is open Sunday afternoons late May until October.

LOCATION: 5085 Martisco Road, Marcellus
WEBSITE: cnynrhs.org/Martisco.html
E-MAIL: martisco@cnynrhs.org

New York Museum of Transportation

The museum exhibits various trolley cars, a steam locomotive, a caboose, and rail artifacts as well as highway and horse-drawn vehicles. Trolley rides from the museum take you to Midway station, where you can connect with a diesel train or track car that takes you to the nearby Rochester & Genesee Valley Railroad Museum. The NYMT is open Sundays year-round.

LOCATION: 6393 E. River Road, Rush
PHONE: 585-533-1113
WEBSITE: nymtmuseum.org
E-MAIL: info@nymtmuseum.org

New York Transit Museum

Located in a 1936 subway station, the New York Transit Museum features restored subway cars and other exhibits related to urban transit. Exhibits highlight elevated rail lines and the construction of New York City's first subway line. The museum also offers special subway tours and events during the year.

LOCATION: Boerum Place at Schermerhorn Street, Brooklyn
PHONE: 718-694-1600
WEBSITE: mta.info/mta/museum

North Creek Railway Depot Museum

Step into the North Creek Depot Museum, and you'll relive a piece of presidential history. The depot is where Theodore Roosevelt learned he had become president at the death of President McKinley. The museum features an exhibit on this event as well as ones on area history, the Adirondack Railroad, and other railroads. The museum complex includes a restored freight house, an engine house, and a working turntable. The Saratoga & North Creek Railway also boards from the depot's platform.

LOCATION: 5 Railroad Place, North Creek
PHONE: 518-251-5842
WEBSITE: northcreekdepotmuseum.com
E-MAIL: director@northcreekdepotmuseum.com

Railroad Museum of Long Island

The Railroad Museum of Long Island has two locations: Greenport and Riverhead. Greenport, situated in a Victorian-style Long Island Rail Road freight station, exhibits photos and artifacts of Long Island rail history. It displays an 1898 snowplow and a 1927 wooden caboose. An operating tower and turntable are also on site. At Riverhead, the museum restores its rolling stock and displays several steam locomotives and various railcars. A miniature train ride also operates around the site. The Riverhead visitor center is located at 416 Griffing Avenue. At times, you can take the LIRR and tour both sites in one day.

LOCATION: 440 Fourth Street, Greenport
PHONE: 631-477-0439 (Greenport) or 631-727-7920 (Riverhead)
WEBSITE: rmli.us
E-MAIL: info@rmli.us

Railroad Museum of the Niagara Frontier

Housed in a restored Erie Railroad freight depot, which was built in 1922, the museum contains a collection of artifacts that recognizes the region's railroading heritage. Also on display are several industrial locomotives, an Erie caboose, and a New York Central caboose.

LOCATION: 111 Oliver Street, North Tonawanda
PHONE: 716-694-9588
WEBSITE: railroadniagara.com
E-MAIL: museum@nfcnrhs.com

Rochester & Genesee Valley Railroad Museum

The Rochester & Genesee Valley Railroad Museum is housed in a restored 1918 Erie Railroad depot. Inside, you'll see the original ticket agent's office, waiting room, and artifacts. You can also inspect various early diesel and steam locomotives, freight cars, and passenger cars. It is open Sundays mid-May through October. Start your visit at nearby New York Museum of Transportation and take a train, trolley, or track-car ride over to the RGVRRM.

LOCATION: 282 Rush-Scottsville Road, Rush
PHONE: 585-533-1431
WEBSITE: rgvrrm.org
E-MAIL: form on website

Roscoe O&W Railway Museum

This museum complex features a station building, a restored Ontario & Western caboose, a Beaverkill trout car, and watchman shanties. The museum specializes in O&W memorabilia and artifacts but also contains other railroad and local historical items.

LOCATION: 7 Railroad Avenue, Roscoe
PHONE: 607-498-4346
WEBSITE: nyow.org

Salamanca Rail Museum

This Buffalo, Rochester & Pittsburgh depot has been fully restored right down to the telegraph key in the ticket office, and it includes a ladies retiring room and a baggage room. Artifacts and photos show the history of railroads in western New York and Pennsylvania. A boxcar, a crew camp car, and two cabooses are on display.

LOCATION: 170 Main Street, Salamanca
PHONE: 716-945-3133
WEBSITE: mysite.verizon.net/bizxyrad/salamancarailmuseumassociation
E-MAIL: salarail@verizon.net

Trolley Museum of New York

The museum operates a trolley ride aboard No. 358, a restored 1925 trolley, from Kingston to the banks of the Hudson River, where you can enjoy a picnic lunch. With a stop at the museum, you can learn about trolleys and see them being restored. The museum's collection dates back to the early 1900s. The museum is open weekends and holidays from Memorial Day weekend to Columbus Day.

LOCATION: 89 E. Strand Street, Kingston
PHONE: 845-331-3399
WEBSITE: tmny.org
E-MAIL: admin@tmny.org

Adirondack Scenic Railroad

LOCATION: 321 Main Street, Utica
PHONE: 800-819-2291 or 315-724-0700
WEBSITE: adirondackrr.com
E-MAIL: info@adirondackrr.com

Karl Zimmermann

The Adirondack Scenic Railroad currently operates excursions over two sections of line—52 miles of the former New York Central's Adirondack Division from Utica to Thendara (plus an additional six miles on to Carter Station) and 10 miles between Lake Placid and Saranac Lake.

CHOICES: For serious riders, the railroad offers all-day excursions from Utica to Thendara two or three days a week from mid-July through October. There is time for visiting the resort town of Old Forge and taking a two-hour cruise on the Fulton Chain of Lakes. Shorter round trips (of 20 miles, either south to Otter Lake or north to Carter Station) are offered from Thendara June through mid-October. Similar trips operate between Saranac Lake and Lake Placid at the other end of the railroad. You can ride in coaches or in open-air cars to soak in the scenery.

WHEN TO GO: The brilliant foliage of fall makes that season a fine time to ride. In late November through mid-December, the railroad offers *Polar Express* trains.

GOOD TO KNOW: The Adirondack Scenic offers a complete smorgasbord of special trains and events throughout the year including dinner, beer and wine-tasting, Halloween, and Doo Wop '50s trains.

WORTH DOING: Thendara, Saranac Lake, and Lake Placid are all deep in the Adirondacks, replete with natural beauty. The region's history is interestingly presented at the Adirondack Museum in Blue Mountain Lake. Adirondack Park offers 2,000 miles of hiking trails and hundreds of miles of kayaking routes.

DON'T MISS: The Adirondack Scenic Railroad shares Utica's grand 1914 Union Station with Amtrak, making it among the few excursion railroads with rail connections. Take time to look through this historic station. An easy walk away is the Hotel Utica, which predates the station by two years. Its restored lobby is also worth a look.

GETTING THERE: Served by multiple Amtrak trains each day, Utica also has excellent highway access, being located right on the New York State Thruway (I-90). The nearest major airport is in Syracuse. Lake Placid is 30 miles from the Adirondack Northway (I-87). Adirondack Regional Airport is in Clear Lake, 15 miles away.

Arcade & Attica Railroad

LOCATION: 278 Main Street, Arcade
PHONE: 585-492-3100
WEBSITE: arcadeandatticarr.com
E-MAIL: form on website

Dave Crosby

When steam engine No. 18 blows its whistle, you get a real blast from the past. The Arcade & Attica Railroad offers the last remaining steam locomotive excursion in New York. This 90-minute scenic ride rolls through countryside that has changed little since the line was formed in the early 1880s.

CHOICES: On the 14-mile round trip, you can ride aboard steel heavyweight coaches that were built around 1915 or an open-air gondola observation car (just watch out for soot). The train may also be pulled by a General Electric 44-ton center cab diesel, either No. 111 or No. 112. No. 111 was originally purchased by the railroad in 1947. In the Arcade station, you can view historic photographs, artifacts, and operating model railroad layouts. A 1920s boxcar and caboose are also on display.

WHEN TO GO: Regular steam excursions run on weekends from Memorial Day through September. During July and August, additional rides take place on Wednesdays and Fridays, and there is a special extended schedule in October for viewing fall foliage. Murder mystery, Halloween, Christmas, and other special trains also run during the season. Diesel locomotives operate after Halloween.

GOOD TO KNOW: Tourist steam excursions began in 1962, and the railroad has been been carrying passengers for 50 years. In 2013, look for dinner theater trains to begin operating.

WORTH DOING: A special Civil War reenactment takes place in August that includes a battle with Union and Confederate troops fighting on and off the train. A free shuttle bus takes you to a park where the troops are encamped, so you can see how soldiers and civilians lived in the 1860s.

DON'T MISS: On the 15-minute stopover at Curriers depot, watch No. 18 run around for the return trip to Arcade. You can even take pictures and talk to the crew. Then, for a unique experience, hop in the gondola, which is now coupled to the front of the engine, for the ride back.

GETTING THERE: Arcade is located about an hour's drive south of Buffalo. The museum is located three miles east of Route 16 on Main Street at Railroad Avenue.

Catskill Mountain Railroad

LOCATION: 5408 Route 28, Mount Tremper
PHONE: 845-688-7400
WEBSITE: catskillmtrailroad.com
E-MAIL: info@catskillmtrailroad.com

Karl Zimmermann

The Catskill Mountain Railroad operates at two locations, both segments of the former Ulster & Delaware Railroad, which later became New York Central's Catskill Mountain Branch. The longer section runs from Mount Tremper to Boiceville, a distance of 2.5 miles. The railroad also operates over 1.5 miles of track in Kingston.

CHOICES: Of the two operations, the more extensive and scenic is the one from Mount Tremper, which runs along Esopus Creek. You can ride in either an open car or a restored 1917 Delaware, Lackawanna & Western coach pulled by an ex-Long Island Rail Road Alco S1 built in 1946. Trains may be boarded at Mount Tremper or Phoenicia for the full round trip. The Kingston City Shuttle, powered by an Alco RS1 built in 1950 for the Illinois Terminal, boards at the Westbrook station.

WHEN TO GO: The fall foliage season is the prime time to ride along the Esopus, although trains operate through the summer as well—and that too is a lovely time to visit the Catskill Mountains. From July through October, the Esopus trains run on weekends, which except in September includes Fridays. The *Twilight Limited* runs on several summer evenings from Mount Tremper for a look at the night sky, with entertainment provided by an excellent string band. The Kingston Shuttle runs on Saturdays in July and August, along with Halloween and winter holiday trains.

GOOD TO KNOW: Tracks are being restored across the Hurley Flats to reach Hurley Mountain Road.

WORTH DOING: When the Catskill Mountain Railroad first opened, its primary function was to haul whitewater inner tubers, rafters, and kayakers upstream along Esopus Creek. These sports remain popular, and the trout fishing is good as well.

DON'T MISS: The restored Phoenicia depot, which opened in 1900 and is now home to the Empire State Railway Museum, is near Mount Tremper. Also just a short drive away is the Delaware & Ulster Railroad, which offers excursions from Arkville.

GETTING THERE: Both sections of the railroad are easily accessible from Exit 19 of the New York State Thruway (I-87). The Kingston Shuttle is virtually right there. For Mount Tremper, follow Route 28 west for roughly 20 miles.

Delaware & Ulster Railroad

LOCATION: 43510 Route 28, Arkville
PHONE: 800-225-4132 or 845-586-3877
WEBSITE: durr.org
E-MAIL: tours@durr.org

Karl Zimmermann

The Delaware & Ulster Railroad's 12-mile excursions, a round trip of just under two hours, run from Arkville north to Roxbury, much of it along the scenic East Branch of the Delaware River, across rolling fields and through small towns in the heart of the Catskill Mountains.

CHOICES: In addition to the scenic excursions aboard open cars or ex-Pennsylvania Railroad coaches, the D&U also operates a luncheon train, the *Rip Van Winkle Flyer*. While the *Flyer* doesn't have a set schedule, operating only if a group has made a booking, the public is welcome on these occasions whenever there's available space, which there most often is. Motive power for the excursion and luncheon trains is generally an Alco RS36 resplendent in its original Delaware & Hudson livery.

WHEN TO GO: The Delaware & Ulster operates on Saturdays and Sundays from Memorial Day through the end of October, with Thursday and Friday trains added in July and August. On the railroad route through the Catskill Mountains, there's no more spectacular time for a visit than during the fall foliage season.

GOOD TO KNOW: The *Rip Van Winkle Flyer* is a handsome, five-car Budd-built streamliner, featuring an ex-New York Central parlor-observation car and a dome diner that began life as a Missouri Pacific dome coach.

WORTH DOING: The Catskill Scenic Trail lies along 26 miles of the former Catskill Mountain Branch Railroad Line. It passes through seven towns and connects with hundreds of miles of other trails. The four-season trail is used by hikers, bicyclists, cross country skiers, and horseback riders.

DON'T MISS: The depots at both Roxbury and Arkville offer displays of photographs and artifacts highlighting the history of the Ulster & Delaware.

GETTING THERE: Arkville is a 43-mile drive on Route 28 from Exit 19 on the New York State Thruway (I-87). Route 28 passes right by the depot.

Medina Railroad Museum

LOCATION: 530 West Avenue, Medina
PHONE: 585-798-6106
WEBSITE: railroadmuseum.net
E-MAIL: office@railroadmuseum.net

Jim Wrinn

The area east of Buffalo provides a pleasant distraction with small towns, farms, and a relaxed existence. Here, you'll find a museum located inside one of the largest surviving wooden freight houses around. You will also have the opportunity to ride a streamlined passenger train.

CHOICES: The old New York Central freight house is huge—301 feet long and 34 feet wide—and contains memorabilia, models, and artifacts. Enter the Union Station archway, and you'll see displays dedicated to the trains, such as the *Empire State Express* and *20th Century Limited*, and railroads, including the Pennsylvania Railroad, that helped develop the area. On a former New York Central main line, you can ride in 1947 Budd coaches pulled by a historic Alco Century diesel locomotive. The two-hour, 34-mile round trip parallels and then crosses the Erie Canal. The trains run on select days. One special is an all-day winery train.

WHEN TO GO: The museum is open year-round Tuesday through Sunday. Fall foliage trips during October and Santa trains during December are very popular train rides.

GOOD TO KNOW: Ask about the bridge at Lockport, which, according to legend, was built upside down so as to limit the size of barge traffic on the competing Erie Canal.

WORTH DOING: For a unique experience, take a one-of-a-kind ride in a mule-drawn packet boat on the Erie Canal.

DON'T MISS: In the museum, watch a large HO scale model railroad in action. The prototypical railroad layout measures 14 feet by 204 feet. Also, take a close look at the lobby, which is refinished as the freight depot office.

GETTING THERE: Medina is situated between Buffalo and Rochester, not far from Lake Ontario. From Buffalo, take I-90 east to Route 77. Continue north on Route 77/63 to downtown Medina. There, turn left onto North Avenue and then turn right onto West Avenue.

Saratoga & North Creek Railway

LOCATION: 3 Railroad Place, North Creek
PHONE: 877-726-7245
WEBSITE: sncrr.com
E-MAIL: info@sncrr.com

Karl Zimmermann

The Saratoga & North Creek Railway operates passenger trains over 56.5 miles of the former Delaware & Hudson Railway's Adirondack Branch, connecting S&NC's namesake cities of Saratoga Springs and North Creek and making seven flag stops in between, thus running as a typical passenger railroad. The northern part of the line follows the Hudson River, which is a scenic, rushing whitewater stream there near its source.

CHOICES: S&NC features two levels of service, coach and first class, the latter offered in full-length dome cars. Depending on departure time, full breakfast, lunch, or dinner menus are offered aboard the domes—on the upper level for passengers with tickets for dome seating and on the lower level for coach passengers.

WHEN TO GO: Trains operate daily from Memorial Day through October, with two trains operating Friday through Monday and one Tuesday through Thursday. The region's brilliant fall foliage makes that the season of choice for excursions. Ski trains also run to Gore Mountain and other resort areas during winter.

GOOD TO KNOW: From Thursday through Monday, the S&NC makes all four connections at Saratoga Springs to and from Albany and New York City with Amtrak's *Adirondack* and *Ethan Allan Express*.

WORTH DOING: Both Saratoga Springs and North Creek offer ample recreational opportunities. Nestled in the Adirondack Mountains, North Creek is a hub for outdoor activities such as hiking and kayaking the Hudson River. Just a few miles away, you'll find the historic Barton Garnet Mines. With its historic downtown, Saratoga Springs is a city of elegant homes and quality restaurants. At its historic track, thoroughbreds race from mid-July through Labor Day.

DON'T MISS: Leave time to visit the North Creek Depot Museum, which contains exhibits about the Adirondack region and Theodore Roosevelt's train ride to be sworn in as President of the United States.

GETTING THERE: Both Saratoga Springs and North Creek are easily accessible from the Adirondack Northway (I-87). The nearest city with a major airport is Albany.

NORTH CAROLINA

Charlotte Trolley Powerhouse Museum

The museum features exhibits devoted to streetcars, including Car 85, which is one of Charlotte's original electric trolley cars. The museum also hosts arts and other special events.

LOCATION: 1507 Camden Road, Charlotte
PHONE: 704-375-0850
WEBSITE: charlottetrolley.org
E-MAIL: info@charlottetrolley.org

Craggy Mountain Line

This new operation offers a ride over three miles of historic track from Asheville to Craggy Branch in a caboose train. Motor car rides are also available. Its collection of equipment includes several restored Southern Railway cabooses, an original 1925 Asheville trolley car, and a Tweetsie gas-powered motor car.

LOCATION: 111 N. Woodfin Avenue, Asheville
PHONE: 828-808-4877
WEBSITE: newtondepot.com
E-MAIL: rocky@craggymountainline.com

Southeastern Narrow Gauge & Short Line Museum

A restored 1924 depot contains displays devoted to narrow gauge and short line railroads. Across from the depot is a newly constructed carbarn that contains a variety of rolling stock including an 1870s boxcar, a 2-6-0 Mogul steam locomotive, and an Alco S3 diesel.

LOCATION: 1123 N. Main Avenue, Newton
PHONE: 828-464-3930
WEBSITE: newtondepot.com

Wilmington Railroad Museum

The museum is housed in an 1880s railroad freight warehouse, where you can view Atlantic Coast Line artifacts and a re-creation of a country station. Outside, you can inspect a 1910 Baldwin steam locomotive, a hobo display in a boxcar, and an Atlantic Coast Line caboose. The museum is open year-round.

LOCATION: 505 Nutt Street, Wilmington
PHONE: 910-763-2634
WEBSITE: wrrm.org
E-MAIL: form on website

Great Smoky Mountains Railroad

LOCATION: 226 Everett Street, Bryson City
PHONE: 800-872-4681 or 828-586-8811
WEBSITE: gsmr.com
E-MAIL: info@gsmr.com

Great Smoky Mountains Railroad

Few mountain railroads in the southeastern United States traverse such splendid scenery as this line does. Created from a portion of Southern Railway's Murphy Branch, the GSMR hugs the Tuckaseegee and Nantahala Rivers, climbs a mountain at Red Marble Gap, and rolls out over a 700-foot-long trestle at Fontana Lake.

CHOICES: GSMR offers a variety of accommodations on two different train rides. The train features open-air cars, traditional coaches, and air-conditioned lounge cars. A 4.5-hour excursion travels to Nantahala Gorge and back and includes a layover at the Nantahala Outdoor Center. The other is a 32-mile round trip along the Tuckasegee River to Dillsboro. Seating options include standard coach, crown class, premium open-air, and first class. First-class service includes lunch options.

WHEN TO GO: The railroad runs year-round. Spring and fall offer mild weather best suited to open cars and being able to see beyond the trees and into the forest. Summer can be humid, and the tremendous foliage of the Southeast can restrict the views.

GOOD TO KNOW: The railroad offers numerous special events throughout the year, including some ideal for kids (Thomas the Tank Engine and the *Polar Express*). Some steam trains may run during the summer schedule.

WORTH DOING: In the area, you can visit several theme parks, discover Cherokee culture, and explore Great Smoky Mountains National Park from the North Carolina side.

DON'T MISS: Try an adventurous combination package in which you ride the train from Bryson City into the Nantahala Gorge and then raft the river for three hours.

GETTING THERE: The railroad is about three hours from Atlanta and one hour from Asheville. Major highways to the area include I-40, Route 19/23, and Route 441. The station in Bryson City is downtown.

New Hope Valley Railway

LOCATION: 5121 Daisey Street, Bonsal
PHONE: 919-362-5416
WEBSITE: triangletrain.com
E-MAIL: info@nhvry.org

Patrick Treadaway Jr.

Operating from the North Carolina Railroad Museum, the New Hope Valley Railway provides an hour-long trip through the scenic pine forests situated south of Raleigh and Durham in central North Carolina.

CHOICES: The railway offers both steam and diesel round trips between Bonsal and New Hill. You can ride in an open-air car, but try a ride in a real caboose. It doesn't get any better than that! The museum features an outdoor exhibit of railroad equipment as well as displays of local rail artifacts. It includes a variety of industrial and short line diesel locomotives.

WHEN TO GO: The railway operates on one Sunday each month from April through December, as well as on other select days, with Halloween and Santa trains scheduled. The North Carolina Railroad Museum is open weekends.

GOOD TO KNOW: The railroad offers the chance to operate a diesel electric or 0-4-0T steam locomotive, which is an oil-burning switcher that began operation in 1941.

WORTH DOING: The American Tobacco Trail runs near the railway. The trail is built over part of an old rail line that carried tobacco. You can hike, bike, and ride horses along the trail. Special events take place in the trail's New Hill parking lot.

DON'T MISS: Kids will especially enjoy the G scale garden railroad that operates on the grounds.

GETTING THERE: Located between Bonsal and New Hill, the railroad is a 30-minute drive from Raleigh along Route 1. Take Exit 89, turn right on New Hill Holleman Road, and then turn left onto old Route 1 for 2.5 miles. The museum is on the right on Daisey Street, and parking for the train rides is on the left on Bonsal Road.

North Carolina Transportation Museum

LOCATION: 411 S. Salisbury Avenue, Spencer
PHONE: 704-636-2889
WEBSITE: nctrans.org
E-MAIL: nctrans@nctrans.org

Jim Wrinn

The state's transportation museum is housed in shop buildings from Southern Railway's largest steam locomotive repair shop that date from before 1900 to 1924. But this is no static museum. Trains run most of the year on 2.5 miles of track, giving visitors the chance to experience a 25-minute train ride that covers most of the 57-acre site.

CHOICES: Among the giant structures you'll see are the nation's largest preserved roundhouse, the 37-stall Robert Julian Roundhouse, which houses railroad displays, a restoration shop, active locomotives, and rolling stock. You will also see the back shop, a 600-foot-long, 80-foot-tall building once used to overhaul steam locomotives. The narrated train rides take place daily during summer, and you can ride in the locomotive cab for an extra fare. You'll get a unique view and a personalized tour. You might even get to blow the horn.

WHEN TO GO: The museum is open Wednesday through Sunday year-round, and any time of the year is enjoyable. Rail Days, the annual railroad festival when all the trains run, is usually held in June. Summer can be sweltering, but fall is long and mild.

GOOD TO KNOW: The visitor center served as a train depot in Barber. The building was cut into three sections and moved to the site in 1980. The Flue Shop, used to repair the flues (pipes) in steam locomotive boilers, houses a collection of antique automobiles.

WORTH DOING: There are plenty of pork barbecue places in the region if you want to sample real Piedmont food.

DON'T MISS: Take a five-minute ride on the turntable. The 100-foot-long lazy Susan is used to turn locomotives at the roundhouse, and it helps define the term *in the round*.

GETTING THERE: About an hour's drive from Charlotte or Winston-Salem, the museum is a few minutes off I-85. Take Exit 79 and then follow the signs to the museum in Spencer.

Tweetsie Railroad

LOCATION: 300 Tweetsie Railroad Lane, Blowing Rock
PHONE: 800-526-5740
WEBSITE: tweetsie.com
E-MAIL: form on website

Tweetsie Railroad

One of the original Wild West theme parks of the 1950s, when TV cowboys were popular, Tweetsie has roots in one of the most famous Southeastern narrow gauge railroads, the East Tennessee & Western North Carolina. The three-mile train ride gives the historic, coal-fired engines a chance to work and show that they are still the real thing.

CHOICES: The train is pulled by steam locomotive No. 12. The native engine worked for the East Tennessee & Western North Carolina and is listed on the National Register of Historic Places. Ride in a coach close to the engine, so you can hear it work up grade and listen to the whistle echo about the mountains.

WHEN TO GO: The park is open April through November. From Memorial Day weekend through mid-August, it is open daily. An annual railfan weekend is held in September, and a ghost train runs in fall.

GOOD TO KNOW: The East Tennessee & Western North Carolina ran from Elizabeth City, Tenn., to Boone, N.C., for many years. Its whistle sounded a "tweet," and from that, locals nicknamed the railroad *Tweetsie*.

WORTH DOING: Visit the Blowing Rock and learn its legend. Hike or drive through the scenic Blue Ridge Mountains. At Grandfather Mountain, you can cross the Mile High Swinging Bridge, a 228-foot long suspension bridge that spans an 80-foot chasm.

DON'T MISS: Bring the entire family along—there's lots to see and do for kids in the park. Admission to the railroad includes amusement rides, live shows, and other attractions.

GETTING THERE: The railroad is west of Winston-Salem in the Blue Ridge Mountains near the Tennessee border. It is located off Route 321 between Boone and Blowing Rock.

NORTH DAKOTA

Bonanzaville USA

The museum features more than 40 historic buildings and 400,000 artifacts that depict life when bonanza homes dotted the Plains. Rail structures include a vintage Northern Pacific train depot, a water tower, and a train shed. The train shed displays an 1883 NP 4-4-0 steam locomotive, a caboose, and a 1930s Pullman car. It is open Memorial Day through September.

LOCATION: 1351 W. Main Avenue, West Fargo
PHONE: 701-282-2822
WEBSITE: bonanzaville.com
E-MAIL: form on website

Fort Lincoln Trolley

The trolley car takes you on a nine-mile excursion along the Heart River from Mandan to Fort Abraham Lincoln State Park and back. The park features several reconstructed buildings that would have been found in the original fort.

LOCATION: 2000 Third Street SE, Mandan
PHONE: 701-663-9018
WEBSITE: realnd.com/fortlincolntrolleyindex.htm

Midland Continental Depot Transportation Museum

The restored depot is the only surviving Midland Continental station and is on the National Register of Historic Places. The first floor houses railroad exhibits and the upper floor, once the agent's living quarters, has exhibits honoring singer Peggy Lee, who lived in the depot when her father was the agent. It is open from Memorial Day to Labor Day.

LOCATION: 401 Railway Street, Wimbledon
PHONE: 701-435-2333
WEBSITE: midlandcontinentaldepot.com
E-MAIL: midlandcontinentaldepot@gmail.com

North Dakota State Railroad Museum

New exhibits to the five-acre museum include an 1890 depot moved from Steele and a 1953 diesel switcher. The main museum building, a former BN yard office, houses artifacts from several railroads. Rolling stock includes cabooses, boxcars, and a tank car. It is open daily Memorial Day through Labor Day, with special events scheduled during the summer.

LOCATION: 3102 37th Street NW, Mandan
PHONE: 701-663-9322
WEBSITE: ndrailroading.coffeecup.com/rrmuseum
E-MAIL: ndstaterrmuseum@gmail.com

Old Soo Depot Transportation Museum

This museum focuses on the transportation history of the American West and includes materials on trains, planes, and automobiles. Located in a completely restored 1912 Soo Line depot, it also offers an excellent location for train-watching. The museum is open Monday through Friday.

LOCATION: 15 N. Main Street, Minot
PHONE: 701-852-2234
E-MAIL: soodepot@srt.com

Railroad Museum of Minot

The Railroad Museum of Minot contains artifacts relating to the Great Northern Railway and other railroads of the area. A Great Northern Railway caboose and a snowplow car are also on display. The museum is open 10-2 on Saturdays.

LOCATION: 19 First Street NE, Minot
PHONE: 701-852-7091
E-MAIL: railroadmuseum@srt.com

OHIO

AC&J Scenic Line

The railway offers a one-hour round trip that takes you over the last remaining portion of the New York Central's Ashtabula-to-Pittsburgh passenger line. On the 12-mile excursion, you'll travel on 1920s passenger cars pulled by a first-generation diesel through scenic forests and farmland and cross two bridges. A multitude of special events, including a steam train weekend, are scheduled throughout the year.

LOCATION: 161 E. Jefferson Street, Jefferson
PHONE: 440-576-6346
WEBSITE: familytrainrides.com
E-MAIL: info@acjrscenic.net

Cincinnati Dinner Train

Operating every Saturday throughout the year, the dinner train travels east from Madisonville to downtown Cincinnati, along the riverfront, and back. You'll enjoy the scenery and a four-course meal during a leisurely three-hour excursion aboard two restored 1940s dining cars or the *Silver Sword*, originally a Chicago, Burlington & Quincy coach.

LOCATION: 4725 Madison Road, Cincinnati
PHONE: 513-791-7245
WEBSITE: cincinnatirailway.com/dinnertrain
E-MAIL: cdt@cincinnatirailway.com

Conneaut Railroad Museum

Located in a Lake Shore & Michigan Southern depot, which was built in 1900, this museum displays railroad memorabilia, photos, and artifacts such as lanterns and timetables. Be sure to climb aboard and inspect the cab of Nickel Plate Berkshire No. 755 displayed outside. It is open Memorial Day weekend through Labor Day.

LOCATION: 363 Depot Street, Conneaut
PHONE: 440-599-7878

Jefferson Depot Village

The Jefferson Depot is more than a depot. It is a small village. In addition to the restored 1872 Lake Shore & Michigan Southern Railroad station, the site features a 1918 caboose and several 19th century buildings including a one-room schoolhouse, a post office, and a church. It is open June through October. The AC&J Scenic Line is right next door.

LOCATION: 147 E. Jefferson Street, Jefferson
PHONE: 440-576-0496
WEBSITE: jeffersondepotvillage.org
E-MAIL: duttonjg@hotmail.com

Lebanon Mason Monroe Railroad

The LM&M runs one-hour excursions through southwestern Ohio from April through October. You can ride in a vintage coach or, on some select dates, a Detroit, Toledo & Ironton caboose. The railroad also offers a mystery dinner train, a Civil War train, and a variety of special events, many geared toward children such as a ride to a pumpkin patch and a visit with Santa.

LOCATION: 127 S. Mechanic Street, Lebanon
PHONE: 513-933-8022
WEBSITE: lebanonrr.com
E-MAIL: info@lebanonrr.com

Marion Union Station

The station contains a museum, and a fully restored Erie Railroad tower is also on site. Located between two diamond crossings, the station is a great place to watch trains from. More than 100 go by daily. The museum is open Tuesdays and Thursdays.

LOCATION: 532 W. Center Street, Marion
PHONE: 740-383-3768
WEBSITE: mariononline.com

Northern Ohio Railway Museum

Numbering more than 40, the museum's collection of streetcars, interurbans, and other railcars continues to grow. It features streetcars and equipment that operated in Cleveland, Shaker Heights, and other cities. You can stop in and take a guided walking tour on Saturdays mid-May through October.

LOCATION: 5515 Buffham Road, Seville
PHONE: 330-769-5501
WEBSITE: trainweb.org/norm
E-MAIL: wstoner001@neo.rr.com

Ohio Railway Museum

This museum displays more than 30 pieces of equipment, including locomotives, passenger cars, and streetcars, with a focus on the Ohio Railway. It offers two-mile streetcar rides as well as some rides in its diesel-pulled passenger car. The museum is open Sunday afternoons.

LOCATION: 990 Proprietors Road, Worthington
PHONE: 614-885-7345
WEBSITE: ohiorailwaymuseum.org
E-MAIL: info@ohiorailwaymuseum.net

Orrville Railroad Heritage Society

The society offers a variety of excursions, including trips on the Wheeling & Lake Erie Railway, fall rides, and holiday trains. Railroad Days in August and other special events take place at the restored Orrville depot.

LOCATION: 145 Depot Street, Orrville
PHONE: 330-683-2426
WEBSITE: orrvillerailroad.com
E-MAIL: questions@orrvillerailroad.com

Toledo, Lake Erie & Western Railway

The TLE&W cancelled its 2012 operations to repair a washed out culvert and make other necessary track improvements. Please check the website or Facebook for the status of the 2013 season.

LOCATION: 49 N. Sixth Street, Waterville
PHONE: 419-878-2177
WEBSITE: tlew.org
E-MAIL: info@tlew.org

Cuyahoga Valley Scenic Railroad

LOCATION: 1630 Mill Street West, Peninsula
PHONE: 800-468-4070 or 330-657-2000
WEBSITE: cvsr.com
E-MAIL: form on website

Mark Perri

The Cuyahoga Valley Scenic Railroad operates over 47 miles of track through northeastern Ohio, from Independence (near Cleveland) through Peninsula and Akron to Canton. Much of the railroad is in the picturesque Cuyahoga Valley National Park, along the Cuyahoga River and the route of the abandoned Ohio & Erie Canal.

CHOICES: The CVSR runs an extensive schedule of regular trains from various boarding stations. In addition, special events run February through November. They include a variety of wine trains, educational trains, and a premier *Polar Express* train. There are several seating options including those in an elevated dome section that offer a panoramic view of the park.

WHEN TO GO: The summer months offer the most extensive schedule of regular trains. Mid-October offers extra trains for viewing the beautiful fall foliage. Trains are less crowded yet still offer spectacular scenery in April and September.

GOOD TO KNOW: The Cuyahoga Valley National Park features the Towpath Trail, which was built along much of the Ohio and Erie Canal Towpath. It is excellent for hiking and biking, and the railroad has an extensive schedule of heavily discounted Bike Aboard fares that cater to bicyclists. Many intermediate flag stops have been added to enable bikers to ride the trail one way and the train the other.

WORTH DOING: Explore many of the restored historical buildings in the national park, including the Canal Visitor Center (accessible by train) that details the canal's history and includes an operating canal lock.

DON'T MISS: The east side of the train generally includes the best views of the Cuyahoga River, which parallels the railroad, especially on the north end from Peninsula up to Independence. Many photo opportunities abound, and the park has re-created the feel of the early 1900s by building many of the railroad's depots and shelters in a style modeled after the railroad's original structures.

GETTING THERE: The Ohio Turnpike crosses the CVSR near Peninsula, and I-77 generally parallels the railroad from Cleveland to Canton.

Dennison Railroad Depot Museum

LOCATION: 400 Center Street, Dennison
PHONE: 877-278-8020 or 740-922-6776
WEBSITE: dennisondepot.org
E-MAIL: director@dennisondepot.org

Mark Perri

This meticulously restored ex-Pennsylvania Railroad depot, built in 1873, houses a comprehensive collection of exhibits highlighting the depot's significance as a World War II serviceman's canteen.

CHOICES: Dennison Railroad Depot Museum offers both guided and self-guided tours. Take time to explore a recent addition, which is made up of five remodeled coaches including a rare hospital car. A variety of interactive exhibits, many designed for children, allows visitors to climb in a caboose, sleep in a Pullman bunk, and send a message by telegraph. The museum also contains local history exhibits, houses a research library, and features a collection of railcars.

WHEN TO GO: The museum is open year-round but is closed on Mondays. It hosts numerous special events including an annual three-day Soldiers Homecoming Festival, complete with reenactors that celebrates the museum's wartime heritage.

GOOD TO KNOW: If you are hungry, a full-service restaurant, Trax Diner, is located in the depot and offers excellent lunches and dinners. Across the street, Dennison Yard, a local bar and grill, features a wonderful home-cooked Italian menu. There is also a picnic area on the museum's platform.

WORTH DOING: Dennison is close to Ohio's Amish Country in the east-central part of the state. The Pro Football Hall of Fame is 45 minutes north in Canton. The museum offers a Golden Triple Ticket, which provides discounted admission to its nearby affiliated museum partners, the Uhrichsville Clay Museum and Historic Schoenbrunn Village.

DON'T MISS: If you would like to see a hand-carved wooden locomotive, Warther Carvings Museum, 15 minutes away near Dover, features an extensive collection of carved railroad pieces in walnut, ebony, and ivory.

GETTING THERE: The nearest cities having air service are Columbus, Akron, and Pittsburgh. By car, Dennison is easily reached from I-77 via Route 250 (from the north) or Route 36 (from the south). Once in Dennison, take Second Street past the tracks and then turn left on Center Street.

Hocking Valley Scenic Railway

LOCATION: 33 E. Canal Street, Nelsonville
PHONE: 800-967-7834 or 740-753-9531
WEBSITE: hvsry.org
E-MAIL: hvsrwy@gmail.com

Mark Perri

The Hocking Valley Scenic Railway offers diesel-powered excursions with vintage open-window coaches between Nelsonville and Logan, over part of the original Hocking Valley Railway's Athens branch. The train takes you through Wayne National Forest, in the foothills of the Appalachians, and along the Hocking River.

CHOICES: The railroad's basic excursions are a 14-mile trip to Haydenville and a 22-mile trip to Logan. The trips are narrated, and you can ride in a 1920s coach, a 1930s heavyweight passenger car, or an open-air car. Along the way, besides enjoying the scenery, you'll see a canal lock, take in historical landmarks, and stop at Robbins Crossing, an 1850s-era log village.

WHEN TO GO: Excursions begin weekends in May and continue through October. To view the stunning fall foliage in the national forest, Thursday and Friday trains are added in October. Holiday and theme trips are scheduled during the year and include Easter, Halloween, and Christmas trains.

GOOD TO KNOW: Once a year, the HVR runs a special caboose train that railfans and photographers will especially enjoy.

WORTH DOING: There is something to do for everyone in Wayne National Forest. It has more than 300 miles of trails for hiking and riding bikes, horses, and ATVs. In Nelsonville, you can explore the Public Square, which contains Stuart's Opera House, the Dew House, and other historic buildings.

DON'T MISS: On your visit to Robbins Crossing, you'll see a group of original log cabins arranged into a historical village. The include a schoolhouse, blacksmith shop, general store, and several homes. Costumed guides offer commentary and demonstrate crafts.

GETTING THERE: Nelsonville is approximately 56 miles from Columbus and about 200 from Cleveland. From Columbus, take Route 33 to Nelsonville. In downtown Nelsonville, take Hocking Parkway south to the depot.

Mad River & NKP Railroad Museum

LOCATION: 253 Southwest Street, Bellevue
PHONE: 419-483-2222
WEBSITE: madrivermuseum.org
E-MAIL: madriver@onebellevue.com

Mark Perri

The Mad River & NKP Railroad Museum opened on our nation's bicentennial in 1976 as a lasting tribute to the transportation industry. The museum has a widely varied collection of railroad locomotives, coaches, freight cars, equipment, and structures.

CHOICES: While the museum focuses on the Nickel Plate Road and its successors, many other unique pieces of equipment, such as CB&Q Silver Dome No. 4714 (the first dome car built in the United States) are present. The museum is comprised of static exhibits. However, many pieces, especially the passenger equipment, have interiors that are open for inspection. In addition, some cars are outfitted with museum displays.

WHEN TO GO: The museum is open daily Memorial Day through Labor Day. In addition, the museum is open weekends in May, September, and October.

GOOD TO KNOW: Bellevue is a thriving, quaint rural Ohio town, with ample amenities for food and lodging, and many other options for tourists such as antique shops and flea markets.

WORTH DOING: Bellevue is a 30-minute drive from Sandusky and the Cedar Point amusement park, which is known for its roller coasters and its steam-powered, narrow gauge railroad.

DON'T MISS: Many opportunities exist for watching and photographing trains from public property around town. It is a major hub for the Norfolk Southern and home of one of the largest classification yards in the eastern United States. Mainline tracks bisect the museum, where you can see Norfolk Southern Heritage units or regional Wheeling & Lake Erie Railway trains.

GETTING THERE: The nearest major airports are Toledo, Cleveland, and Detroit. Amtrak's *Lakeshore Limited* and *Capitol Limited* stop in Toledo. For those driving, Bellevue is 20 minutes from the Ohio Turnpike off Exit 110.

OKLAHOMA

Frisco Depot Museum

Once a main hub for the Frisco, the depot in Hugo is now a museum. Listed on the National Register of Historic Places, the museum features preserved Harvey Girl rooms, railroad artifacts, and displays on local history. It also includes a restored and operational Harvey House restaurant. Outside the museum, the depot park contains a narrow gauge steam locomotive and picnic areas.

LOCATION: 307 N. B Street, Hugo
PHONE: 580-326-6630
WEBSITE: friscodepot.org
E-MAIL: friscodepot@live.com

Heritage Express Trolley

This 25-minute trolley ride is the only rail-based trolley in operation in Oklahoma. It runs from Heritage Park to downtown El Reno. Heritage Park is also home of the Canadian County Museum, which is based in a historical Rock Island train depot.

LOCATION: 300 S. Grand Avenue, El Reno
PHONE: 405-262-5121
WEBSITE: elreno.org
E-MAIL: info@elreno.org

Oklahoma Railway Museum

The museum possesses an interesting collection of equipment that includes a Santa Fe FP45 with a warbonnet paint scheme. It also operates a variety of train rides and special events. The museum's newest display features the 1879 Santa Fe steam locomotive, Frisco caboose, and track speeder that were displayed at the Oklahoma State Fairgrounds since the 1950s. It is open Thursday through Saturday, with train rides taking place April to October.

LOCATION: 3400 NE Grand Boulevard, Oklahoma City
PHONE: 405-424-8222
WEBSITE: oklahomarailwaymuseum.org
E-MAIL: drake@oklahomarailwaymuseum.org

Railroad Museum of Oklahoma

Located in a former Santa Fe freight house, this museum houses a large collection of railroad artifacts and memorabilia including a replica Pullman car interior. In the yard, you can climb aboard a 1925 Baldwin 4-8-2 steam locomotive, wander through cabooses from nine different railroads, and view an assortment of freight cars. The museum also sponsors several all-caboose excursions. It is open Tuesdays through Sundays year-round.

LOCATION: 702 N. Washington Street, Enid
PHONE: 580-233-3051
WEBSITE: railroadmuseumofoklahoma.org
E-MAIL: railroad_museum@att.net

Route 66 Village

In the village, you'll see the restored Frisco 4500 *Meteor* steam engine along with a passenger coach, tank car, caboose, and trolley car. A 154-foot oil derrick stands next to the railcars. It also features indoor historical exhibits related to Route 66 and Tulsa.

LOCATION: 3770 Southwest Boulevard, Tulsa
WEBSITE: route66village.org

Santa Fe Depot Museum

This 1905 Santa Fe depot has been restored and now contains a collection of railroad photos and other local historical artifacts. On display are 1907 Baldwin steam locomotive Santa Fe No. 1951, a coal tender, and a caboose. The museum is open Tuesday through Saturday, and it features a convenient picnic area. A toy and action figure museum is also located in Pauls Valley.

LOCATION: 204 S. Santa Fe Street, Pauls Valley
PHONE: 405-238-2244
WEBSITE: paulsvalley.com

Waynoka Air-Rail Museum

The Waynoka Station complex includes a restored 1910 Santa Fe depot and Harvey House, 1918 section foreman's house, water tower, and diesel locomotive. The museum contains displays on Fred Harvey, the Santa Fe Railroad, Waynoka transportation history, and other subjects.

LOCATION: 1386 S. Cleveland Street, Waynoka
PHONE: 580-824-1886
WEBSITE: waynoka.org
E-MAIL: waynokahs@hotmail.com

OREGON

Ashland Historic Railroad Museum

The museum preserves Ashland's railroad history through exhibits, photos, talks, and films. It also conducts walking tours of the city's railroad district and presents Tombstone Tales during the summer. It is open Tuesday through Saturday year-round.

LOCATION: 258 A Street, Ashland
PHONE: 541-261-6605
WEBSITE: ashlandrrmuseum.org

Canby Depot Museum

The Canby Depot Museum is housed in what could be the oldest railroad station in Oregon, which has been around since at least 1873. The museum's displays provide a look at 19th century life of this historic community and include a Union Pacific caboose and other rail items. It is open Thursday through Sunday March through December.

LOCATION: 888 NE Fourth Avenue, Canby
PHONE: 503-266-6712
WEBSITE: canbyhistoricalsociety.org
E-MAIL: depotmusuem@canby.com

Oregon Rail Heritage Center

The Oregon Rail Heritage Center houses three historical steam locomotives: Oregon Railroad & Navigation 197, Southern Pacific 4449, and Spokane, Portland & Seattle 700. SP 4449 and SP&S 700 pull the Holiday Express along the Wilamette River through the Oaks Bottom Wildlife Refuge in December. The center is open Thursday through Sunday.

LOCATION: 2250 SE Water Avenue, Portland
PHONE: 503-680-8895
WEBSITE: orhf.org

Mount Hood Railroad

LOCATION: 110 Railroad Avenue, Hood River
PHONE: 800-872-4661 or 541-386-3556
WEBSITE: mthoodrr.com
E-MAIL: form on website

Mount Hood Railroad

The Columbia River Gorge is filled with magnificent scenery, and the area around Mount Hood especially so because of its abundant orchards and vineyards. The Mount Hood Railroad offers a 44-mile round trip to Parkdale that features spectacular views of its namesake mountain.

CHOICES: The four-hour excursion departs in the morning and follows the valley between the Columbia River and Mount Hood, providing views of Mount Adams as well. Aboard the Fruit Blossom excursion, the train stops en route at The Fruit Company, allowing you to visit the Fruit Heritage Museum. In addition, the railroad schedules train robberies and brunch trains every Sunday as well as regular wine trains and a variety of dinner trains.

WHEN TO GO: Trains run April through October, operating Wednesday through Saturday during summer (July and August). Otherwise, trains run several times weekly depending on the time of year.

GOOD TO KNOW: The railroad still carries a limited amount of freight, so don't be surprised if you see a boxcar somewhere along the line. Not far out of the Mount Hood depot, the train traverses a switchback, where it zigzags up the side of the mountain to gain elevation quickly. The rear of the train becomes the front for the rest of the trip into Parkdale.

WORTH DOING: There is much to do in the area. Sample apples and pears from orchards, visit a local winery, or watch wind surfers try to master the winds from the Columbia River Gorge. You can also take a drive on the Mount Hood Loop, which gives you a view of many scenic waterfalls.

DON'T MISS: Try first-class seating in the upper level of the dome car and get the same view as the engineer. Premium seating is available in the lower level of the dome car, and regular coach seating is found in other cars.

GETTING THERE: The Mount Hood Railroad is located 60 miles east of Portland off I-84. In Hood River, take Exit 63 to reach the depot. If driving from the south, Highway 35 also goes to Hood River.

Oregon Coast Scenic Railroad

LOCATION: 403 American Way, Garibaldi
PHONE: 503-842-7972
WEBSITE: ocsr.net
E-MAIL: info@ocsr.net

Martin Hansen

Experience the Pacific Ocean on a 10-mile, 90-minute excursion along the shores of Tillamook Bay. The train is pulled by a 1910 Heisler or a 1925 Baldwin 2-6-2 and runs between Garibaldi and Rockaway Beach.

CHOICES: On your trip along the coast, you can ride in a flatcar, in the restored Southern Pacific 1924 *Wilson River* coach, or for an extra fee, in the steam locomotive's cab. Wherever you sit, find a seat on the left side of the train. It's on the ocean side, and the views are spectacular. Dinner trains operate throughout the year, a special fireworks train runs in July, and the Candy Cane Express runs in December.

WHEN TO GO: Regular excursions operate on weekends from Memorial Day through September, with daily service in July and August.

GOOD TO KNOW: Look for OCSR to expand service as it has leased 46 miles of Port of Tillamook Bay Railroad track along the former Southern Pacific Tillamook branch, which is famous for its grades and bridges in the Salmonberry River canyon.

WORTH DOING: Oregon's dairy industry is based in Tillamook, and it produces some of the best cheese and ice cream in North America. Be sure to stop at the Tillamook Cheese factory in nearby Tillamook. In addition, the area features an aviation museum housed in a World War II blimp hanger. You can also view numerous lighthouses along the Pacific shore.

DON'T MISS: There is a layover between each run that provides the opportunity to explore Garibaldi or Rockaway Beach, get a bite to eat, or just enjoy the oceanside.

GETTING THERE: The railroad is located along the Oregon coast, 10 miles north of Tillamook, in Garibaldi just off Highway 101. From Portland, take Highway 26 west to Highway 6 at Banks and follow Highway 6 over the forested Coast Range Mountains to Tillamook. At Tillamook, take Highway 101 north to Garibaldi. In Garibaldi, turn left on Third Street to Lumberman's Park, where the train boards.

Sumpter Valley Railroad

LOCATION: Highway 7, Sumpter
PHONE: 800-523-1235 or 866-894-2268
WEBSITE: sumptervalleyrailroad.org
E-MAIL: info@sumptervalleyrailroad.org

Dave Crosby

A five-mile portion of one of the most charming narrow gauge lines of the Pacific Northwest has been re-created amid forests and the spoils of a former gold-mining dredge operation. It is a good approximation of a remote steam line in eastern Oregon, where snowcaps rise in the distance even in June.

CHOICES: The railway runs between McEwen and Sumpter. Both round-trip and one-way excursions are available at either station. Locomotives currently operating are a wood-burning W.H. Eccles Lumber Co. two-truck Heisler and oil-burning Sumpter Valley Railway 2-8-2 No. 19. Train robberies and special events take place throughout the season.

WHEN TO GO: The railway is open on weekends and holidays from Memorial Day through September. A special fall foliage photography train runs in October, and Christmas trains run in December.

GOOD TO KNOW: The Sumpter depot is a replica of the original depot. Located on the Elkhorn Scenic Byway, Sumpter is surrounded by the Elkhorn Mountains. The area is filled with history, and nearby Baker City boasts at least 60 restored buildings.

WORTH DOING: Near the Sumpter station, in the Sumpter Valley Dredge State Heritage Area, visit the historic gold dredge that churned up all the rocks the railroad runs through—it's as big as a house and a monster of a machine well worth touring.

DON'T MISS: Cab rides aboard the steam locomotive are available.

GETTING THERE: The railway is about 330 miles from Portland in northeast Oregon. From Portland, take I-84 to Baker City and then take Highway 7 south 22 miles to McEwen.

PENNSYLVANIA

Allegheny Portage Railroad

This national historic site preserves the remains of the Allegeny Portage Railroad that operated from 1834 to 1854. You can explore the 900-foot Staple Bend Tunnel, the first railroad tunnel built in the United States, visit the engine house, or take a hike. The Staple Bend Tunnel is about 25 miles southwest from the site's main location. From the parking lot, it is a two-mile hike or bike ride to the tunnel. The site conducts a large number of special events.

LOCATION: 110 Federal Park Road, Gallitzin
PHONE: 814-886-6150
WEBSITE: nps.gov/alpo
E-MAIL: form on website

Electric City Trolley Museum

Located on the grounds of the Steamtown National Historic Site, the museum is housed in a restored mill building. In addition to displaying vintage regional trolleys, the museum features a unique under-the-skin look at a restored trolley and other interactive exhibits. Ten-mile trolley excursions travel through a 4,747-foot interurban tunnel.

LOCATION: 300 Cliff Street, Scranton
PHONE: 570-963-6590
WEBSITE: ectma.org
E-MAIL: webmaster@ectma.org

Franklin Institute Science Museum

The museum features the Train Factory, a permanent, interactive exhibit showcasing Baldwin's experimental locomotive No. 60000, which has been at the museum since 1933, and two other locomotives. You'll explore past and present railroad technology as you journey through the exhibit and even take No. 60000 for a test run. The museum is open year-round.

LOCATION: 222 N. 20th Street, Philadelphia
PHONE: 215-448-1200
WEBSITE: fi.edu
E-MAIL: guestservices@fi.edu

Friends of the East Broad Top Museum

Located at the former southern operating terminus of the East Broad Top Railroad, the museum includes two historic buildings, an EBT station and a post office, both constructed around 1915. Exhibits illustrate the history of the railroad and the people who constructed, maintained, and operated it. The museum is open on the first and third weekends May through October.

LOCATION: 550 Main Street, Robertsdale
PHONE: 412-441-7881
WEBSITE: febt.org
E-MAIL: vckeller@comcast.net

Greenville Railroad Park and Museum

This railroad museum displays Union Railroad 0-10-2 No. 604. Built in 1936, it is the largest steam switcher built. Several railcars are also on display. Museum exhibits highlight a CTC panel from Bessemer Railroad, Empire cars, and the invention of the parachute. It is open weekends during May, September, and October. During summer months, the museum is open Tuesday through Sunday.

LOCATION: 314 Main Street, Greenville
PHONE: 724-588-4009
WEBSITE: greenvilletrainmuseum.org
E-MAIL: greenvillerailroadpark@gmail.com

Harris Tower Museum

Visitors to the switch tower can operate an actual interlocking machine and model board that controls virtual trains from the 1940s. Throw any of the 113 levers on the interlocking machine, which controlled track switches and signals, and watch the model board light up to show what would happen. The tower is next to operating tracks, so railfans can watch Norfolk Southern and Amtrak trains go by. It is open Saturdays late May through October.

LOCATION: 637 Walnut Street, Harrisburg
PHONE: 717-232-6221
WEBSITE: harristower.org
E-MAIL: harristower@verizon.net

Kiski Junction Railroad

This freight-hauling railroad also hauls passengers. From June to October, on Tuesdays, Fridays, and Saturdays, it offers train rides along the scenic Kiski River to Bagdad and back. You can ride aboard a caboose, coach, or open-air car. Special fall and Christmas trains also run.

LOCATION: 130 Railroad Street, Schenley
PHONE: 724-295-5577
WEBSITE: kiskijunction.com
E-MAIL: info@kiskijunction.com

Ligonier Valley Rail Road Museum

The Ligonier Valley Rail Road Museum is housed in the restored Darlington station, and its exhibits show the history of the Ligonier Valley Rail Road. It is open Wednesday through Saturday April through February and Saturdays in March.

LOCATION: 3032 Idlewild Hill Lane, Ligonier
PHONE: 724-238-7819
WEBSITE: lvrra.org
E-MAIL: info@lvrra.org

Newtown Square Railroad Museum

At this museum, you'll see a restored 1895 freight station, Alco steam locomotive, 1907 boxcar, 1950 caboose, and 1902 PRR passenger coach, which is being restored. It is open weekends June through September.

LOCATION: West Chester Pike in Drexel Lodge Park, Newtown Square
PHONE: 610-688-6262 or 610-459-4183
WEBSITE: newtownsquare-railroadmuseum.org
E-MAIL: info@jaychild.com

Pennsylvania Trolley Museum

A visit to the museum includes a trolley ride and guided tours of the trolley display building, where you will see about 10 trolleys, and the restoration shop. In the visitor center, you can view a video on trolleys and examine photograph displays. For an added fee, you can take an in-depth, behind-the-scenes tour of the trolley display building. Special events are scheduled throughout the year.

LOCATION: 1 Museum Road, Washington
PHONE: 724-228-9256
WEBSITE: pa-trolley.org
E-MAIL: ptm@pa-trolley.org

Pioneer Tunnel Coal Mine & Steam Train

Take a scenic ride along Mahanoy Mountain as you hear stories about mining, bootlegging, and the Centralia Mine fire. A 1927 narrow gauge 0-4-0 steam locomotive takes you around the mountain. You can also tour a real anthracite coal mine in open mine cars. It is open April through October.

LOCATION: 19th Street and Oak Street, Ashland
PHONE: 570-875-3850
WEBSITE: pioneertunnel.com

Portage Station Museum

The museum is located in a restored Pennsylvania Railroad train station, originally built in 1926. The first floor contains a stationmaster's office and items from the Pennsylvania Railroad, and on the second floor, there is a display of mining artifacts and a large model train that depicts railroading of the area, which runs the first Saturday of each month.

LOCATION: 400 Lee Street, Portage
PHONE: 814-736-9223
WEBSITE: portagepa.us
E-MAIL: ihuschak@comcast.net

Reading Railroad Heritage Museum

You can't take a ride on the Reading Railroad, but you can discover its heritage in this museum. You can tour the museum's large outdoor collection of vintage Reading Railroad cars and locomotives. Inside, you can view a 1930s station agent's office, photographs, and artifacts.

LOCATION: 500 S. Third Street, Hamburg
PHONE: 610-562-5513
WEBSITE: readingrailroad.org
E-MAIL: info@readingrailroad.org

Rockhill Trolley Museum

The museum offers a three-mile ride aboard a vintage electric trolley car from its Meadow Street platform to Blacklog Narrows. Along the way, you can hop off and take photographs and catch a later trolley. You can also tour the museum's collection, which includes city trolleys, high-speed interurban cars, and other vehicles. It is open Saturdays and Sundays Memorial Day weekend through October with special events in November and December.

LOCATION: 430 Meadow Street, Rockhill Furnace
PHONE: 814-447-9576
WEBSITE: rockhilltrolley.org
E-MAIL: form on website

Tunnels Park & Museum

From the nearby Jackson Street Bridge, you get a great view of the twin tunnels, which are 3,605 feet long. The site also features a museum and a restored 1942 Pennsylvania Railroad caboose. The museum includes railroad artifacts and photos. It is open Tuesday through Sunday.

LOCATION: 411 Convent Street, Gallitzin
PHONE: 814-886-8871
WEBSITE: gallitzin.info
E-MAIL: info@gallitzin.info

West Chester Railroad

The railroad offers a variety of special excursions during the year, starting with Easter and going to Christmas, which includes summer picnics and fall foliage runs. The 90-minute round trip runs from West Chester to Glen Mills, following scenic Chester Creek. For history buffs, Valley Forge National Historical Park is less than 20 miles away.

LOCATION: 230 E. Market Street, West Chester
PHONE: 610-430-2233
WEBSITE: westchesterrr.com
E-MAIL: info@westchesterrr.com

Horseshoe Curve National Historic Landmark

LOCATION: Burgoon Road, Altoona
PHONE: 888-425-8666 or 814-946-0834
WEBSITE: railroadcity.com
E-MAIL: form on website

Jim Wrinn

Horseshoe Curve is an engineering marvel completed in 1854 as part of the Pennsylvania Railroad's main line over the Allegheny Mountains. By curving the track across the face of a mountain, builders were able to gain elevation without making the grade too steep for trains to climb. Today, the curve is as vital as ever, serving as a key link in the Norfolk Southern system, with more than 50 trains passing over its three tracks each day.

CHOICES: Attractions at Horseshoe Curve consist of a visitor center at ground level and the trackside park, which is accessible by a 194-step walkway or by a funicular railway. First-timers will want to tour the visitor center, ride the funicular up to track level for some train-watching, and perhaps take the stairway back down. The best show at the curve is the passage of a heavy westbound train, laboring up the grade with helper engines on the front and/or rear. Try to stay long enough to catch this spectacle.

WHEN TO GO: The visitor center and funicular are open from early April through mid-November. In October, the fall colors can be brilliant. Freight traffic tends to build toward the end of each week, so there may be more trains to see on Thursday, Friday, and Saturday.

GOOD TO KNOW: The site is managed by the Altoona Railroaders Memorial Museum in downtown Altoona. Combined admission tickets are available.

WORTH DOING: Continue west on Kittanning Point Road to Gallitzin and visit the small park at the west portal of one of the tunnels the railroad uses to pierce the spine of the Alleghenies. Cresson, a little further west is also a good place to watch trains. Both towns have trackside, railfan-oriented lodging.

DON'T MISS: The longer you stay at Horseshoe Curve, the greater the chances of seeing two or even three trains rounding the curve simultaneously, a thrilling occurrence.

GETTING THERE: Horseshoe Curve is located five miles west of Altoona. Altoona is on I-99, 33 miles north of I-70/76. Amtrak's New York-Philadelphia-Pittsburgh *Pennsylvanian* stops at Altoona daily.

Lake Shore Railway Museum

LOCATION: 31 Wall Street, North East
PHONE: 814-725-1911
WEBSITE: grape-track.org
E-MAIL: lsrhs31@gmail.com

Jim Wrinn

On the grounds of a former New York Central passenger depot, you'll find a museum that maintains a collection focused on General Electric, Heisler, and Pullman equipment as well as on local railroads.

CHOICES: The restored New York Central passenger station houses numerous artifacts, and 24 pieces of rolling stock are displayed outdoors. A freight station built in 1869 by the Lake Shore & Michigan Southern also sits on the grounds. View fireless 0-6-0 No. 6, one of 29 such Heisler locomotives built between 1934 and 1941. Demonstrations of the locomotive occur on select weekends.

WHEN TO GO: From Memorial Day through Labor Day, the museum is open Wednesdays through Sundays. The grounds are accessible all year. Enjoy Christmas at the Station on weekends following Thanksgiving with caboose rides and other activities.

GOOD TO KNOW: The museum hosts occasional lunches or dinners in the diner, wine tastings, and other events.

WORTH DOING: Time your visit with the cherry festival in July or the wine festival in September. There are five wineries in or near North East. You can also drive along Lake Erie and stop at one of the local beaches. Also, in December, look for the town's Sugar Plum Weekend.

DON'T MISS: CSX's Chicago-New York main line and Norfolk Southern's line to Buffalo run beside the museum. You can watch 60–80 trains each day from the platform, including Amtrak's *Lake Shore Limited* passenger train.

GETTING THERE: The museum is located about 15 miles east of Erie, Pa., near the New York state border. From Erie, take Route 20 to North East, where it becomes Main Street. Turn right on Clinton, right on Mill Street, and then left on Wall.

Lehigh Gorge Scenic Railway

LOCATION: 2 Susquehanna Street, Jim Thorpe
PHONE: 570-325-8485
WEBSITE: lgsry.com
E-MAIL: info@lgsry.com

Dave Crosby

This 16-mile round trip into the Lehigh Gorge is among the most beautiful in Pennsylvania, a state blessed with numerous great tourist railroads and museums because of its abundant railroad development. Trains run on the tracks of the Reading & Northern regional railroad, paralleling a bike path into an isolated, narrow chasm.

CHOICES: The one-hour, narrated excursion follows the winding Lehigh River, curve after curve, and crosses it in several places, until it reaches Old Penn Haven. Leaving from the renovated, distinct Central Railroad of New Jersey depot, you can ride behind a diesel locomotive in a vintage 1920s coach, an open-air car, or a first-class car, from which you can stand on the rear platform.

WHEN TO GO: The railway operates on Saturdays and Sundays mid-May through mid-December. The mountains present a new look for each season, but fall offers beautiful foliage and an extended schedule in October. Santa trains run in December.

GOOD TO KNOW: In 1953, the towns of Mauch Chunk and East Mauch Chunk merged into one town with the name of Jim Thorpe when that famous athlete was buried there. Looking for a place that would help develop a memorial for her husband, who had no previous ties to the area, Thorpe's widow found assistance from the two towns.

WORTH DOING: Explore the town of Jim Thorpe, a charming village of shops, stores, and B&Bs, many featuring Victorian architecture. The town was once known as the Switzerland of America for its steep hillsides, narrow streets, and terraced gardens.

DON'T MISS: The railroad, from time to time, fires up and uses 4-6-2 No. 425, a steam locomotive built for passenger service on the Gulf, Mobile & Northern in 1928.

GETTING THERE: Located in the heart of the Poconos, Jim Thorpe is approximately 90 miles from Philadelphia. From there, take I-476 to Exit 74. Then take Route 209 south into Jim Thorpe, where it becomes Susquehanna Street, and follow it to the railway.

Middletown & Hummelstown Railroad

LOCATION: 136 Brown Street, Middletown
PHONE: 717-944-4435
WEBSITE: mhrailroad.com
E-MAIL: form on website

Middletown & Hummelstown Railroad

If you're looking for that relaxed train ride in central Pennsylvania, here's your ride. The M&H provides a trip along the Swatara Creek that travels past the ruins of a canal and makes a dramatic bridge crossing of a creek on an 11-mile round trip.

CHOICES: The M&H offers plenty of different trips, from scenic outings to murder mystery barbecues. Trains depart from the 1891 freight station in Middletown. Aboard the train's Delaware, Lackawanna & Western coaches, you'll hear informative narration about the area, and be prepared to sing some railroading songs on the return trip. Caboose rides also take place.

WHEN TO GO: Excursions begin Memorial Day weekend and end in October. They run Thursdays, Saturdays, and Sundays during summer and weekends during the remaining schedule. There are numerous special events, including a Civil War reenactment, during the year. Festive Christmas trains begin running in November.

GOOD TO KNOW: Formerly part of the Reading Railroad, the M&H also provides freight service. At the Middletown yard, the railroad displays a collection of rolling stock that includes a wooden boxcar, a trolley freight car, and other assorted trolleys and streetcars.

WORTH DOING: Top off your relaxing train ride with a stop in Middletown at the Cone-A-Cabana for ice cream. In Hershey, you can hop on more than 60 rides, including roller coasters and water rides, at Hersheypark amusement park.

DON'T MISS: Tour nearby Indian Echo Caves for an interesting underground outing.

GETTING THERE: Middletown is situated between Harrisburg and Hershey, both 10 miles away, and 100 miles from Philadelphia. From Philadelphia, take I-76 to Route 283. Exit at Middletown and from Main Street, turn left on Pine Street, and then left on Brown Street to get to the station.

New Hope & Ivyland Railroad

LOCATION: 32 W. Bridge Street, New Hope
PHONE: 215-862-2332
WEBSITE: newhoperailroad.com
E-MAIL: info@newhoperailroad.com

Jim Wrinn

The New Hope & Ivyland Railroad provides a scenic, 45-minute trip through the rolling hills and valleys of Bucks County, leaving from the quaint resort village of New Hope on the Delaware River.

CHOICES: There are lots of trains to ride, from scenic excursions to murder mysteries and dinner trains, as well as story and sing-along rides for children. You can board regular excursion trains at either New Hope or Lahaska. The 1920s vintage passenger coaches are pulled by steam engine No. 40, a 1925 Baldwin-type 2-8-0, or a diesel locomotive. Try out open-air car No. 1525 and enjoy the breeze—and unobstructed views. The former Reading car was built in 1925.

WHEN TO GO: The New Hope & Ivyland operates year-round. From January through March, excursions run on Saturdays and Sundays. In April, May, and November, Friday runs are added to the weekend schedule. And beginning Memorial Day weekend, excursions operate daily through the end of October. Special trains operate throughout the year, and December is filled with holiday trains.

GOOD TO KNOW: The restored Victorian station at New Hope has been in operation since 1891. An original "witch's hat" station, it once housed the railroad's telegraph operator.

WORTH DOING: History buffs can visit Valley Forge National Historical Park, which is about 40 miles from New Hope.

DON'T MISS: You can get off at either station and take a later train back to the originating station. At Lahaska, you can enjoy a family picnic, and in New Hope, you can take a mule-drawn boat ride in the Delaware Division of the Pennsylvania Canal or stroll along the Delaware River.

GETTING THERE: New Hope is 45 miles northeast of Philadelphia. From Philadelphia, take the Pennsylvania Turnpike east to the Willow Grove exit. Then take Route 611 to Route 202. Turn north on Route 202 and go 10 miles to Route 179, which leads you into New Hope. In town, take a left onto Bridge Street to the station. Lahaska is five miles southwest of New Hope, and the station is on Street Road one mile east of Route 202.

Oil Creek & Titusville Railroad

LOCATION: 409 S. Perry Street, Titusville
PHONE: 814-676-1733
WEBSITE: octrr.org
E-MAIL: ocandt@usachoice.net

Oil Creek & Titusville Railroad

The Oil Creek & Titusville Railroad follows Oil Creek through the nation's first oil patch, where oil was discovered by Col. Edwin L. Drake in 1859. Along the way, the train passes a number of ghost towns that sprang up during the oil boom and just as quickly disappeared when the rush faded.

CHOICES: Much of the route along the three-hour excursion runs through Oil Creek State Park, a popular venue for camping, fishing, and kayaking. Along the way, tour guides tell stories about Oil Country. You don't have to make the return trip right away. You may visit Drake Well Park, ride one way and bike the other, or kayak down Oil Creek and then ride the train back. For a more comfortable rider, try first-class seating in the *Wabash Cannonball*.

WHEN TO GO: The Oil Creek & Titusville operates weekends June through October, with select weekdays added in July, August, and October. The fall foliage season is spectacular in the area and is a favored time to visit.

GOOD TO KNOW: At various times throughout the year, murder mystery dinner trains, Peter Cottontail trains, and Santa trains operate. A highlight is Speeder Day, when visitors have an opportunity to ride small railway maintenance cars along part of the line.

WORTH DOING: Stopping at Drake Well Park gives you a chance to see a replica of the very first oil well in the United States, from which oil still flows today. The park also displays a large collection of machinery and equipment used to produce oil.

DON'T MISS: The OC&TR operates the only Railway Post Office in regular service in the United States. Postcards mailed on the train will receive the official "Oil Creek & Titusville R.P.O." cancellation, which is valued by collectors.

GETTING THERE: Titusville is in the forested mountains of northwestern Pennsylvania. From I-80, take Exit 29 and then Route 8 north through Oil City to Titusville. From Erie and I-90, take Route 97 south to its junction with Route 8 and then follow Route 8 to Titusville.

Railroad Museum of Pennsylvania

Pennsylvania

LOCATION: 300 Gap Road, Strasburg
PHONE: 717-687-8628
WEBSITE: rrmuseumpa.org
E-MAIL: info@rrmuseumpa.org

Rob McGonigal

The Railroad Museum of Pennsylvania boasts one of the top rolling stock collections in the United States. The highlight is a dozen steam locomotives preserved by the Pennsylvania Railroad in the 1950s; very few PRR engines exist elsewhere. The collection also includes about 100 other locomotives and cars from the PRR and other railroads serving the state, many displayed in a 100,000-square-foot exhibition hall.

CHOICES: Go up, down, and out: an elevated walkway gives a fine view of the Rolling Stock Hall, a pit between the rails allows inspection of the underside of one of the locomotives, and tours of the rolling stock yard are sometimes available. Be sure to see PRR 4-4-2 No. 7002, a beautiful example of a high-wheeled passenger speedster from the early 20th century; PRR GG1 No. 4935, the best-preserved example of the most famous class of electric locomotives; and PRR E7 No. 5901, the only surviving example of General Motors' top-selling passenger diesel.

WHEN TO GO: The museum is open every day except for certain major holidays and most Mondays November through March. A variety of special events are scheduled throughout the year.

GOOD TO KNOW: The famous "Lindbergh Engine," PRR class E6s Atlantic No. 460, is undergoing a full cosmetic overhaul in the museum's restoration shop. If you would like to see trains on a smaller scale, the National Toy Train Museum is also located in Strasburg.

WORTH DOING: Spend part of the day at the museum and then take a ride on a steam train on the Strasburg Rail Road, located right across the road. Combined admissions are available.

DON'T MISS: Grab the controls of a diesel locomotive with the museum's cab simulator and feel the thrill of operating a locomotive on a trip from Lancaster to Harrisburg.

GETTING THERE: The museum is on Route 741 (Gap Road) one mile east of Strasburg, which is about 15 minutes from Lancaster, one hour from Harrisburg or Reading, and 90 minutes from Philadelphia. Most folks take Route 30 to Route 896 south to Route 741.

Pennsylvania

Railroaders Memorial Museum

LOCATION: 1300 Ninth Avenue, Altoona
PHONE: 888-425-8666 or 814-946-0834
WEBSITE: railroadcity.com
E-MAIL: form on website

Railroaders Memorial Museum

Of all the places in the United States deserving a first-rate railroad museum, Altoona is certainly at the top of the list. The museum here is among the best when it comes to providing an interactive experience and telling the story of this shop town that in the 1920s employed more than 15,000 Pennsylvania Railroad workers. Today, Altoona is still a shop city for Norfolk Southern, and the museum tells the story of how it became so important and the people who made it so.

CHOICES: Be sure to step into the re-created community bar to hear all about the lives of railroaders as they sit and sip a cold one. Also look at the exhibit on the PPR's testing and research lab. Their efforts were astounding.

WHEN TO GO: The museum is open daily May through October and Friday through Sunday in November and December.

GOOD TO KNOW: The museum is housed in the Pennsylvania Railroad's former master mechanic's building, which was built in 1882. The museum completed a new roundhouse in 2012.

WORTH DOING: The Allegheny Portage Railroad National Historic Site and Staple Bend Tunnel are both within 25 miles of Altoona.

DON'T MISS: Take a day and spend half of it in the museum and the other half watching trains at Horseshoe Curve. Combined admission tickets are available.

GETTING THERE: Altoona is about 95 miles east of Pittsburgh. From Pittsburgh, take Route 22 to I-99 north. Take Exit 33, 17th Street, and a right turn on Ninth Avenue takes you to the museum.

Steamtown National Historic Site

LOCATION: Lackawanna Avenue and S. Bridge Avenue, Scranton
PHONE: 888-693-9391 or 570-340-5200
WEBSITE: nps.gov/stea

Dave Crosby

The former Delaware Lackawanna & Western railroad shop complex is home to one of the East's most complete railroad history exhibits. Housed in several buildings on the site of the Lackawanna's roundhouse, Steamtown provides a shrine to steam-era railroading in the northeastern United States. It also offers both short and long train rides. The real treat is a walk through the active portion of the roundhouse, where steam locomotives are still maintained.

CHOICES: The site includes both a steam history museum as well as a technology museum. The orientation movie, hands-on exhibits about workers as well as hardware, and equipment displays are excellent. Demonstrations of the turntable and shop tours are also conducted. For a brief visit, you can walk through the exhibits and take the *Scranton Limited*, a half-hour ride on vintage commuter coaches. If you have time, schedule your visit when you can spend a day with the exhibits and then ride a longer steam excursion train to Moscow, a two-hour trip that includes a climb up the Poconos, or through the countryside to Tobyhanna.

WHEN TO GO: Steamtown is open year-round. Summer can be sultry, but spring and fall are pleasant. Winter sees less activity. The *Scranton Limited* runs on select days late April through November. Most Moscow excursions operate on Saturdays beginning in July, and special trains on select days.

GOOD TO KNOW: Monthly tour and *Scranton Limited* schedules are posted online about a week before the beginning of each month. The 45-minute shop tour, offered regularly, provides a good behind-the-scenes look at heavy-duty restoration work underway on several locomotives.

WORTH DOING: Nearby, you can view the Scranton Iron Furnaces or tour a coal mine.

DON'T MISS: The Union Pacific Big Boy is one of the largest steam locomotives ever built. It is the only one of its type on exhibit in the eastern United States.

GETTING THERE: From I-81, take Exit 185. Stay in the left lanes to downtown Scranton and turn left at first traffic light. Follow Lackawanna Avenue to Bridge Avenue, where the park entrance is located.

Strasburg Rail Road

LOCATION: 301 Gap Road, Strasburg
PHONE: 717-687-7522
WEBSITE: strasburgrailroad.com
E-MAIL: srrtrain@strasburgrailroad.com

Dave Crosby

The nine-mile, 45-minute round trip from Strasburg to Paradise through Amish farmland aboard authentic 19th century wooden coaches being pulled by a steam locomotive recalls travel before automobiles. Narration provides an entertaining and educational ride.

CHOICES: Different types of service are available on regular excursions, and you can ride in a coach, open-air car, dining car, or first-class car. Get off the train at Groffs Grove for a picnic or to just watch the action, which in the busy season includes a meet between two trains every half hour. Lunch, dinner, wine and cheese, and other special trains are also offered. Tours of the shop and engine house are available.

WHEN TO GO: Steam trains run every day nearly all year, and in summer, two trains run simultaneously. A rare, wooden self-propelled doodlebug from a long-abandoned Lancaster County short line runs several days in March and in November. Strasburg's Thomas the Tank Engine events draw immense crowds.

GOOD TO KNOW: Locomotives pull trains tender-first on the outbound trips and engine-first on the return. Sit on the right-hand side of the train out of Strasburg for the best view of the locomotive changing ends at Paradise. The Strasburg Rail Road occasionally runs genuine steam-powered freight trains, usually on Friday mornings. For an interesting overnight experience, you can stay in one of 38 cabooses at the nearby Red Caboose Motel.

WORTH DOING: Take a drive through the heart of scenic Pennsylvania Dutch Country, one of the largest Amish communities in America. Buggy rides are offered by various enterprises.

DON'T MISS: View the Railroad Museum of Pennsylvania's world-class collection, which is right across the road (a combo pass is available), or take in the nearby Toy Train Museum.

GETTING THERE: The railroad is on Gap Road (Route 741) one mile east of Strasburg.

Tioga Central Railroad

LOCATION: 11 Muck Road, Wellsboro
PHONE: 570-724-0990
WEBSITE: tiogacentral.com
E-MAIL: form on website

Sam Botts

Here's a short railroad that still carries freight on its 34-mile route but also knows how to have some fun. The ride takes you along Crooked Creek, through forests, and to Lake Hammond, a large reservoir. It's a good trip at a brisk pace behind rare Alco diesels.

CHOICES: The Tioga Central, in addition to operating its regular, 24-mile, 90-minute excursions, offers a variety of special trains, including a Friday night ice cream train, dinner and brunch trains, and a Happy Hour Express. Ride the train's open-air car and keep a lookout for wildlife such as osprey, blue heron, deer, and even bald eagles.

WHEN TO GO: The railroad offers regular excursions Thursdays through Sundays from Memorial Day weekend into October. In fall, to take advantage of the spectacular foliage, added excursions operate.

GOOD TO KNOW: The railroad owes its good views of Lake Hammond, which it parallels for much of its journey, to a dam project that almost resulted in the railroad's abandonment. Fortunately, the railroad was relocated to the side of the reservoir.

WORTH DOING: Explore the nearby Pine Creek Gorge however you like. You can take a hike, ride a bike, or raft a river. Called the Grand Canyon of Pennsylvania, the 1,000-foot-deep gorge winds its way through acres of scenic landscape. Various parks provide breathtaking views of the canyon from hiking trails. You can also bike the Pine Creek Trail, a former rail line, through the canyon. Rafting is best in spring.

DON'T MISS: At the station, take a look at the railroad's oldest piece of rolling stock. Now an office, Car 54 was originally a double-ended, open-platform paymaster car built in 1894 for the Grand Trunk Western.

GETTING THERE: Wellsboro is in north-central Pennsylvania, 50 miles north of Williamsport. Trains leave from Wellsboro Junction, which is about three miles north of Wellsboro on Route 287.

Wanamaker, Kempton & Southern Railroad

LOCATION: 42 Community Center Drive, Kempton
PHONE: 610-756-6469
WEBSITE: kemptontrain.com
E-MAIL: info@kemptontrain.com

Wayne Laepple

While it's short on mileage, the Wanamaker Kempton & Southern, known as the Hawk Mountain Line, is long on atmosphere. For 50 years, this little line has operated in the relaxed style of a country branch line railroad, with authentically painted and lettered equipment.

CHOICES: Diesel locomotives power trains on the 40-minute round trip, with hourly departures on operating days. In addition to regular excursions, a variety of events take place throughout the season, including Easter Bunny, Harvest Moon, Halloween, and Santa specials, as well as murder mystery, wine and cheese, and fall foliage trains.

WHEN TO GO: WK&S operates Sundays May through September with Saturdays and Sundays in Otober. Passing prosperous farms and crossing Ontelaunee Creek, the excursion takes riders through beautiful scenery at any time of year. The fall colors in late September and early October on the surrounding mountains are breathtaking.

GOOD TO KNOW: The WK&S celebrates its 50th anniversary in 2013, with special operations on June 30, followed by an evening concert. Three trains will be in operation on that weekend.

WORTH DOING: A visit to WK&S can easily be combined with a trip to other rail attractions such as Steamtown National Historic Site and Pioneer Tunnel Coal Mine. Also close by are the Mid-Atlantic Air Museum, Crystal Cave, Hawk Mountain Raptor Sanctuary, the Appalachian Trail, and Roadside America, where you can see 200 years of American life depicted in miniature.

DON'T MISS: Ride the left side of the train for the best views of Ontelaunee Creek and vistas of the nearby mountains, orchards, and farms. Be sure to leave the train during the layover at Wanamaker for a quick look at the original station and the old-fashioned general store just a few steps away.

GETTING THERE: WK&S is located in east-central Pennsylvania, five miles north of I-78, just off Route 737 in Kempton. Follow signs to the station, which is a short distance north of the village.

RHODE ISLAND

Newport Dinner Train

Aboard the Newport Dinner Train, you can enjoy lunch or dinner in elegantly restored 1940s Budd dining cars. The 22-mile round trip takes you along scenic Narragansett Bay. The menu offers several entree choices including the train's specialty, baby back ribs. The Islander Touring Train offers 90-minute scenic train excursions aboard self-propelled commuter cars. Special packages are offered, some featuring boat cruises of Newport Harbor.

LOCATION: 19 America's Cup Avenue, Newport
PHONE: 800-398-7427 or 401-841-8700
WEBSITE: newportdinnertrain.com
E-MAIL: info@newportdinnertrain.com

Old Colony & Newport Railway

Enjoy a unique 80-minute train ride along the shores of Narragansett Bay. The ride provides views of various craft plying the bay, rocky beaches, and wildlife. First-class service is available aboard an 1884 parlor car, and coach passengers ride in a 1904 open-platform coach. The railway operates Sundays mid-January to mid-November. A special holiday train runs the last week of December. The railway may also offer several North End Specials during the year.

LOCATION: 19 America's Cup Avenue, Newport
PHONE: 401-849-0546
WEBSITE: ocnrr.com
E-MAIL: info@ocnrr.com

SOUTH CAROLINA

Best Friend of Charleston Railway Museum

Built in 1830, the *Best Friend of Charleston* was an early steam locomotive used for passenger service. A full-size replica of the engine was built, and it is currently on loan to Norfolk Southern for display. Located in the Citadel Mall, the museum contains artifacts, videos, and an operating model of the train. The museum is open Tuesday and Thursday evenings and Saturday and Sunday afternoons.

LOCATION: 2070 Sam Rittenberg Drive, Charleston
WEBSITE: bestfriendofcharleston.org
E-MAIL: bfoc1830@yahoo.com

Railroad Historical Center

A walk-through display of rolling stock includes a 1906 2-8-2 steam engine, Pullman cars, and Piedmont & Northern cars. It is operated in partnership with The Museum in Greenwood, located four blocks north, which features a wide range of historical exhibits and educational programs. The Railroad Historical Center is open Saturdays April through October.

LOCATION: 908 S. Main Street, Greenwood
PHONE: 864-229-7093
WEBSITE: emeraldtriangle.sc/museum
E-MAIL: themuseum@greenwood.net

South Carolina Railroad Museum

LOCATION: 110 Industrial Park Road, Winnsboro
PHONE: 803-635-9893
WEBSITE: scrm.org
E-MAIL: info@scrm.org

South Carolina Railroad Museum, Bill White

A slice of Southeastern shortline history awaits visitors to the South Carolina Railroad Museum. Located on the former Rockton & Rion Railway, a granite quarry short line, this museum brings the experience of a casual Southeastern short line to life through a 10-mile, one-hour ride, interesting exhibits, and rolling stock displays.

CHOICES: The Rockton, Rion & Western Railroad runs west past antebellum plantation remains and through pine forests on the trip to Rion. You can enjoy the ride in a dining car, coach, open-air car, or caboose. The museum's collection showcases South Carolina's railroad heritage and includes exhibits of track tools, artifacts, and photographs. Rolling stock features passenger cars, freight cars, cabooses, and other equipment from the Lancaster and Chester, Norfolk Southern, CSX, and other railroads. Steam trains may operate on a limited schedule.

WHEN TO GO: The museum is open several Saturdays each month June through October, with regular train rides scheduled on those days. It also hosts a variety of special events throughout the year, including Santa trains.

GOOD TO KNOW: The railroad is more than a hundred years old and is listed on the National Register of Historic Places. The museum's 100-ton General Motors diesel saw action during the Korean War.

WORTH DOING: Wet a fishing line in one of the state's top fishing lakes. Lake Wateree has more than 13,700 acres and contains bream, catfish, crappie, and bass. Dammed in 1919, it is also one of the oldest manmade lakes in the state. Lake Wateree State Recreation Area also includes a nature trail for a short hike.

DON'T MISS: Take a look at steam locomotive 4-6-0 No. 44 from the Hampton & Branchville, which is in process of being restored. It is one of the few steam locomotives on display in South Carolina.

GETTING THERE: About 30 miles from Columbia, Winnsboro is between Columbia and Rock Hill, just off I-77. Take Exit 34 and follow Route 34 about five miles and turn left at the steam locomotive that marks the museum's entrance.

SOUTH DAKOTA

Prairie Village

Prairie Village is a collection of restored buildings, rail equipment, and farm machinery that preserves the past. Rail structures include several historical depots, a roundhouse, and an operating turntable. On Saturdays, you can take a two-mile train ride around the village. Several steam and diesel locomotives, various cabooses, and a unique chapel car are featured. Railroad Days take place in July.

LOCATION: Highway 34, Madison
PHONE: 800-693-3644 or 605-256-3644
WEBSITE: prairievillage.org
E-MAIL: info@prairievillage.org

South Dakota State Railroad Museum

The museum contains artifacts and rolling stock related to the railroads that have served South Dakota since 1872. It also features additional displays and seasonal activities including the annual Trees and Trains exhibit. The museum is located next to the Black Hills Central Railroad.

LOCATION: 222 Railroad Avenue, Hill City
PHONE: 605-574-9000
WEBSITE: sdsrm.org
E-MAIL: sdsrrm@gmail.com

Black Hills Central Railroad

South Dakota

LOCATION: 222 Railroad Avenue, Hill City
PHONE: 605-574-2222
WEBSITE: 1880train.com
E-MAIL: office@1880train.com

Dave Crosby

This railroad gives you a chance to ride on a real mountain railroad with its steep grades, mines, and scenic hills. Situated close to Mount Rushmore, the Black Hills Central, also known as the 1880s Train, carries riders between Keystone and Hill City.

CHOICES: The two-hour, 20-mile round trip is a beautiful journey through the historic, rugged landscape of the Black Hills. You can ride in a coach or pile into the drover's car, believed to be one of only two left from the Chicago & North Western Railroad and the only one in use. Cattlemen lived in these cars while following their herds to market. Fitting for the area, Wild West shootouts take place during several special events.

WHEN TO GO: With a few exceptions, trains operate daily between May and into October, departing from both Keystone and Hill City. Trains make several trips a day from late May through September. Some last-train departures from Keystone are one-way trips only.

GOOD TO KNOW: Keystone is rich in tourist offerings including restaurants, shows, and shops. Hill City has amenities but without the tourist hubbub.

WORTH DOING: The Black Hills area is filled with must-see activities, including a trip to Mount Rushmore. You can experience the rugged beauty of the Badlands, see bison in Custer State Park, and visit the Wild West town of Deadwood.

DON'T MISS: Try to ride behind steam locomotive No. 110, the nation's only operating Mallet locomotive. What makes this engine special is that it has two sets of cylinders and drivers, and the exhaust steam from the back set of cylinders moves the front set of drivers. It is like having two smaller engines under one boiler. The locomotive is impressive as it tackles grades as steep as 5 percent for almost a mile but never breaks a sweat.

GETTING THERE: Whether traveling east or west, I-90 gets you to the train. To reach Keystone from Rapid City, take Highway 16 to Highway 244. To reach Hill City from Deadwood, take Highway 385.

TENNESSEE

Casey Jones Railroad Museum

At Casey Jones Village, you can learn about the life and legend of this famous engineer by touring his family home and a replica of No. 382, Casey's engine. The museum, a re-created 1890s train station, contains related displays and artifacts as well as those of Jackson's railroad history. Be sure to treat yourself to a fountain favorite in village's old-fashioned ice cream parlor, tour the historic Providence House, or walk through the *Judge Milton Brown* Pullman railcar.

LOCATION: 30 Casey Jones Lane, Jackson
PHONE: 877-700-7942 or 731-668-1222
WEBSITE: caseyjones.com
E-MAIL: caseyjonesmuseum@gmail.com

Cookeville Depot Museum

The railroad museum is housed in a Tennessee Central Railway depot. Built in 1909, the building is listed on the National Register of Historic Places. Inside, there are changing displays of railway artifacts and photos highlighting local railroad history. A renovated caboose contains additional exhibits, and a Tennessee Central locomotive, tender, and caboose are on display. It is open year-round Tuesday through Saturday.

LOCATION: 116 W. Broad Street, Cookeville
PHONE: 931-528-8570
WEBSITE: cookevilledepot.com
E-MAIL: form on website

Cowan Railroad Museum

Featured in this century-old depot are displays, photographs, and artifacts relating to Cowan and the railroads around the city. Led by a 1920 Porter locomotive, a complete train is displayed next to the museum. Also on display are a GE diesel switcher and several motor cars. Located near the CSX main line, train-watching opportunities exist at the museum.

LOCATION: 108 Front Street, Cowan
PHONE: 931-967-3078
WEBSITE: cowanrailroadmuseum.org
E-MAIL: secretary@cowanrailroadmuseum.org

Little River Railroad Museum

The museum holds a number of tools, artifacts, and photographs dedicated to the Little River Railroad and the lumber company it served. It displays a restored 1909 Shay locomotive, several pieces of rolling stock, logging equipment, and a water tower. It is open April through November.

LOCATION: 7747 E. Lamar Alexander Parkway, Townsend
PHONE: 865-448-2211
WEBSITE: littleriverrailroad.org
E-MAIL: president@littleriverrailroad.org

Lynnville Railroad Museum

The museum features a 1927 2-6-2 Baldwin steam locomotive and a replica depot that contains a two-ton scale model of a locomotive and rail artifacts. The museum is open daily and usually has several special events scheduled during the year.

LOCATION: 162 Mill Street, Lynnville
PHONE: 931-478-0880
WEBSITE: lynnvillerailroadmuseum.com
E-MAIL: tim@lynnvillerailroadmuseum.com

Monterey Depot Transportation Museum

The museum, a replica of the town's earlier Tennessee Central depot, preserves transportation-related items, which include artifacts from the Tennessee Central and other railroads that operated in the area. The museum is open daily.

LOCATION: One Depot Street, Monterey
PHONE: 931-839-2111
WEBSITE: montereydepot.com
E-MAIL: kenhall@montereydepot.com

Nashville, Chattanooga & St. Louis Depot and Railroad Museum

The museum houses a collection of artifacts, photographs, and memorabilia associated with railroad and local history. The grounds feature a dining car and two cabooses. Built in 1907, the depot is listed on the National Register of Historic Places. It is open year-round, Monday through Saturday.

LOCATION: 582 S. Royal Street, Jackson
PHONE: 731-425-8223
WEBSITE: jacksonrecandparks.com
E-MAIL: thedepot@cityofjackson.net

Tennessee

Southern Appalachia Railway Museum

LOCATION: Highway 58, Oak Ridge
PHONE: 865-241-2140
WEBSITE: techscribes.com/sarm

David P. Oroszi

For many years, the government did not acknowledge the existence of the huge nuclear research lab at Oak Ridge or the railroad that served it. Now that the lab is closed, the railroad to "Secret City" is now a tourist attraction, giving visitors some insight into this unusual bit of railroading as well as a nice ride through the east Tennessee hills.

CHOICES: Pulled by a variety of EMD, GE, and Alco diesels, the 12-mile, 60-minute round trip takes you through the former secret atomic facility. Once outside the Secret City, the train enters the countryside, where it crosses Poplar Creek and follows this stream along a rural valley before returning. Two-hour dinner trains are scheduled from February to September.

WHEN TO GO: Excursions run several Saturdays a month from April through September. A full slate of fall foliage trains run throughout October. Halloween, Thanksgiving, and Santa trains also run.

GOOD TO KNOW: There are restrictions on non-U.S. citizens riding the train, which you can find out by checking with the museum.

WORTH DOING: To learn more about the secrets of atomic power, you can visit the American Museum of Science & Energy in Oak Ridge or take a self-guided auto tour of some Manhattan Project sites in the area.

DON'T MISS: When the train leaves, it passes through an enclosure used to check railcars for hobos, and it still provides a way to screen the train from unwanted spies. The boarding station is a former guardhouse.

GETTING THERE: Oak Ridge is about 30 miles west of Knoxville, and the Heritage Center is situated between Oak Ridge and I-40 on Route 58. To get there from Knoxville, take I-40 west to Exit 356. Turn right and travel north on Route 58 approximately five miles to the Heritage Center. Turn left into the main entrance and take the first left inside the plant.

Tennessee Central Railway Museum

LOCATION: 220 Willow Street, Nashville
PHONE: 615-244-9001
WEBSITE: tcry.org

Ralcon Wagner

The museum offers day trips on a streamlined passenger train through scenic middle Tennessee over the tracks of the Nashville & Eastern Railroad to various destinations. Duration of excursions range from two to 12 hours.

CHOICES: Excursions leaving from the Nashville station travel to Watertown, Baxter, Lebanon, Cookeville, and Monterey. Passengers have a choice of coach, first-class, or dome seating. Dome seating is limited and sells out early on most trips. All trains feature a special theme—from onboard train robberies and murder mysteries to seasonal Easter Bunny or North Pole Express trips. Wine trains to the Delmonico winery are popular and sell out quickly, and rides behind Thomas the Tank Engine are always a big hit with kids of all ages.

WHEN TO GO: The museum is open Monday through Saturday year-round. Excursions run on select Saturdays throughout the year. The longer trips to Cookeville or Monterey take place in the fall when the foliage is most brilliant. In September, kids of all ages can ride with Thomas the Tank Engine.

GOOD TO KNOW: The museum is housed in the former Tennessee Central Railway's master mechanic's office, and it includes a large collection of Tennessee Central artifacts. It also features a collection of locomotives and railcars.

WORTH DOING: Only minutes away are numerous downtown attractions that will appeal to the entire family. These include the Country Music Hall of Fame and Museum, Bicentennial Capitol Mall State Park, Historic Ryman Auditorium, Tennessee State Capitol building, and Riverfront Park.

DON'T MISS: Tour Nashville's historic 113-year-old restored Union Station, which is now an upscale hotel. Ride Nashville's *Music City Star* commuter train from downtown's Riverfront Station.

GETTING THERE: The museum is located a mile east of downtown Nashville. From I-40, take Exit 212 and turn left. Go a block to Hermitage Avenue (Highway 70) and turn left. Turn right at Fairfield Avenue which becomes Willow Street. Follow signs to the museum, which is located at bottom of the hill on the left.

Tennessee Valley Railroad

LOCATION: 4119 Cromwell Road, Chattanooga
PHONE: 423-894-8028
WEBSITE: tvrail.com
E-MAIL: form on website

Dave Crosby

If you were to take a major steam railroad from the 1920s, shrink it and preserve it, you'd have the Tennessee Valley Railroad. It offers a steam-powered train ride that leaves from a magnificent station, crosses a high trestle and other bridges, and passes through a pre-Civil War tunnel before it reaches the terminal at the opposite end of the run.

CHOICES: The railroad offers a variety of excursions. You can take the *Missionary Ridge Local* on a six-mile round trip between Grand Junction and East Chattanooga, traveling through a unique horseshoe tunnel as you do. On the *Chickamauga Turn*, a six-hour ride takes you to Chickamauga and back. Departing out of Etowah, the railroad offers a trip through the Hiwassee River Gorge that rides to the top of the Great Hiwassee Loop. Mainline excursions on Norfolk Southern are also offered.

WHEN TO GO: Excursions run every month, and except for some Mondays, there is a train running almost every day mid-March through October, with dinner trains and other specials scheduled throughout the year. Anytime the steam train is running is a good time to go. Railfest takes place over Labor Day weekend.

GOOD TO KNOW: If you want an all-railroad experience, stay at the Chattanooga Choo Choo, a Holiday Inn in the former terminal station. You can eat at the station complex in one of several venues, including a real railroad dining car, and sleep on a train car.

WORTH DOING: In Chattanooga, activities include visiting the Tennessee Aquarium and taking a riverboat cruise on the Tennessee River. History buffs can explore both the Lookout Mountain and Chickamauga battlefields.

DON'T MISS: At East Chattanooga, a guided tour of the shop and turntable is included with the *Missionary Ridge Local*. The shop features one of the few complete wheel shops in the country, and on any given visit, there's no telling what set of wheels from what engine is there for repairs.

GETTING THERE: The railroad is in the northeast section of Chattanooga. To get there, take Route 153 to Exit 3. At the end of the exit ramp, turn left over Route 153 and turn right onto Cromwell Road.

Three Rivers Rambler

LOCATION: Volunteer Landing on Neyland Drive, Knoxville
PHONE: 865-524-9411
WEBSITE: threeriversrambler.com
E-MAIL: karen@threeriversrambler.com

Dave Crosby

There are few perfect chances to ride a steam train in a beautiful part of the Appalachians, leaving from one of the more pleasant areas of a small city like Knoxville. But the *Three Rivers Rambler* offers just such an outing. From its departure point on the Tennessee River, it makes its way into the country to its namesake point: the confluence of the Holston and French Broad Rivers that creates the mighty Tennessee. The train bridges this point on a magnificent trestle that puts an exclamation point on the trip.

CHOICES: On the 90-minute round trip, you'll ride in a coach or an open-air car. Two steam engines or a diesel locomotive provide the power. No. 203 is a 1925 Baldwin steam engine and No. 154, an 1890 steam engine.

WHEN TO GO: Excursions operate around holidays and special events during the year, with an extended schedule for Christmas trains. Since the *Rambler* hauls freight Monday through Friday, most passenger trains run on weekends.

GOOD TO KNOW: Before its return to the rails, former Southern Railway steam engine No. 154, a 2-8-0 Consolidation built by Schenectady Locomotive Works, had been on display since 1953 in Knoxville's Chilhowee Park. It is oldest Southern Railway locomotive in operation.

WORTH DOING: The departure point on the Tennessee River is adjacent to the university in an area with several good restaurants. Sports fans could try and catch a University of Tennessee football or basketball game or visit the Women's Basketball Hall of Fame.

DON'T MISS: Along the way, feel free to ask the conductor or volunteer staff questions about the train or local history.

GETTING THERE: From I-40, take Exit 386B to Neyland Drive and turn left. Drive two miles to the parking lot on your left and look for signs. After parking, cross under Neyland Drive and proceed left down the riverwalk to the train at Volunteer Landing.

TEXAS

History Center
The History Center features indoor and outdoor interpretive exhibits. Permanent displays include a 1920 Baldwin 4-6-0 from Texas Southeastern Railroad on which you can ring its bell and blow its whistle, a log car, and a caboose. The center contains a large number of photos on east Texas railroading and logging operations.

LOCATION: 102 N. Temple Drive, Diboll
PHONE: 936-829-3543
WEBSITE: thehistorycenteronline.com
E-MAIL: info@thehistorycenteronline.com

Lehnis Railroad Museum
This railroad museum displays an AT&SF steam locomotive, a business car, and a caboose. It includes a collection of railroad china, lanterns, equipment, and photos. From the train-watching platform, you can look for passing BNSF trains. Located next to a Harvey House and Santa Fe depot, the museum is open Tuesdays through Saturdays.

LOCATION: 700 E. Adams Street, Brownwood
PHONE: 325-643-6376
WEBSITE: ci.brownwood.tx.us/LRM
E-MAIL: kpeterson@ci.brownwood.tx.us

New Braunfels Railroad Museum
Housed in the restored 1907 International & Great Northern depot, the museum displays a 0-6-0 Porter oil-fired steam locomotive, a Missouri Pacific caboose, and numerous railroad artifacts. It is open Thursday through Monday.

LOCATION: 302 W. San Antonio Street, New Braunfels
PHONE: 830-627-2447
WEBSITE: newbraunfelsrailroadmuseum.org
E-MAIL: info@newbraunfelsrailroadmuseum.org

Railroad & Heritage Museum

Housed in a 1910 Santa Fe depot, the museum features exhibits related to the Santa Fe Railway and the city of Temple including those on Harvey Houses, the Santa Fe Hospital, and railroad lanterns. Outdoor displays feature a variety of cars, a steam locomotive, and a diesel engine. The museum is open Tuesday through Saturday.

LOCATION: 315 W. Avenue B, Temple
PHONE: 254-298-5172
WEBSITE: rrhm.org
E-MAIL: form on website

Railroad and Transportation Museum of El Paso

A restored 1857 4-4-0 locomotive and other railroad exhibits are on display in the Transit Terminal of Union Plaza. One exhibit covers urban transit from the mule car through streamlined Art Deco streetcars. It is open Tuesday through Sunday.

LOCATION: 400 W. San Antonio Avenue, El Paso
PHONE: 915-422-3420
WEBSITE: elpasorails.org
E-MAIL: form on website

Railway Museum of San Angelo

Located in a historic Kansas City, Mexico & Orient depot, which was completed in 1910, the museum highlights local railroad history. It features a large collection of railroad photos by Allen Johnson. Static displays include two diesel locomotives and a Santa Fe boxcar and caboose. It is open on Saturdays. For a unique special event for kids, try Fry an Egg on the Track Day in August.

LOCATION: 703 S. Chadbourne Street, San Angelo
PHONE: 325-486-2140
WEBSITE: railwaymuseumsanangelo.homestead.com
E-MAIL: railmuseum@gmail.com

Rosenberg Railroad Museum

The museum features Tower 17, the last manned interlocking tower in Texas. Inside the fully restored tower, you can work the interlocking machine. Also on display are the *Quebec*, an 1879 business car, and a Missouri Pacific caboose. The museum building, modeled after the city's original depot, contains signaling, station agent, and telegraph artifacts.

LOCATION: 1921 Avenue F, Rosenberg
PHONE: 281-633-2846
WEBSITE: rosenbergrrmuseum.org
E-MAIL: form on website

Texas Transportation Museum

The museum displays automobiles, fire trucks, and carriages as well as a variety of railroad structures and equipment including two steam locomotives, two diesel engines, and rolling stock. It features a Southern Pacific depot built in 1913 that was moved from Converse. The two-room building contains memorabilia from the railroads that served San Antonio. The museum operates a short train ride on weekends. It also offers rides on antique vehicles when available.

LOCATION: 11731 Wetmore Road, San Antonio
PHONE: 210-490-3554
WEBSITE: txtransportationmuseum.org
E-MAIL: form on website

Wichita Falls Railroad Museum

The museum's collection includes a Fort Worth & Denver steam locomotive, a Missouri-Kansas-Texas switch engine, a 1913 Pullman all-steel sleeper, troop sleepers, cabooses, and other cars. Artifacts center on the railroads that served Wichita Falls. The museum is open Saturdays year-round.

LOCATION: 500 Ninth Street, Wichita Falls
PHONE: 940-723-2661
WEBSITE: wfrrm.com
E-MAIL: wfrrm@hotmail.com

Austin Steam Train

LOCATION: 401 E. Whitestone Boulevard, Cedar Park
PHONE: 512-477-8468
WEBSITE: austinsteamtrain.org
E-MAIL: info@austinsteamtrain.org

J. Parker Lamb

This tourist line was formed in 1989 to provide weekend service over a portion of a 167-mile route purchased from Southern Pacific. The train operates out of Cedar Park and rolls through the scenic Texas Hill Country—and history.

CHOICES: The railroad's operating hub is in Cedar Park, 19 miles from downtown Austin. The *Hill Country Flyer* makes a 66-mile round trip between Cedar Park and Burnet, and the trip includes a leisurely layover. On the 46-mile round trip aboard the *Bertram Flyer*, you'll leave Cedar Park, cross the South San Gabriel River, and arrive in Bertram. Rolling stock consists of six vintage Pennsylvania P70 coaches, along with three first-class parlor cars of Santa Fe, Nickel Plate Road, and Missouri Pacific heritage. You have a choice of riding coach, excursion, or first class (either in coach or lounge). Coach cars have opening windows while the other cars are climate-controlled.

WHEN TO GO: Excursions run weekends all year. Many visitors choose to ride during the spring and fall and bypass the summer heat. Murder mystery and evening trains also operate, as do holiday specials such as the *North Pole Flyer*.

GOOD TO KNOW: Trains are pulled by an Alco RSD15, a unit originally built for Santa Fe, that's been repainted in an SP-inspired "black widow" scheme. Namesake motive power 786, an ex-SP Mikado, is due to be operational again by 2015.

WORTH DOING: Both Cedar Park and Burnet have numerous lodging and dining options for visitors, while Austin is famous for its museums, entertainment, scenic drives, and area lakes.

DON'T MISS: In September, you can catch the *Oatmeal Flyer*, which takes you to Bertram's Oatmeal Festival in time to view the festival parade, complete with raining oatmeal.

GETTING THERE: Cedar Park can be reached from the north by leaving I-35 at Round Rock and using Highway 45 westward, while visitors arriving from the south will travel northward though Austin on I-35 and connect directly with Highway 183. Cedar Park also is served by Capital Metro, the city's transit authority, whose MetroRail trains utilize the line as far as Leander.

Galveston Railroad Museum

LOCATION: 2602 Santa Fe Place, Galveston
PHONE: 409-765-5700
WEBSITE: galvestonrrmuseum.com
E-MAIL: galvrrmuseum@sbcglobal.net

Tom Kline

Housed in the former Santa Fe station on Galveston Island's east end, the museum features a yardful of fascinating rolling stock, including a pair of EMD F7s painted in AT&SF's classic warbonnet scheme.

CHOICES: After a tour of the static displays, take a trip on the Harborside Express, a 15-minute excursion aboard a ex-Missouri Pacific caboose that runs several times most Saturdays. The museum also boasts one of the largest collections of railroad china and dininerware in the United States. In the station's waiting room, you'll see Ghosts of Travelers Past, full-sized plaster figures of people congregating there as it appeared in 1932. With the touch of a button, you can operate a $40,000 model train layout.

WHEN TO GO: The museum is open daily year-round, but summers on the Texas Gulf Coast tend to be hot and humid. The other three seasons are usually more pleasant when spending time outdoors.

GOOD TO KNOW: Hurricane Ike, the costliest hurricane in Texas history, did lots of damage to the museum's collection of equipment and railroadiana. Four years and $4 million later, the museum held a grand reopening in November 2012.

WORTH DOING: Like in New Orleans to the east, Mardi Gras is a big deal on the island. The center of all the activity takes place near the museum on The Strand, Galveston's historic downtown district. Another popular destination is Moody Gardens, which contains a rain forest pyramid, aquarium, and other attractions.

DON'T MISS: No trip to the island would be complete without a visit to a beach. Galveston features 32 miles of beaches and most operated by the city. If you want to get away from the crowds but still enjoy the surf, head to the island's west end to Galveston Island State Park, a 2,000-plus-acre site that offers camping, bird-watching, hiking, mountain biking, fishing, and swimming.

GETTING THERE: Fron Houston, take I-45 south to Exit 1C. Turn left onto Harborside Drive, then turn right on 25th Street/Rosenberg Street, turn right on Santa Fe, and then right again to the museum.

Grapevine Vintage Railroad

LOCATION: 705 S. Main Street, Grapevine
PHONE: 817-410-3123 or 817-410-8136
WEBSITE: grapevinetexasusa.com

J. Parker Lamb

Grapevine operates the only 19th century steam locomotive in Texas. Based at the restored 1888 Cotton Belt depot in downtown Grapevine, the railroad runs over 21 miles of ex-Cotton Belt track into the famous Fort Worth Stockyards Mall. It also includes a six-mile branch line running south from the mall across the Trinity River.

CHOICES: The railroad's 75-minute ride takes you from Grapevine to the Stockyards, and the two-hour layover allows ample time for exploring the mall's many offerings. The Trinity River run passes through Trinity Park and the Fort Worth Zoo along a segment of the famous Chisholm Trail. *Puffy*, an 1896 Cooke 4-6-0 steam locomotive, was used for decades by the Southern Pacific in fire service on Donner Pass and alternates its duties with *Vinny*, a former AT&SF Electro-Motive GP7. Trains carry four 1925-era day coaches (19th century décor) plus a pair of open-air excursion coaches.

WHEN TO GO: Regular excursions run February through November. In June, July, and August, they operate Friday through Sunday. Frequency is reduced to two days (Saturday and Sunday) during the rest of the season. A shorter run from Grapevine operates on Saturdays only. The line offers numerous special events including train robberies and wine tastings, as well as numerous holiday trains.

GOOD TO KNOW: Grapevine is close to the Texas Rangers ballpark at Arlington, Dallas Cowboys stadium, and Six Flags Over Texas. The Fort Worth Stockyards complex includes the Texas Cowboy Hall of Fame and weekend rodeo shows. Just north of the city is Grapevine Lake, a mecca for water sports.

WORTH DOING: True to its name, Grapevine is home to numerous wineries with regular tours and a special Grapefest celebration in September.

DON'T MISS: For maximum mileage, passengers can board at Grapevine, travel to the Fort Worth Stockyards, and then ride the Trinity River run, which connects with the return train to Grapevine.

GETTING THERE: The city of Grapevine is adjacent to the northwest corner of DFW Airport. Three highways (114, 121, and 360) intersect at Grapevine, with I-30 being a few miles south of the airport and I-35E a few miles east.

McKinney Avenue Trolley

LOCATION: McKinney Avenue, Dallas
PHONE: 214-855-0006
WEBSITE: mata.org
E-MAIL: ask_mata@yahoo.com

Ralcon Wagner

Vintage electric trolley cars take riders back in time during a 3.5-mile ride down McKinney Avenue and other streets in the historic Uptown neighborhood.

CHOICES: The heritage trolley route, referred to locally as the M-Line, has become increasingly popular with tourists and commuters alike. An extension down Olive Street should be open by summer 2013. Additional cars will be added to the roster as part of the expansion, including at least one PCC car. Most of the cars are air-conditioned. Because of the historical nature of the trolleys, cars are not equipped for handicapped boarding. Since the trolley line is operated as a nonprofit organization, there is no fare.

WHEN TO GO: Trolleys operate year-round and run every 15 to 25 minutes from morning through the evening with extended hours on Fridays and Saturdays.

GOOD TO KNOW: Most of the cars trundling down the M-Line were built between 1909 and 1925 by a variety of builders. As a result, each car is unique in appearance and design, while sporting names such as *Rosie, Petunia,* and *Matilda.*

WORTH DOING: There are a variety of things to do along the McKinney Avenue corridor, such as dining at one of the many restaurants and sidewalk cafes and browsing through art galleries, boutiques, and antique shops. The Dallas World Aquarium and Museum of Art are a short walk from the trolley line.

DON'T MISS: Only minutes away, Dallas Union Station is an architectural gem that serves as a transportation hub for DART light rail, Trinity Railway Express commuter trains, and Amtrak. Take a stroll down the nearby Katy Trail, a scenic rail-trail along the former Missouri-Kansas-Texas Railroad right-of-way.

GETTING THERE: You can park on Cityplace West Boulevard or any cross street and board the trolley at the blue waiting shelter or the Uptown Station. If using public transit, ride any DART light rail Blue, Red, or Orange Line train to the Cityplace/Uptown subway station. Take the west exit to the surface to board the trolley.

Museum of the American Railroad

LOCATION: 6299 Cotton Gin Road, Frisco
PHONE: 214-428-0101
WEBSITE: historictrains.org
E-MAIL: form on website

Museum of the American Railroad

Texas

The museum features more than 40 pieces of vintage equipment. The museum contains an eclectic mix of all types of locomotives from both the United States and Canada. It features one of the nation's largest collections of pre-World War II heavyweight passenger equipment. It also has a variety of lightweight passenger cars, freight cars, and cabooses.

CHOICES: The collection includes a rare unrestored Santa Fe Alco PA1 that was donated from the Smithsonian, two of the Union Pacific's largest locomotives (a Big Boy 4-8-8-4 steam locomotive and a Centennial DDA40X diesel), and a Pennsylvania GG1 electric. Other engines range in size from a giant Frisco 4-8-4 down to a diminutive 0-6-0 from the Dallas Union Terminal. Also on display are historic structures and a 1941 Ford truck used by the Railway Express Agency. Structures include a Santa Fe tower and a Houston & Texas Central station.

WHEN TO GO: The museum is open Wednesdays through Sundays. Special events include a Day Out with Thomas at Grapevine Vintage Railroad. Additional events will be offered as the museum gets more settled into its new home.

GOOD TO KNOW: After a two-year move from Dallas, the museum has opened in its new location. Please check the museum's website for the most current information on the opening of new exhibits.

WORTH DOING: While Dallas and all its attractions are a half hour away, Frisco has activities and attractions as well. You can visit the Texas Sculpture Garden, Sci-Tech Discovery Center, and Frisco Heritage Museum.

DON'T MISS: For a ride on a steam train, the Grapevine Vintage Railroad is 30 miles southwest of Frisco.

GETTING THERE: The easiest route to Frisco from Dallas is on the Dallas North Tollway. Although when traffic is bad, the 30-mile drive may take an hour.

Texas State Railroad

LOCATION: Highway 84 and Park Road 76, Rusk
PHONE: 888-987-2461 or 903-683-2561
WEBSITE: texasstaterr.com
E-MAIL: info@texasstaterr.com

Tom Kline

The Texas State Railroad offers a relaxing, enjoyable ride through the piney woods region of east Texas between the small towns of Rusk and Palestine. Locomotives with regional history pull the trains through tall stands of timber in the I.D. Fairchild National Forest, giving riders a glimpse into the railroad's origin of hauling agricultural and timber products in the early 20th century.

CHOICES: Currently, all excursions are steam powered but diesels are also available. On your 25-mile round trip, you have several seating options. For standard seating, you can sit in a coach with cushioned seats and open windows or sit in an open-air coach with bench seats. Lone Star service offers climate-controlled seating in either an adult-only car or a family car. A box lunch or supper is provided for both levels of service.

WHEN TO GO: Trains operate weekends during late spring, summer, and fall. Texas summers can be hot so book early for air-conditioned Lone Star seating. Dinner trains and various special events, including military reenactments, the *Polar Express*, and some featuring Peanuts characters, are offered. Also, keep an eye open for a masked man as the Lone Ranger rides again at the Texas State Railroad.

GOOD TO KNOW: Trains leave from each depot. The Victorian-styled stations also contain historical exhibits and displays that highlight the railroad's role in various move and TV productions. Adjacent to each depot, you'll find picnic areas as well as camp sites.

WORTH DOING: Palestine features many restored Victorian homes, historic buildings from the early 1800s, and the Dogwood Trails Festival in March.

DON'T MISS: RailFest takes place in May, and activities includes a steam excursion, a shop tour, and special photo-taking opportunities. Check to see if tours of Texas & Pacific 2-10-4 No. 610 housed in the shop at Palestine are available.

GETTING THERE: Major airlines to Dallas or Houston provide the closest air transportation. From there, a leisurely three-hour drive is required to reach the two east Texas towns.

UTAH

Tooele Valley Railroad Museum

Housed in the old Tooele Valley depot, built in 1909, the museum tells the story of the area's colorful mining and smelting years. Tooele Valley Railway steam locomotive No. 11 is the museum's No. 1 attraction. The 1910 Alco 2-8-0 consolidation-type engine is displayed with two wood cabooses and other rolling stock. Open Tuesday through Saturday, Memorial Day through September, the museum runs a miniature train on Saturdays.

LOCATION: 35 N. Broadway Street, Tooele
PHONE: 435-882-2836 or 435-843-2143
WEBSITE: tooelecity.org

Western Mining and Railroad Museum

Museum exhibits feature the Denver & Rio Grande Western and other railways. Located in the old Helper Hotel, which was completed in 1914, the museum contains four floors of artifacts. The third floor contains a railroad office and two rooms of railroading artifacts. A 100-year-old caboose is also on display. Other exhibits, including a simulated coal mine, focus on the mining industry and its workers. It is open year-round.

LOCATION: 296 S. Main Street, Helper
PHONE: 435-472-3009
WEBSITE: wmrrm.org
E-MAIL: helpermuseum@helpercity.net

Golden Spike National Historic Site

LOCATION: Golden Spike Drive, Promontory
PHONE: 435-471-2209
WEBSITE: nps.gov/gosp
E-MAIL: form on website

Jeff Terry

The construction of the transcontinental railroad is one of the pivotal events in the nation's history. Completed May 10, 1869, at this remote spot northwest of Ogden, the National Park Service does justice to the event by running replica locomotives and conducting reenactments.

CHOICES: Reenactments of the Last Spike Ceremony, complete with dignitaries in period dress, take place on Saturdays and holidays May through Labor Day. The two steam locomotive replicas, the coal-burning Union Pacific No. 119 and the wood-burning Central Pacific *Jupiter*, are accurate reproductions and fully functional. The visitor center offers informative films and exhibits.

WHEN TO GO: Except for Thanksgiving, Christmas, and New Year's Day, the visitor center is open. Between May and Labor Day, the steam locomotives are on display and conduct demonstrations. During winter, when the locomotives are being maintained, engine house tours are available.

GOOD TO KNOW: The correct name for the location of Golden Spike National Historic Site is Promontory Summit, not Promontory Point, which is 35 miles to the south. The summit is the highest point of Promontory Pass. For some reason, the wrong location was reported in some records in 1869 and perpetuated throughout history.

WORTH DOING: Drive through Brigham City and view the interesting Box Elder Tabernacle, and stop at the restored early 20th century train depot.

DON'T MISS: The Big Fill Loop Trail (1.5-mile round trip) takes you out on the original Central Pacific grade and back on the Union Pacific grade. You'll see the site of the Union Pacific's trestle, go through cuts, and see drill marks where workers blasted away rock.

GETTING THERE: Golden Spike National Historic Site is in northern Utah, 32 miles west of Brigham City. From Brigham City, take Highway 83 to the entrance, which is Golden Spike Drive. The area is still very rugged and sparsely populated. Food and fuel are available in Brigham City.

Heber Valley Railroad

LOCATION: 450 S. 600 West, Heber City
PHONE: 800-888-8499 or 435-654-5601
WEBSITE: hebervalleyrr.org
E-MAIL: info@hebervalleyrr.org

Jeff Terry

This railroad offers a scenic ride beside Deer Creek Reservoir and into Provo Canyon with the Wasatch Mountains as a backdrop over a line that began operating in 1899.

CHOICES: Heber Valley offers several regular excursions in the shadow of 12,000-foot Mount Timpanogos aboard vintage coaches. The *Provo Canyon Limited* is a three-hour round trip that runs to Vivian Park and back. The 90-minute *Deer Creek Express* goes to Deer Creek Reservoir and returns. The *Lakeside Limited* is a scenic two-hour ride along Deer Creek Reservoir and the base of Mount Timpanogo. Summer excursion packages combine river rafting, horseback riding, or ziplining with a train ride. Numerous special events take place, from sunset barbecues to the *North Pole Express*.

WHEN TO GO: The railroad operates late May through December. Summer is especially beautiful in Utah, but winter excursions offer a unique look at a snowy wnderland. The *Provo Canyon Limited* runs summer and early fall, the *Lakeside Limited* from late fall through December, and the *Deer Creek Express*, the entire season.

GOOD TO KNOW: Trains are currently operating under diesel power, and steam operations are scheduled to return with the restoration of 2-8-0 No. 75, possibly in 2013.

WORTH DOING: Take a scenic drive along the Provo Canyon Scenic Byway (Highway 189) that runs between Heber Valley and Provo. A short side trip on the Alpine Scenic Loop (Highway 92) takes you past Robert Redford's Sundance Resort.

DON'T MISS: For a high-flying adventure, try combining a wilderness zip line with a train ride. The adventure begins with a train ride through Heber Valley, and if you make it through without running into Black Jack Raven and his gang of train robbers, you'll be driven into the Wasatch Mountains to the zip line drop-off, where you'll zip over the scenery.

GETTING THERE: The railroad is located between Salt Lake City and Provo. From Salt Lake City, take I-80 east to Exit 148 and then follow Highway 40 into Heber City. Turn right on W. 300 S and then left on S. 600 West to the station.

Ogden Union Station

LOCATION: 2501 Wall Avenue, Ogden
PHONE: 801-393-9886
WEBSITE: theunionstation.org
E-MAIL: museums@theunionstation.org

Dave Crosby

Built in 1924, Ogden Union Station now houses a variety of museums and galleries, including the Utah State Railroad Museum and Eccles Rail Center. The museum contains artifacts of Utah railroading, and the rail center displays historic pieces of equipment. Other museums in the station focus on history, firearms, gems, classic cars, and the arts.

CHOICES: You can browse an extensive collection of rolling stock that is displayed outside the station or go inside. You'll see locomotives and cars from the big Class I railroads that served Utah, including Union Pacific, Southern Pacific, and Rio Grande. Interactive exhibits bring to life the story of the first transcontinental railroad, which was completed nearby at Promontory Summit, just west of Ogden. You'll also pass under timbers used to construct the historic Lucin trestle across the Great Salt Lake. A model railroad depicts scenery from across Utah.

WHEN TO GO: The museum is open Monday through Saturday year-round, but the outdoor railroad exhibits are accessible anytime. Many special events take place at the station, some relating to railroading.

GOOD TO KNOW: UP 4-8-4 No. 833, representing the zenith of steam passenger and freight power, was one of the last big steam locomotives built in America

WORTH DOING: There are numerous hiking trails in and around Ogden, on which you can see mountains, waterfalls, forests, and wildlife. In scenic Ogden Valley, you can ski on the same slopes as Olympic skiers did or just enjoy the scenery. In Ogden, you can take in a show or film at Peery's Egyptian Theater, with its restored Egyptian look.

DON'T MISS: View the Union Pacific cauldron car, which carried the Olympic flame during the 2002 Winter Olympics that were held in Utah and based in Salt Lake City. The unique car carried the flame more than 3,200 miles across 11 states.

GETTING THERE: From Salt Lake City, take I-15 north to Exit 341 and follow Highway 79 east. Turn left onto Wall Avenue. The museum is in downtown Ogden and directions are well marked.

VERMONT

Shelburne Museum

Outside the museum, you'll see the 1890 Shelburne passenger station, locomotive No. 220, which pulled the trains of four presidents, and an 1890 private luxury car. Other historic buildings, a steamship, and more than 200 horse-drawn vehicles are displayed at the museum.

LOCATION: 6000 Shelburne Road, Shelburne
PHONE: 802-985-3346
WEBSITE: shelburnemuseum.org
E-MAIL: info@shelburnemuseum.org

Green Mountain Railroad

LOCATION: 102 Railroad Row, White River Junction
PHONE: 800-707-3530 or 802-463-3069
WEBSITE: rails-vt.com
E-MAIL: form on website

Kevin Burkholder

Green Mountain Railroad operates both regular excursions and special trains over the Vermont Rail System.

CHOICES: On its two-hour round trip from White River Junction to Thetford, the *White River Flyer* rolls along the Connecticut River and provides a view of New Hampshire's White Mountain foothills. It also pauses at the Montshire Museum of Science. Easter, hobo, fireworks, pumpkin, murder mystery, Taste of Vermont, and other theme trains run during the year. In fall, the *Green Mountain Flyer* operates between Bellows Falls and Chester Depot. The ride follows the Connecticut and Williams Rivers, taking you past covered bridges and a deep gorge at Brockways Mills. Special trains periodically run on other sections of the VRS, including Burlington and St. Johnsbury.

WHEN TO GO: The *White River Flyer* runs Thursday through Sunday during July and August with service expanding to Tuesday to Sunday in September and October. The *Green Mountain Flyer* runs in September and October for the fall foliage season.

GOOD TO KNOW: Train operations and special offerings change from year to year, so be sure to check the website for the most current information.

WORTH DOING: The historic Hotel Coolidge operates across from the White River Junction depot, and Calvin Coolidge's boyhood home is preserved in a state historic site in Plymouth Notch. Other nearby attractions include the Quechee Gorge area and Dartmouth College's Hood Museum of Art in Hanover, N.H.

DON'T MISS: Former Rutland Railroad Alco RS1 No. 405, which has operated in Vermont since it was built in 1951, makes regular appearances on Green Mountain passenger trains. Boston & Maine 4-4-0 steam engine No. 494 and a restored wooden caboose are on display at the White River Junction depot.

GETTING THERE: Near the Vermont–New Hampshire border, White River Junction is at the intersection of I-89 and I-91. Railroad Row and the station can be accessed from Main Street and Joe Reed Drive or from Bridge Street.

VIRGINIA

C&O Railway Heritage Center

A restored 1895 C&O freight depot exhibits the history of the Chesapeake & Ohio Railway. The center also displays a restored 1949 C&O caboose, dining car, and combination car. You can also climb into a replica signal tower and watch trains roll by.

LOCATION: 705 Main Street, Clifton Forge
PHONE: 540 862 8653 or 540-862-2210
WEBSITE: candoheritage.org
E-MAIL: cohs@cohs.org

Crewe Railroad Museum

Housed in a rail station, the museum features memorabilia from the Norfolk & Western Railroad and a display of the Crewe roundhouse. The yard contains a steam locomotive, diesel engine, caboose, and several boxcars. The museum is open Thursday through Sunday year-round.

LOCATION: 111 West Virginia Avenue, Crewe
PHONE: 434-645-9868 or 434-645-9650
WEBSITE: crewerailroadmuseum.org

Eastern Shore Railway Museum

The museum is housed in a restored 1906 Pennsylvania Railroad passenger station. On the siding are two cabooses, a baggage car, a Pullman sleeper, a Budd dining car, and a touring car. The museum also includes an 1890s maintenance-of-way tool shed, a crossing guard shanty, and various railroad artifacts. It is open year-round.

LOCATION: 18468 Dunne Avenue, Parksley
PHONE: 757-665-7245
WEBSITE: chincoteaguechamber.com/i-rail.html

Fairfax Station Railroad Museum

At the Fairfax museum, visitors can learn about the Orange & Alexandria Railroad and Civil War history. Stations on the site played a role in several Civil War battles, and Clara Barton tended to wounded soldiers here. The current building is a restored 1903 station, and a Norfolk Southern caboose is also on display. The museum is open Sunday afternoons.

LOCATION: 11200 Fairfax Station Road, Fairfax
PHONE: 703-425-9225
WEBSITE: fairfax-station.org
E-MAIL: fxstn@fairfax-station.org

Rappahannock Railway Workers Museum

Only at this museum can you ride the Little Yellow Train, a maintenance train composed of a speeder and various track cars, and learn more about working on the railroad. The museum contains dining car china, uniforms, lanterns, and other items. Also on display are several cabooses, a Pennsylvania baggage car, and a boxcar. It is open Saturdays mid-March through October.

LOCATION: 11700 Main Street, Fredericksburg
WEBSITE: rcnrhs.com
E-MAIL: form on website

Richmond Railroad Museum

With its exhibits, the museum highlights the railroads that served central Virginia. The restored Southern Railway passenger station includes a stationmaster's office and a freight room containing artifacts. Guided tours are available, and excursions are offered several times a year. On display outside are a steam saddle locomotive, baggage car, and caboose. It is open Saturdays and Sundays year-round.

LOCATION: 102 Hull Street, Richmond
PHONE: 804-231-4324 or 804-233-6237
WEBSITE: richmondrailroadmuseum.org
E-MAIL: chefwrg@aol.com

Suffolk Seaboard Station Railroad Museum

The restored Victorian Seaboard Air Line passenger station features items from Seaboard, Virginian, Norfolk & Western, and Atlantic & Danville railroads. It is also home to a two-room HO scale model of Suffolk in 1907 and a caboose originally built for the Nickel Plate Line. It is open Wednesday through Sunday.

LOCATION: 326 N. Main Street, Suffolk
PHONE: 757-923-4750
WEBSITE: suffolktrainstation.org
E-MAIL: trainstation@exis.net

O. Winston Link Museum

LOCATION: 101 Shenandoah Avenue NE, Roanoke
PHONE: 540-982-5465
WEBSITE: linkmuseum.org

O. Winston Link Museum

Only two photographers in the United States have their own museums. One belongs to noted landscape photographer Ansel Adams. The other is O. Winston Link. A commercial photographer, Link was fascinated with steam locomotives and made a pilgrimage to record the last of these on the Norfolk & Western in the late 1950s.

CHOICES: The museum is housed in the former Norfolk & Western passenger station in downtown Roanoke. The station was the departure point for many of the trains Link photographed, making it an excellent departure point for a world of Link's photography. More than 300 of Link's photographs are on display. The museum includes interactive exhibits, Link's photography equipment, and his railroad sound recordings. Be sure to watch the documentary film on Link's life. It's an excellent look at the man and his work through his voice and those of many others.

WHEN TO GO: The museum is open daily except for Easter, Thanksgiving, Christmas, and New Year's Day. Fall and spring in the Blue Ridge Mountains are magnificent and wonderful times to explore the area.

GOOD TO KNOW: Famous for his nighttime scenes that record the passing railroad as well as slices of rural life, Link took many photos of the region in the late '50s and early '60s. For years, Link's work languished, but in the 1980s, his career rebounded as the art world discovered his genius of capturing steam at night in (mostly) black and white.

WORTH DOING: The Hotel Roanoke, directly behind the museum, is a former railroad hotel and a great place to spend the night. Spend some time on the front lawn and watch the coal trains lumber by as they have for more than 120 years.

DON'T MISS: The former station is a Virginia Historic Landmark and is listed on the National Register of Historic Places. It is one of several renovated railroad buildings in the area. Another is the Virginia Museum of Transportation, which is a short walk away. The two museums offer a combined admission.

GETTING THERE: Roanoke is about 190 miles west of Richmond and near West Virginia and North Carolina. To reach the museum from I-81, take I-581 south and exit at Williamson Road and turn right on Shenandoah Avenue.

Virginia Museum of Transportation

LOCATION: 303 Norfolk Avenue SW, Roanoke
PHONE: 540-342-5670
WEBSITE: vmt.org
E-MAIL: info@vmt.org

Jim Wrinn

Roanoke was once synonymous with the best steam locomotives in the land. The Norfolk & Western built many of them right here, just a few blocks away. While the museum's scope is the broad subject of transportation, with more than 50 pieces of rolling stock, its heart is in railroading.

CHOICES: The museum is housed in a historic rail setting, the city's old N&W freight station. Through exhibits and rolling stock displays, you'll learn a lot about how people got around in the Old Dominion State. It displays steam and diesel locomotives, antique automobiles, trucks, and even a post office bus. The red, white, and blue bicentennial SD45, No. 1776, makes a splashy display!

WHEN TO GO: The museum is open daily, except for some holidays and during inclement weather, throughout the year.

GOOD TO KNOW: Joint admissions are available with the O. Winston Link Museum and the History Museum of Western Virginia. Discounts are also available for members of several other rail-heritage organizations in western Virginia.

WORTH DOING: Stroll along the rail walk that connects the museum with the O. Winston Link Museum and Hotel Roanoke. The walk parallels the Norfolk Southern's mainline track and features displays and interactive exhibits along the way.

DON'T MISS: Climb into the crew cab of the streamlined Norfolk & Western 4-8-4 Class J. Built in 1950, No. 611 is the last of its kind, one of 13 that pulled the railroad's named trains. Capable of sprinting faster than 100 mph or climbing the mountains of West Virginia, these locomotives were considered to be among the best in the nation. You can stand in the cab and see the gauges, handles, and levers that made it all happen. Next door to No. 611 is No. 1218, a Class A. Built in 1943, this articulated locomotive features two sets of drivers and cylinders.

GETTING THERE: Situated in the Blue Ridge Mountains, Roanoke is served by a regional airport and several major highways. The museum is located downtown on Norfolk Avenue between Second and Fifth Streets.

WASHINGTON

Bellingham Railway Museum

This small museum displays a collection of lanterns as well as photographs and artifacts that highlight the history of railroading in the area. It also has railroad history walks, presentations, and motor car rides on Saturdays. The museum offers train rides in conjunction with Lake Whatcom Railway in Wickersham. It is open Tuesdays through Saturdays.

LOCATION: 1320 Commercial Street, Bellingham
PHONE: 360-393-7540
WEBSITE: bellinghamrailwaymuseum.org
E-MAIL: brm@integra.net

Cashmere Museum & Pioneer Village

The pioneer village features 20 historical structures, dating back to the late 1800s. Railroad displays include a Great Northern section house, ticket office, caboose, equipment, and artifacts. The museum also includes exhibits regarding pioneer and Native American history. It is open March through October.

LOCATION: 600 Cotlets Way, Cashmere
PHONE: 509-782-3230
WEBSITE: cashmeremuseum.org
E-MAIL: info@cashmeremuseum.org

Dayton Historical Depot

Built in 1881, this is the oldest surviving railroad station in Washington. The stylish Stick/Eastlake building is now a museum of local history. It includes artifacts from the Union Pacific and the Oregon Railroad and Navigation Company, and a UP caboose is also on display. It is open year-round.

LOCATION: 222 E. Commercial Street, Dayton
PHONE: 509-382-2026
WEBSITE: daytonhistoricdepot.org
E-MAIL: info@daytonhistoricdepot.org

Issaquah Depot Museum and Trolley

The museum displays a variety of railcars including several from Weyerhaeuser Company and a World War II kitchen car that contains logging, mining, and railroad artifacts. The historic depot includes a station agent's office with railroad and local history displays. The Issaquah Valley Trolley runs from the depot to a bridge across the East Fork of Issaquah Creek. It was built in 1925 for service in Lisbon, Portugal, and is powered by a generator car. The museum is open Friday, Saturday, and Sunday with extra hours added during summer.

LOCATION: 150 First Avenue NE, Issaquah
PHONE: 425-392-3500
WEBSITE: issaquahhistory.org
E-MAIL: info@issaquahhistory.org

Lake Whatcom Railway

This 90-minute train ride takes you from the shores of Lake Whatcom into the wooded countryside and back. The vintage coaches and diesel locomotive were all used on the Northern Pacific. A 100-year-old steam engine and wooden Great Northern freight cars are also on site. For a good workout, you can try your hand at riding a handcar. Excursions run during summer and for special events.

LOCATION: Highway 9 and NP Road, Wickersham
PHONE: 360-595-2218
WEBSITE: lakewhatcomrailway.com

Northern Pacific Railway Museum

The 1911 Northern Pacific Railway depot in Toppenish now serves as a museum to that railroad. The site's freight house has been converted to an engine house, where several steam locomotives are being restored. The museum offers caboose rides during special events throughout the year. It is open Tuesday through Sunday May through October.

LOCATION: 10 S. Asotin Avenue, Toppenish
PHONE: 509-865-1911
WEBSITE: nprymuseum.org

Ritzville Railroad Depot History Museum

The brick mission-style depot was built in 1910. The building is on the National Register of Historic Places and retains many of its original features, including floor scales that you can try out. The museum contains railroad memorabilia, a telegraph machine, and local historical items. The museum is open Tuesdays through Saturdays Memorial Day through Labor Day.

LOCATION: Railroad Avenue and Washington Street, Ritzville
PHONE: 509-659-1656
WEBSITE: museums.goritzville.com
E-MAIL: museums@goritzville.com

Washington State Railroads Historical Society Museum

The museum features equipment, artifacts, and photos of the railroads involved in the state. Outdoors, it displays a variety of locomotives, passenger cars, freight cars, and cabooses. It is open on Thursdays, Fridays, and Saturdays.

LOCATION: 122 N. Tacoma Avenue, Pasco
PHONE: 509-543-4159
WEBSITE: wsrhs.org
E-MAIL: email@wsrhs.org

Yakima Valley Trolleys

Yakima Valley trolleys have been operating for more than 100 years. You can ride along the historic line weekends and holidays from Memorial Day to Labor Day. Railcars used on the line date between 1910 and 1930. Trolleys leave from the carbarn.

LOCATION: S. Third Avenue at W. Pine Street, Yakima
PHONE: 509-249-5962
WEBSITE: yakimavalleytrolleys.org
E-MAIL: yakimavalleytrolleys@hotmail.com

Chehalis-Centralia Railroad

LOCATION: 1101 Sylvenus Street, Chehalis
PHONE: 360-748-9593
WEBSITE: steamtrainride.com
E-MAIL: info@steamtrainride.com

Chehalis-Centralia Railroad, Dave LaClair

In the shadow of Mount Saint Helens, this relaxing train ride takes you into the forests of western Washington. You'll ride behind a steam locomotive that saw many years of service logging these very forests.

CHOICES: The railroad offers two different excursions. The 12-mile Milburn run takes you through forests and countryside. A longer 18-mile round trip to Ruth extends the ride by following the Chehalis River. The railroad's brunch and dinner trains follow the Ruth route and serve meals in a refurbished 1920s dining car.

WHEN TO GO: Summer steam train rides begin Memorial Day weekend and operate Saturdays and Sundays through September. Murder mystery trains, holiday trains, and other special events are scheduled throughout the year.

GOOD TO KNOW: For an extra fee, you can experience what it is like to ride in the cab of a working steam locomotive with a cab ride in No. 15, a 2-8-2 Mikado type steam engine.

WORTH DOING: Take time to visit Mount Saint Helens National Volcanic Monument and view the dramatic changes the area has undergone since the 1980 eruption. The 110,000-acre site contains hiking trails, several visitor centers, and an observatory.

DON'T MISS: On summer Saturdays, the railroad usually makes an early 12-mile run to Milburn and then follows up with an 18-mile run to Ruth later in the afternoon. You can catch the early run, take pictures with Mount Saint Helens as a backdrop, and return on the later trip.

GETTING THERE: The railroad is about a 90-minute drive from either Portland or Seattle. From I-5, take Exit 77 (Main Street) into Chehalis. Turn left on Riverside Drive and then left again on Sylvenus Street. Nearby Centralia is also served by Amtrak.

Chelatchie Prairie Railroad

LOCATION: 207 N. Railroad Avenue, Yacolt
PHONE: 360-686-3559
WEBSITE: bycx.com
E-MAIL: admin@bycx.com

Chelatchie Prairie Railroad, Will Pickering

The train runs on a remote former logging railroad line in western Washington from Yacolt to Lucia. The eight-mile route includes a 330-foot-long tunnel carved from solid rock, a trestle over the Lewis River, and a half-hour layover at Moulton Falls.

CHOICES: You can enjoy the scenic ride by traveling in a coach car, open observation car, circus car, or caboose. Trains are powered by a 1941 Alco diesel or a 1929 steam locomotive. On the layover in Moulton Falls Park, you can have a picnic and take in two waterfalls and a tall arched bridge.

WHEN TO GO: The railroad operates May through December. It runs on various weekends and offers train robberies, wine trains, and fall color excursions as well as other specials throughout the year, including those for Mother's Day, Father's Day, Halloween, and Christmas.

GOOD TO KNOW: The railroad offers a unique Christmas tree and train experience for families. After taking the train to Moulton, you can visit with Santa, enjoy some cookies and hot chocolate, and pick out your Christmas tree. The locally grown tree is loaded into a 1912 heavyweight boxcar for the return trip to Yacolt.

WORTH DOING: A half hour may not be enough time to see Moulton Falls Park. The park contains a hiking trail and volcanic rock formations. It also connects to Lucia Falls Park and the Bells Mountain Trail. Mount Saint Helens is about an hour's drive north of Yacolt.

DON'T MISS: BYCX's coach car No. 60 has seen many changes since being built by the Pullman Company in 1918 as a 12-section sleeping car. It was later converted to a tourist sleeper and then in 1948 remodeled into a baggage car. No. 60 was put in maintenance-of-way service (and first painted mineral red and white) and in 1975, became a kitchen/bunk car. Now it is back in passenger service.

GETTING THERE: The railroad is located an hour's drive from Vancouver, Wash., and Portland. From I-5, take Exit 16 through Fargher Lake or Exit 9 through Battle Ground to Yacolt. In Yacolt, the station is on Railroad Avenue at Yacolt Road.

Mount Rainier Scenic Railroad

LOCATION: 54124 Mountain Highway East, Elbe
PHONE: 888-783-2611 or 360-492-5588
WEBSITE: mrsr.com
E-MAIL: admin@mrsr.org

Jim Wrinn

Here's a chance to experience a real Pacific Northwest logging railroad at work. The locomotives, the setting, and the route all have the feel of a working railroad. Adjacent to its shop facility, the railroad's logging museum and forestry interpretive center is scheduled to open in June 2013.

CHOICES: A pure steam experience, a 2-8-2T logging engine usually pulls the passenger coaches through the foothills of Mount Rainier on a two-hour round trip. You'll ride out over creeks, through forests, and across bridges to Mineral. The railroad offers all three major types of geared logging locomotives as possible power: a Shay, a Climax, and a Heisler. You can choose to ride in a coach or an open car.

WHEN TO GO: The railroad operates weekends May, June, September, and October, with daily excursions during the busy months of July and August. The Santa Express runs weekends during November and December.

GOOD TO KNOW: The railroad operates a rare Willamette-type geared steam locomotive. Built in 1929 in Portland, Ore., engine No. 2 was one of only 33 manufactured for use on logging railroads in the Pacific Northwest.

WORTH DOING: Mount Rainier National Park offers scenic drives and hikes around the 14,410-foot active volcano. Most roads are open from late May to October. Hiking, biking, and climbing are all fun activities.

DON'T MISS: In Mineral, while the steam engine takes water from a rebuilt logging-era water tank, you have the opportunity to visit a reconstructed logging camp, inspect a variety of logging equipment, and view the railroad's collection of steam locomotives.

GETTING THERE: Elbe is located in western Washington near Mount Rainier National Park, approximately 75 miles south of Seattle and 125 miles north of Portland. From the Seattle area, take I-5 to Highway 512 and then exit on Highway 7, which is also Mountain Highway.

Northwest Railway Museum

LOCATION: 38625 SE King Street, Snoqualmie
PHONE: 425-888-3030
WEBSITE: trainmuseum.org
E-MAIL: info@trainumseum.org

Northwest Railway Museum

The museum is home to more than 70 pieces of rolling stock, the bulk of it from the Pacific Northwest. The museum also includes a collection of dining car china, tools, signs, and lanterns. It offers a short train ride from either Snoqualmie or North Bend.

CHOICES: The museum is headquartered at Snoqualmie depot, a restored 1890 Queen Anne-style building that is on the National Register of Historic Places. It features exhibits inside the depot and outdoor displays of restored equipment including steam locomotives, passenger cars, freight cars, and maintenance equipment. It offers 10-mile round trips to Snoqualmie Falls in restored heavyweight coaches pulled by first-generation diesel locomotives.

WHEN TO GO: The museum is open daily year-round except for Thanksgiving, Christmas, and New Year's Day. It offers train rides on weekends April through October, with Day Out with Thomas and other special events scheduled during the year. Railroad Days take place in August. Santa trains sell out quickly and run for four weekends.

GOOD TO KNOW: The museum has restored a unique logging caboose. Built by White River Lumber Company in 1945, the caboose is just 24 feet long. Because of wartime shortages of raw materials, the caboose was made of wood and recycled parts.

WORTH DOING: View Snoqualmie Falls, one of the state's most popular attractions. The waterfall cascades down 270 feet, which is 100 feet more than Niagara Falls.

DON'T MISS: Check out the nine steam locomotives in the collection, including the unusual Mallet engines that were used for logging—they're basically two locomotives under one boiler.

GETTING THERE: The museum is 30 miles east of Seattle on I-90. From I-90 east, take Exit 25. Heading north, follow Snoqualmie Ridge Parkway for approximately four miles to Highway 202. Turn right on Highway 202 and proceed a half-mile to the Snoqualmie depot on your right. To get to the North Bend depot, take Exit 31 off I-90. Follow Bendigo Street into North Bend and turn right on North Bend Way.

WEST VIRGINIA

Princeton Railroad Museum

The museum is a replica of the Virginian Railway station that stood in Princeton for 70 years. It features exhibits devoted to the Virginian and Norfolk & Western Railways. It contains art, lanterns, and other artifacts. A Virginian caboose is also on display.

LOCATION: 99 Mercer Street, Princeton
PHONE: 304-487-5060
WEBSITE: princetonrailroadmuseum.com
E-MAIL: form on website

Cass Scenic Railroad State Park

LOCATION: Highway 66, Cass
PHONE: 800-225-5982 or 304-456-4300
WEBSITE: cassrailroad.com
E-MAIL: form on website

Cass Scenic Railroad

The Cass Scenic Railroad is as close as you'll ever come to experiencing a mountain logging railroad—because it once was one. Leaving from the mill town of Cass along the beautiful Greenbrier River, trains climb steep grades out of the Leatherbark Creek area, negotiate two switchbacks, and hug hillsides to gain elevation. It was all about getting to the timber 100 years ago. Today, it's all about getting above it all. And Cass does that.

CHOICES: Got only a little time? Ride a two-hour trip to Whitaker station and back for a taste. Got plenty of time? Sink your teeth into a half-day trip to Bald Knob and back. At Whittaker, all trains pause for servicing, and you can inspect a re-created railroad logging camp. Continuing on, trains powered by unusual geared steam locomotives work their way to Bald Knob, which, at 4,880 feet, is the second highest point in West Virginia. The view there is spectacular, and the trains climb an 11 percent grade to reach the summit.

WHEN TO GO: The railroad runs Memorial Day through October, with heavy passenger counts during the colorful autumn. It schedules several special events during the season including a train with a barbecue dinner and bluegrass music.

GOOD TO KNOW: In spring, the railroad's support organization, the Mountain State Railroad & Logging Historical Association, holds a railfan weekend when all the Shay geared locomotives run. This event covers tracks not normally used by Cass trains.

WORTH DOING: Near Cass, there are several state parks and forests, including Droop Mountain Battlefield State Park, the site of the state's last major battle during the Civil War. The Greenbrier River Trail is a biking and hiking trail that runs along the river for many of its 78 miles.

DON'T MISS: Ticket price also includes admission to the logging museum, Cass Showcase diorama, camp tour, and shop tour.

GETTING THERE: Cass Scenic Railroad is located in eastern West Virginia, and I-64 is the closest major road. From there, narrow, winding two-lane roads are the rule, so take plenty of time and watch for deer. Route 66 connects to Route 219 at Slatyfork.

Durbin & Greenbrier Valley Railroad

LOCATION: 315 Railroad Avenue, Elkins
PHONE: 877-686-7245 or 304-636-9477
WEBSITE: mountainrailwv.com
E-MAIL: ticketinfo@mountainrail.com

Durbin & Greenbrier Valley Railroad

The Durbin & Greenbrier Valley Railroad operates three separate and distinct railways over 135 miles of scenic railroad through the Mountain State. The *Cheat Mountain Salamander* offers a ride into the high country of Cheat Mountain, the *Durbin Rocket* operates a 1910 Climax locomotive, and the *New Tygart Flyer* is a diesel-powered train that pulls coaches and first-class cars through the wilderness.

CHOICES: This railroad is all about choices. The *Salamander* offers a 6.5-hour round trip that features a stop at Cheat Bridge and one at the High Falls of the Cheat, an impressive waterfall that puts an exclamation point on the journey. The *Rocket* is a two-hour ride aboard a caboose, coach, or open gondola behind a Climax geared steam locomotive along the unspoiled Greenbrier River. The *Flyer* provides a dramatic four-hour round trip through a curved tunnel, across a deep canyon, and over a rushing river. A mountain dinner train also operates.

WHEN TO GO: The trains operate June through October, with murder mystery, *Polar Express*, and other special trains scheduled in addition to the regular excursions.

GOOD TO KNOW: The *Flyer* and the *Salamander* board in Elkins. The *Rocket* takes off from the restored C&O Railway depot in Durbin. To get a closer view of nature, you can spend one or more nights along the Greenbrier River in the Castaway Caboose, a restored Wabash caboose, which you travel to in the *Durbin Rocket*.

WORTH DOING: In the surrounding Monongahela National Forest, you can go rock climbing, view waterfalls, and see trees that are more than 300 years old.

DON'T MISS: The railroad's location is close to the Cass Scenic Railroad, enabling you to visit four great railroads in one impressive mountain setting.

GETTING THERE: Route 250 connects the railroad's locations. You'll find the Elkins station downtown near the river. Durbin is 35 miles south of Elkins at the base of Cheat Mountain, and the *Rocket* leaves from the station at 3 E. Main Street.

New River Train

LOCATION: Memorial Boulevard and 14th Street West (outdoor museum), Huntington
PHONE: 866-639-7487 or 304-523-0364
WEBSITE: newrivertrain.com
E-MAIL: newrivertrain@aol.com

CPH, Joe Rosenthal

The Collis P. Huntington Railroad Historical Society sponsors the New River Train, which runs all-day excursions during October to view autumn foliage. The society also maintains an outdoor museum and sponsors trips to other locations during the year.

CHOICES: The New River Train travels over the former C&O main line from Huntington to Hinton. You'll go under the New River Gorge Bridge, the largest arch bridge in the country, and enjoy a spectacular view of it. Other sights along the way include Kanawha Falls, Hawks Nest Dam, and Stretcher Neck Tunnel. You'll also roll past ghost towns and old mining sites. Seating choices are coach, premium, and dome. You can board the Amtrak-powered train at Huntington, St. Albans, or Montgomery. The outdoor museum displays ex-Chesapeake & Ohio Class H-6 articulated No. 1308, a saddle-tank switcher, a restored B&O section house, and other items.

WHEN TO GO: The New River Train runs two October weekends during the peak fall foliage season. The museum is open Sundays June into September.

GOOD TO KNOW: The society maintains a museum at its headquarters (1323 Eighth Avenue) in Huntington. The town and society were named for Collis P. Huntington, who helped develop the transcontinental railroad and the Chesapeake & Ohio.

WORTH DOING: While in Huntington, stop by the Cabell-Huntington Convention & Visitors Bureau. The bureau is housed in a former B&O passenger station, and out front are two pieces of vintage equipment donated by the society: former Elk River Coal & Lumber Co. No. 10 and former Southern Railway sleeper *John W. Arrington*.

DON'T MISS: Huntington is two hours away from the New River Gorge National Park, which contains the bridge. You can plan a trip to the park by driving or by Amtrak's *Cardinal*. The third Saturday of October is Bridge Day, the only day you are allowed to walk across the bridge—or parachute from it.

GETTING THERE: To reach the outdoor museum, take I-64 to Exit 6. Follow Highway 52 north toward the Ohio River and get off at the first exit, Madison Avenue. Go east on Madison Avenue about three blocks to 14th Street West, turn right, and go south three more blocks and through the CSX underpass. The museum is on the right.

Potomac Eagle Scenic Railroad

LOCATION: Route 28 North, Romney
PHONE: 304-424-0736
WEBSITE: potomaceagle.info

Mark Perri

Here's a three-hour train ride that goes in search of bald eagles down a remote stretch of the Potomac River just inside West Virginia.

CHOICES: All trains depart from the Wappocomo station, just north of Romney. The 40-mile excursion travels along the South Branch of the Potomac River and through the six-mile Trough, a narrow mountain valley where eagles are often seen. You can ride in open-air coaches. Historic narration adds extra insight into the journey. EMD F units in striking C&O and B&O heritage schemes provide power for most of the trains.

WHEN TO GO: Trains run mid-May through the beginning of November. Departures are on Saturdays with a few Sundays sprinkled in. Autumn makes an especially great time to visit this railroad, and it offers trips almost daily during October.

GOOD TO KNOW: The railroad says eagles are spotted on 90 percent of its trains. As it enters the most remote and steepest portion of the valley, the train pauses, so you can find a seat in the open gondola for the best views.

WORTH DOING: Explore Romney, which includes numerous historic homes and buildings. Possibly the oldest town in West Virginia, it is said to have changed hands 56 times during the Civil War.

DON'T MISS: The railroad offers an occasional 70-mile, all-day trip down the length of the railroad; often this is a special photographer's trip usually the first weekend in November.

GETTING THERE: Romney is located on Route 50 in the northeast corner of the state. It is about 25 miles south of Cumberland, Md. Route 28 takes you to the station, which is 1.5 miles north of Romney.

WISCONSIN

Brodhead Historical Society Depot Museum

This restored Chicago, Milwaukee & St. Paul depot, built in 1881, houses a permanent railroad display with rotating historical displays. Milwaukee Road Fairbanks-Morse switch engine No. 701 and caboose No. 01900 stand alongside the depot. It is open on Wednesdays, Saturdays, and Sundays between Memorial Day and Labor Day.

LOCATION: 1108 First Center Avenue, Brodhead
PHONE: 608-897-4150
WEBSITE: brodheadhistory.org
E-MAIL: info@brodheadhistory.org

Colfax Railroad Museum

This museum includes a large collection of railroad memorabilia and an outdoor display of locomotives and rolling stock that features a Soo Line GP30 diesel engine, a wooden Soo caboose, a heavyweight coach, and other pieces of rolling stock. It is open May through September.

LOCATION: 500 E. Railroad Avenue, Colfax
PHONE: 715-962-2076
WEBSITE: colfaxrrmuseum.org
E-MAIL: form on website

Historical Village

The village features a restored C&NW depot and several other historical structures, including an octagon house. Built in 1923, the depot is authentically furnished and contains railroad artifacts. It also displays a 1941 diesel engine, a Soo caboose, and a C&NW caboose. The museum is open during summer and takes part in Heritage Days & Rail Fest.

LOCATION: 900 Montgomery Street, New London
PHONE: 920-982-8557 or 920-982-5186
WEBSITE: historicalvillage.org

Mineral Point Railroad Museum

The museum is housed in a stone Milwaukee Road depot, which is the oldest depot building in the state. It contains exhibits on the two Mineral Point railroads as well as others. A interactive diorama of the area around 1920 is a popular attraction. The museum is open Thursdays through Sundays May through October.

LOCATION: 11 Commerce Street, Mineral Point
PHONE: 608-987-2695
WEBSITE: mineralpointrailroads.com
E-MAIL: form on website

Railroad Memories Museum

This museum contains 12 rooms filled with railroad memories. Artifacts include lanterns, track equipment, photos, and other items. Housed in a former C&NW depot, it is located next to the Wisconsin Great Northern Railroad. The museum is open Memorial Day weekend through Labor Day.

LOCATION: 424 Front Street, Spooner
PHONE: 715-635-3325 or 715-635-2752
WEBSITE: railroadmemoriesmuseumspooner.org
E-MAIL: info@railroadmemoriesmuseumspooner.org

Camp Five

LOCATION: 5068 Highway 8, Laona
PHONE: 715-674-3414
WEBSITE: camp5museum.org
E-MAIL: info@lumberjacksteamtrain.com

Jeff Terry

Camp Five offers a steam train powered by a vintage 2-6-2 type logging locomotive. It takes you to the site of a timber company's 1914 farm camp, where you can tour a logging museum.

CHOICES: After boarding at an 1880s Soo Line depot, you ride the steam train 2.5 miles to the museum. You can ride in a passenger coach, an open-air car made from a boxcar, or a cupola caboose. At Laona, you can climb a set of steps to inspect the engine's cab.

WHEN TO GO: Camp Five has a short season. It is open Monday through Saturday, starting in June and running through August. It is also open several days in fall.

GOOD TO KNOW: The railroad crosses the Rat River on a bridge. Lumber men who worked this river, floating giant rafts of logs together, became known as river rats. At the farm camp, the lumber company raised meat, produce, and horses to supply other camps as they set up in the forest.

WORTH DOING: Forest County is filled with lakes and covered by the Nicolet National Forest, so there are plenty of opportunities for fishing, hiking, and other recreational activities.

DON'T MISS: There is plenty to do at Camp Five. You can view exhibits on forestry, examine logging equipment, visit a nature center, or take an ecology walking tour. At the logging camp's blacksmith shop, watch a smithy pound and shape horseshoes over the original forge.

GETTING THERE: Camp Five is located off Highway 8 west of Laona, about two hours north of Green Bay. From Green Bay, take Highway 141 north to Highway 64. Follow Highway 64 west to Highway 32. Continue on Highway 32 and turn left on Highway 8.

Wisconsin

East Troy Electric Railroad

LOCATION: 2002 Church Street, East Troy
PHONE: 262-642-3263
WEBSITE: easttroyrr.org
E-MAIL: info@easttroyrr.org

Matt Van Hattem

Interurban railroads once plied much of the Midwest, moving passengers easily from farm to city and vice versa. Today, a sprig of that heritage remains at the East Troy Electric Railroad, where electric trains run through the scenic countryside.

CHOICES: On a 10-mile round trip, the railroad offers a variety of cars to ride that includes trolleys, electric freight motors pulling a caboose, and electrically powered traditional coaches from the famous South Shore Line. Trains depart from both East Troy and Mukwonago. The railroad also offers dinner trains that run to Phantom Lake and back. After viewing the exhibits in the depot, you can walk two blocks to the shops and look at the equipment being refurbished.

WHEN TO GO: Regular weekend excursions run Memorial Day weekend through October. From mid-June through August, trains also operate on Wednesdays, Thursdays, and Fridays (and Fridays in September and October). There is a slate of special events during the year including a Christmas Express.

GOOD TO KNOW: Sheboygan car No. 26 is a 1908 interurban built by the Cincinnati Car Company for Sheboygan Light, Power and Railway. No 26 later became a summer cottage until it was restored.

WORTH DOING: Regular excursions operate from East Troy to the Elegant Farmer near Mukwonago. What's an Elegant Farmer? It makes a great destination as the Farmer provides a deli, greenhouse, and market all in one. Be sure and try the award-winning apple pie baked in a bag.

DON'T MISS: You can explore the substation in East Troy, which is the heart of the operating gear for the electric railroad.

GETTING THERE: East Troy is located in southeastern Wisconsin, about 35 miles from Milwaukee and 15 miles from Lake Geneva. From Milwaukee, take I-43 south to Exit 38. Take Highway 20 to Main Street. Follow Main Street to Church Street and turn right to the museum.

270

Mid-Continent Railway Museum

LOCATION: E8948 Museum Road, North Freedom
PHONE: 800-930-1385 or 608-522-4261
WEBSITE: midcontinent.org
E-MAIL: inquiries@midcontinent.org

Dave Crosby

One of the best museums for the preservation of wooden railroad cars, Mid-Continent features numerous exhibits and a large collection of rolling stock, much of it kept indoors. The museum also offers a train ride. It's all aimed at re-creating the experience of a branch or short line between 1885 and 1915.

CHOICES: Leaving from a restored 1894 C&NW depot, the seven-mile, 50-minute ride takes you through the rolling countryside. You can ride the restored 1915 steel coaches, but you can also get a ticket for the locomotive cab or the caboose.

WHEN TO GO: The railway operates from May into October and also includes a variety of special events. After Memorial Day until Labor Day, it is open daily, other times on weekends only. Fall color, pumpkin, and Santa specials operate as does a snow train.

GOOD TO KNOW: More than 100 pieces of equipment are on display. One is an office car of Great Northern Railway founder James J. Hill's son that included space for hauling an automobile. Structures include a water tower, a crossing shanty, a section shed, a crossing tower, and a freight house.

WORTH DOING: Explore Devil's Lake State Park near Baraboo. This large park features 500-foot cliffs, hiking trails, and kayaking.

DON'T MISS: Make sure you go into the coach shed to see some of the finest wood craftsmanship around when it comes to railroad cars and also check out the engine house, where craftsmen are restoring three steam locomotives for operation.

GETTING THERE: The scenic route from Madison is along Highway 12 going north. Turn left on Highway 36 and then left again on Highway PF to North Freedom. In North Freedom, follow Walnut Street west to the museum.

National Railroad Museum

LOCATION: 2285 S. Broadway Street, Green Bay
PHONE: 920-437-7623
WEBSITE: nationalrrmuseum.org
E-MAIL: form on website

Jim Wrinn

Begun in 1956 by a group wishing to preserve a steam locomotive, the museum has grown to encompass more than 70 pieces of rolling stock, a seasonal train ride, and an unmatched collection of drumheads, the illuminated signs seen on the rear of many passenger trains.

CHOICES: Explore the museum on your own and then take a train ride. During the 25-minute train ride, the conductor provides information about railroad history and museum exhibits. Highlights include a Union Pacific Big Boy, a 1950s Aerotrain, and a Pennsylvania Railroad GG1 electric locomotive. The command train for General Dwight D. Eisenhower is also located at the museum. Guided group tours are also available.

WHEN TO GO: The museum is open daily year-round, except for Mondays January through March and several holidays. Train rides operate May through October, and numerous special events are scheduled during the year.

GOOD TO KNOW: The museum's exhibit on Pullman porters, "From Service to Civil Rights" provides an excellent understanding of the role of these workers on board the rolling luxury hotels of their day. Using a computer generated porter, visitors can learn about all aspects of these workers' lives.

WORTH DOING: Take the kids to Bay Beach Amusement Park for some old-fashioned fun on classic midway rides. Football fans can visit the Green Bay Packers Hall of Fame and tour historic Lambeau Field.

DON'T MISS: Climb to the top of the 85-foot-tall observation tower for a bird's-eye view of the museum.

GETTING THERE: Green Bay is two hours north of Milwaukee. From Milwaukee, take I-43 to Exit 180. Take Highway 172 west and exit at Ashland Avenue. Bear right on Pilgrim Way and then turn left on Broadway Street.

Osceola & St. Croix Valley Railway

LOCATION: 114 Depot Road, Osceola
PHONE: 715-755-3570
WEBSITE: mtmuseum.org
E-MAIL: contact@mtmuseum.org

Steve Glischinski

The Minnesota Transportation Museum's Osceola & St. Croix Valley Railway offers diesel-powered train rides through the scenic St. Croix River Valley along the Wisconsin–Minnesota border.

CHOICES: You can take two regular excursions from Osceola. One heads west 10 miles to Marine on St. Croix, Minn. This highly recommended trip follows the beautiful St. Croix Valley for its entire length. The other trip goes east to Dresser, Wis., a former Soo Line junction town that contains its original wooden depot. A third trip operates on a limited schedule, and this 2.5-hour round trip takes passengers farther down the valley to Withrow, Minn. You can ride in either air-conditioned or open-window coaches. Dinner trains, brunch trains, pizza trains, and fall color trains also run.

WHEN TO GO: Trains operate weekend and holidays from May to October. For the best views of the St. Croix River, May is the time to ride before the leaves have a chance to obstruct views of the river. Early October provides the chance to view the autumn colors before the long northern winter begins.

GOOD TO KNOW: Osceola's downtown contains many examples of late 19th and early 20th century architecture. The St. Croix National Scenic Riverway includes 154 miles of the river and offers recreational opportunities on and off the river.

WORTH DOING: You can take the train to Marine to ride over the Cedar Bend swing bridge across the St. Croix River from Wisconsin into Minnesota. While the bridge doesn't swing open any more, it's a classic steel structure complete with telltales on each end to warn brakemen of close clearances.

DON'T MISS: Watch ex-Northern Pacific Railway post office-baggage-coach combine No. 1102 pick up the mail on the fly from a mail crane at Osceola's restored depot, one of the few places where this once common occurrence can be seen.

GETTING THERE: Osceola is about an hour's drive from Minneapolis. For a scenic drive, follow Highway 95 along the east bank of the St. Croix from Stillwater north to Osceola. Once in Osceola, you'll come to Highway 35. Turn right and proceed under the railroad bridge and immediately turn right again onto Depot Road.

Wisconsin Great Northern Railroad

LOCATION: 426 N. Front Street, Spooner
PHONE: 715-635-3200
WEBSITE: spoonertrainride.com
E-MAIL: info@spoonertrainride.com

Steve Glischinski

The Wisconsin Great Northern Railroad operates excursion and dinner trains on approximately nine miles of former Chicago & North Western track between Spooner and Veazie Springs, just east of Trego, Wis.

CHOICES: In addition to 90-minute sightseeing excursions, the Wisconsin Great Northern offers a variety of regularly scheduled dinner trains that include elegant dining, pizza, and Sunday brunches. The railroad also operates a bed & breakfast train. Passengers board a sleeping car, which is coupled to the dinner train. You can enjoy drinks, dinner, and dessert and then settle in your private bedroom for the night. The next morning, a hot breakfast is served.

WHEN TO GO: Sightseeing excursions run Saturdays and some weekdays May through October. Summer and early fall are great times to ride. The cars are ex-Duluth, Missabe & Iron Range Railway heavyweights with windows that can be opened, and it's a delight to take in the sights during these times.

GOOD TO KNOW: Former Milwaukee Road SW1 No. 862, painted in a scheme resembling that of the former Great Northern Railway pulls the trains.

WORTH DOING: While Spooner is off the beaten path, there is much to do in the area, such as fishing, hiking, biking, camping, and tubing. You can also take a drive 30 miles to Hayward, which is the site of the annual Lumberjack World Championships and the Chequamegon Fat Tire Festival, the largest mass start mountain bike race in the United States.

DON'T MISS: Adjacent to the railroad's ticket office, the independent Railroad Memories Museum contains lanterns, track equipment, photos, and other railroad memorabilia.

GETTING THERE: The Wisconsin Great Northern is about 90 minutes from Eau Claire and two hours from Minneapolis and St. Paul. After you enter Spooner on Highway 70, turn left onto Front Street. Travel four blocks north on Front Street and then look for signs to the depot.

WYOMING

Cheyenne Depot Museum

Cheyenne's architectural jewel is a major landmark in the city. Built in 1886, the Union Pacific depot houses a museum that details the history of the building, the operation of the railroad, and founding of the city. Depot Days take place in May.

LOCATION: 121 W. 15th Street, Cheyenne
PHONE: 307-632-3905
WEBSITE: cheyennedepotmuseum.org
E-MAIL: info@cheyennedepotmuseum.org

Douglas Railroad Interpretive Center

The Douglas Railroad Interpretive Center is housed in a restored 1886 passenger depot belonging to the Fremont, Elkhorn & Missouri Valley Railroad. It displays a 1940 Chicago, Burlington & Quincy steam locomotive and seven railcars. The building is listed on the National Register of Historic Places.

LOCATION: 121 Brownfield Road, Douglas
PHONE: 307-358-2950
WEBSITE: jackalope.org
E-MAIL: chamber@jackalope.org

Union Pacific Roundhouse and Turntable

One section of the 28-bay roundhouse and the machine shop have been restored. (Check with the city for tour information.) In front, the large turntable is still operational. Nearby Railroad Park holds a 1915 steam engine and two boxcars. The Joss House Museum tells the story of the area's Chinese immigrants.

LOCATION: 1440 Main Street, Evanston
PHONE: 307-783-6320 or 307-783-6309
WEBSITE: etownchamber.com
E-MAIL: jlaw@evanstonwy.org

Union Pacific Railroad

LOCATION: UP Steam Shop, Cheyenne
PHONE: 307-778-3214
WEBSITE: uprr.com/aboutup

Union Pacific Railroad

This Class I mainline railroad maintains the only steam locomotive never retired, No. 844, a 4-8-4 built in 1944. Rebuilt between 1999 and 2004, it is used on occasional excursions and display tours.

CHOICES: Home for the locomotive is a nonpublic shop in Cheyenne, where the Union Pacific also maintains steam engine 4-6-6-4 No. 3985, believed to be the largest operational steam locomotive. Departures for No. 844 occur from the UP rail yards as well as from the Cheyenne Depot Museum.

WHEN TO GO: Schedules and routes vary from year to year. One annual outing is the Denver Post Frontier Days excursion train from Denver to Cheyenne for the big rodeo event.

GOOD TO KNOW: The Union Pacific provides a GPS trace system for its steam train at uprr.com/aboutup. Tours of the UP steam shop may be available by calling 307-778-3339 (in advance of your visit).

WORTH DOING: In July, you can take part in Frontier Days, a 10-day rodeo event that celebrates the West and features entertainment and other activities.

DON'T MISS: Visit the Cheyenne Depot Museum in the restored UP depot. Two historic engines are displayed in Cheyenne parks: a Big Boy engine in Holliday Park and the state's oldest steam locomotive, No. 1242, in Lions Park.

GETTING THERE: Cheyenne is in southeast Wyoming, about 90 minutes from Denver on I-25.

ALBERTA

Alberta Railway Museum

The museum's collection of railway equipment and buildings focuses on the Canadian National Railway and the Northern Alberta Railway. It includes more than 75 locomotives and cars, three stations, a telegraph office, and a water tank. The museum is open weekends from Victoria Day through Labor Day. You can take a walking tour, ride a speeder, and on long holiday weekends, ride a passenger train.

LOCATION: 24215 34th Street, Edmonton
PHONE: 780-472-6229
WEBSITE: albertarailwaymuseum.com
E-MAIL: info@albertarailwaymuseum.com

Edmonton Radial Railway

The Edmonton Radial Railway operates streetcars in Fort Edmonton Park and in Old Strathcona. At Fort Edmonton Park, the one-mile streetcar rides are included with admission. In Old Strathcona, the trolley crosses High Level Bridge over the North Saskatchewan River. The Strathcona streetcar barn contains exhibits on streetcar history.

LOCATION: 103rd Street and 84th Avenue, Edmonton
PHONE: 780-437-7721 or 780-496-1464
WEBSITE: edmonton-radial-railway.ab.ca
E-MAIL: info@edmonton-radial-railway.ab.ca

Fort Edmonton Park

Nestled in Edmonton's river valley, Fort Edmonton Park is a living history museum that represents four historical periods between 1840 and 1920. It contains more than 75 buildings. A 1919 steam train takes you through the park, and caboose rides are available. A streetcar also travels along the historic streets.

LOCATION: Fox Drive and Whitemud Drive, Edmonton
PHONE: 780-442-5311
WEBSITE: fortedmontonpark.ca
E-MAIL: attractions@edmonton.ca

Royal Canadian Pacific

The Royal Canadian Pacific, an arm of the passenger department of Canadian Pacific Railway, offers periodically scheduled all-inclusive luxury-train ride packages on CPR's route through the spectacularly scenic Canadian Rockies. Ride aboard vintage, heavyweight CPR sleeping, observation, and dining cars with lavishly restored interiors.

LOCATION: 201 Ninth Avenue SW, Calgary
PHONE: 877-665-3044 or 403-508-1400
WEBSITE: royalcanadianpacific.com
E-MAIL: form on website

Alberta Prairie Railway Excursions

Alberta

LOCATION: 4611 47th Avenue, Stettler
PHONE: 800-282-3994 or 403-742-2811
WEBSITE: absteamtrain.com
E-MAIL: info@absteamtrain.com

John Godfrey

A trip aboard the Alberta Prairie conjures up visions of what a central Alberta wheat line must have been like 100 years ago. Traveling from the well-developed community of Stettler, it passes through forests and fields before reaching Big Valley, where the ruins of a roundhouse and a restored depot remain.

CHOICES: The railroad offers an extensive schedule of excursions and specials throughout the year. All excursions include a buffet meal, which is served in Big Valley or Stettler, onboard entertainment, and possibly a train robbery. Specially themed rides include murder mystery, Christmas, family, and teddy bear trains. During winter, fine-dining trains provide a five-course meal and entertainment. The trains are pulled by Baldwin 2-8-0 steam engine No. 41 or by General Motors diesel No. 1259. Several times a year, usually for special events, such as on Canada Day, historic steam engine No. 6060 is in operation.

WHEN TO GO: Summer excursions begin in May and continue until mid-October each year.

GOOD TO KNOW: The railway was once part of a vast grain railroad network belonging to the Canadian Northern. Be sure to chat with the train crew. Many of the veteran railroaders on this line have great stories. And if you get the right conductor, he might just sing you a song or recite a poem for you en route.

WORTH DOING: In Big Valley, the restored station and several railcars display railroad and local history artifacts. You can take a self-guided tour of the five-stall roundhouse remains and former rail yards, view a wooden grain elevator, and visit the Jimmy Jock Boardwalk, which is modeled after a frontier town's street.

DON'T MISS: For an added prairie experience, you can take a 20-mile covered wagon trip along historic rail rights-of-way.

GETTING THERE: Stettler is about three hours northeast of Calgary on Highway 12.

Heritage Park Historical Village

LOCATION: 1900 Heritage Drive SW, Calgary
PHONE: 403-268-8500
WEBSITE: heritagepark.ca
E-MAIL: info@heritagepark.ab.ca

John Godfrey

Discover what life was like in the Canadian West between 1864 and 1914 by visiting this re-created village framed by the Rockies. More than 150 exhibits, including many buildings transplanted from Calgary and other locations throughout Alberta, bring the past to the present.

CHOICES: The park includes a roundhouse and turntable along with more than 20 locomotives and cars. A train ride is an excellent way to see the park. Make a day of your visit and wander from building to building, paying particular attention to the transplanted railway stations, rolling stock, and re-created carbarn. If it's too hot, take a cruise on the water aboard the replica sternwheeler SS *Moyie*. Heritage Town Square represents a street scene from the 1930s to '50s, complete with an automobile museum and a replica train station.

WHEN TO GO: Heritage Park is open daily from mid-May until October. Unlike the rest of the park, Heritage Town Square is open year-round.

GOOD TO KNOW: A short streetcar line connects the outer parking area to the main entrance. It's well worth it to park out there, view ex-CPR 2-10-4 No. 5931 and S2 No. 7019, and then ride over to the gate in a replica Calgary or Winnipeg trolley. Many photographic opportunities are available around the park's railway loop.

WORTH DOING: Calgary's 10-day annual Stampede, which can draw more than one million people, is the world's largest rodeo. The event also features chuck wagon racing, agricultural exhibits, entertainment, and a parade.

DON'T MISS: During Railway Days in September, the park celebrates Canadian railways and rolls out much of its collection. Steam doubleheaders often operate for this event, and ex-CP Car 76, present at the driving of the last spike on the CPR in Craigellachie in 1885, may be rolled out.

GETTING THERE: Heritage Park is approximately a 20-minute drive southwest from downtown Calgary. A shuttle service operates during park hours from the Heritage light rail stop. Calgary is serviced by scheduled bus and air service.

VIA Jasper-Prince Rupert Route

LOCATION: 607 Connaught Drive, Jasper
PHONE: 888-842-7245
WEBSITE: viarail.ca/en/trains/rockies-and-pacific/jasper-prince-rupert
E-MAIL: form on website

VIA Rail

The VIA Rail Canada train between Jasper and Prince Rupert, British Columbia, is one of the scenic highlights of any trip to western Canada. The two-day, 725-mile trip, which includes an overnight stop in Prince George, takes you from the Rocky Mountains in Jasper National Park to the Pacific coast.

CHOICES: Travelers can opt for either economy or touring accommodation classes. Budget-minded vacationers can relax in the leg-rest seats found in economy class. Those with a voracious appetite for scenery may want to spend a little more for touring class which puts you in a dome car with its upper observation deck and panoramic views. Touring class also provides meals. During off-peak operation (mid-September through the end of May), the dome car is accessible in economy class.

WHEN TO GO: The train operates Wednesday, Friday, and Sunday year-round. The shorter days and deep snows of winter give way to a plethora of spring flowers in May. Hot summer days morph into colorful, cool fall days by October. Economy class is offered year-round, and touring class is available only from mid-June through September.

GOOD TO KNOW: Don't forget to book a hotel room for your overnight stay in Prince George. When arriving in Prince George, you may want to take a taxi, even though accommodations are a few blocks away as the area around the VIA station may be considered rough.

WORTH DOING: In Jasper, you can explore Jasper National Park, the northernmost park in the Rocky Mountains, and leave feeling hot or cold. You can experience a glacier close up and soak in a hot spring. In Prince Rupert, you can visit the Kwinitsa Railway Museum and the First Nation Carving Shed, where artists produce works in wood and metal.

DON'T MISS: Just west of Jasper, Mount Robson, the highest peak in the Canadian Provinces, is visible from the train for only a few cloudless days a year. You may also see moose, bear, elk, wolves, seals, and eagles along the way.

GETTING THERE: VIA Rail operates the Vancouver-Toronto *Canadian* twice a week through Jasper in each direction. Jasper is also served by bus from Edmonton and other points. Scheduled air service operates from Prince Rupert.

BRITISH COLUMBIA

BC Forest Discovery Centre

The most relaxing, and most scenic, way to take in this 100-acre site is by riding the train, which is pulled by a steam-powered 1910 locomotive or a gas-powered locomotive. The site's collection features Shay, Climax, and Vulcan locomotives. Other exhibits include an operating sawmill, a lookout tower, and antique logging trucks.

LOCATION: 2892 Drinkwater Road, Duncan
PHONE: 250-715-1113
WEBSITE: discoveryforest.com
E-MAIL: info.bcfdc@shawlink.ca

Fort Steele Heritage Town

Fort Steele Heritage Town is a restored 1890s pioneer town complete with railway. The railway operates during summer, and unlimited-ride tickets can be purchased. A Montreal Locomotive Works 2-6-2 prairie-type locomotive takes you on a 20-minute scenic ride. Rail equipment is displayed by the engine house, and roundhouse tours are available upon request.

LOCATION: 9851 Highway 93/95, Fort Steele
PHONE: 250-417-6000 or 250-426-7352
WEBSITE: fortsteele.bc.ca
E-MAIL: form on website

Kwinitsa Railway Station Museum

Located in Prince Rupert's waterfront park, this restored station house is an excellent example of the small stations once found along Canada's northern railway line. Photographs, videos, and detailed restorations depict the life of station agents and linemen who worked for the Grand Trunk Railway at the turn of the 20th century. It is open daily June through August.

LOCATION: Bill Murray Way and First Avenue, Prince Rupert
PHONE: 250-624-3207
WEBSITE: museumofnorthernbc.com
E-MAIL: mnbc@citytel.net

Nelson Electric Tramway

Streetcar 23 runs from the park to Prestige Lakeside Resort along the beautiful west arm of Kootenay Lake. The 2.5-mile round trip takes about 20 minutes and includes some street running. The streetcar operates from May into October. Car 23 ran in Nelson more than 60 years ago and was restored after being turned into a dog kennel (and a chicken coop).

LOCATION: Rotary Lakeside Park, Nelson
PHONE: 250-367-9564
WEBSITE: nelsonstreetcar.org
E-MAIL: info@nelsonstreetcar.org

Railway & Forestry Museum

The museum displays historic railway and forestry exhibits in a park-like setting. The extensive rail collection dates to 1899 and includes two stations and a turntable. It also contains both steam and diesel locomotives and more than 40 pieces of rolling stock.

LOCATION: 850 River Road, Prince George
PHONE: 250-563-7351
WEBSITE: pgrfm.bc.ca
E-MAIL: trains@pgrfm.bc.ca

Revelstoke Railway Museum

This railway museum focuses on the history of the Canadian Pacific Railway in western Canada. You can walk through Business Car No. 4 and view steam locomotive No. 5468, various railcars, and artifacts. The museum also operates a small facility at Craigellachie, 28 miles west of Revelstoke, where the last spike of the Canadian Pacific Railway was driven. The museum is open year-round.

LOCATION: 719 Track Street West, Revelstoke
PHONE: 877-837-6060 or 250-837-6060
WEBSITE: railwaymuseum.com
E-MAIL: railway@telus.net

Alberni Pacific Railway

LOCATION: 3100 Kingsway Avenue, Port Alberni
PHONE: 250-723-2118
WEBSITE: alberniheritage.com
E-MAIL: info@alberniheritage.com

Alberni Pacific Railway, Ken Rutherford

The Alberni Pacific offers passengers a chance to visit the former McLean Paper Mill, six miles east of Port Alberni over the former Canadian Pacific Railway Port Alberni Subdivision. The mill is a National Historic Site that now commemorates the history of logging and milling in British Columbia.

CHOICES: Trains to the mill are pulled by a 1929 Baldwin 2-8-2T steam locomotive, and passengers ride in converted former Canadian National transfer cabooses, three of which are open and two are covered. The 35-minute trips leave (and return) from a restored 1912 CPR station. Cab rides in No. 7 are also available.

WHEN TO GO: Runs are made over this scenic trackage Thursdays through Sundays between the end of June until September. Special events occur throughout the year including special steam trains in fall as well as wine trains, train robberies, and Santa trains.

GOOD TO KNOW: The McLean Mill is the only steam-operated sawmill in Canada. This historic site and the railway are part of the Alberni Valley Heritage Network that celebrates the area's history and culture. Also included are the Alberni Valley Museum and Maritime Discovery Centre.

WORTH DOING: Visit Port Alberni's quaint harbor, which offers a mix of restaurants, galleries, tours, and shops. You are also within minutes of numerous outdoor activities including seeing Delta Falls, the tallest waterfall in Canada.

DON'T MISS: At the mill, you can explore the site on your own or take a guided tour. It has been laid out as early 20th century logging camp with restored buildings and original pieces of logging equipment, including an operating steam donkey.

GETTING THERE: Bus service is available from Vancouver Island to Port Alberni. Scheduled air service is available from Victoria to the south. Ferry service operates between the mainland and various points on Vancouver Island including Port Alberni.

Canadian Museum of Rail Travel

LOCATION: 57 Van Horne Street South, Cranbrook
PHONE: 250-489-3918
WEBSITE: trainsdeluxe.com
E-MAIL: mail@trainsdeluxe.com

Canadian Museum of Rail Travel

The Canadian Museum of Rail Travel is a magnet for anyone interested in Canadian passenger rail travel as it once was. It is home to the only surviving train set of equipment from the 1929 Trans-Canada Limited as well as the beautifully reconstructed Royal Alexandra Hall.

CHOICES: Visitors can choose from several different guided tours that examine the trains in the museum's collection, including the *Soo-Spokane Train Deluxe, Trans Canada Limited, Pacific Express,* and *Chinook.* Various business cars, cars of state, and historic structures are also included. Guides explain the history of the equipment and bring to life the beautifully restored railcar interiors. Be prepared to walk. Depending on the tour, you could cover a half mile or more.

WHEN TO GO: The museum is open to the public daily from Victoria Day weekend to Canadian Thanksgiving in October. During the remainder of the year, it is open Tuesday through Saturday.

GOOD TO KNOW: Cranbrook is a gateway to the Canadian Rockies, which are a short drive away. Enjoy the sun and a hot soak. Situated at an elevation of 3,000 feet, Cranbrook also is one of the sunniest spots in Canada. After a walking tour of the museum, you can soak in several hot springs in the area.

WORTH DOING: Fort Steele is less than 20 minutes away. Once a thriving mining town, Fort Steele became a ghost town when the railroad bypassed it for Cranbrook. It is now a heritage town, where visitors can experience its boom-town history.

DON'T MISS: Tour the exquisitely re-created Royal Alexandra Hall from the Canadian Pacific Railway's Royal Alexandra Hotel that once stood near that road's Winnipeg Station. The hall was the grand café of the hotel and features Edwardian architectural style.

GETTING THERE: Air service to Cranbrook is available with direct flights from Vancouver and Calgary. Greyhound also operates daily scheduled service to the city. It is about a 3.5-hour drive from Spokane, Wash.

Kamloops Heritage Railway

LOCATION: 510 Lorne Street, Kamloops
PHONE: 250-374-2141
WEBSITE: kamrail.com
E-MAIL: info@kamrail.com

Kamloops Heritage Railway

This steam-powered tourist line's regular excursion is a seven-mile round trip on the Canadian National's Okanagan Subdivision that features mountain vistas, lakeside scenery, and an occasional train robbery.

CHOICES: On the *Spirit of Kamloops'* 70-minute excursion, you can ride in a restored 1930s air-conditioned coach or in an open-air car. Along the way, masked riders reenact the famous 1906 train robbery by the Bill Miner gang. The train departs from a restored 1927 CN station and crosses the South Thompson River over a 1927 steel trestle bridge, where the train stops and allows you to photograph the scenery.

WHEN TO GO: The *Spirit of Kamloops* operates Monday, Tuesday, and Friday evenings and during the day on Saturdays in July and August. Illuminated with hundreds of lights, the *Spirit of Christmas* is a one-hour holiday special, complete with candy canes, hot chocolate, and caroling. Ghost trains also operate.

GOOD TO KNOW: Kamloops is a regional center that has a wide range of accommodations to choose from, as well as all the services one would expect in a small-sized city, including city bus service. The former courthouse, where train robber Bill Miner was tried and convicted, is now a popular hostel.

WORTH DOING: At the Secwepemc Museum in Kamloops, you can discover the history of the Shuswap people. Visit Heritage Park and go through the incredible 2,000-year-old winter village and the summer pit houses.

DON'T MISS: Railway Heritage Park is the base of operations for the passenger train, and you can view equipment on display in the yard and take a guided tour of the backshop. You may even get an up-close look at locomotive 2141.

GETTING THERE: Kamloops is about a 3.5-hour drive from Vancouver. You can follow the Trans Canada Highway east or take the scenic Fraser Canyon route but allow time for viewing the vistas along the way. There are direct flights from Vancouver and Calgary. Kamloops is also available by bus or VIA Rail. The ticket office is located just outside the main door of the station building at Station Plaza.

Kettle Valley Steam Railway

LOCATION: 18404 Bathville Road, Summerland
PHONE: 877-494-8424 or 250-494-8422
WEBSITE: kettlevalleyrail.org
E-MAIL: kvr@telus.net

Kettle Valley Steam Railway

The Kettle Valley Steam Railway operates over the only preserved portion of the famed Kettle Valley Railway, which was completed in 1915. Passengers can enjoy the rural landscapes of Summerland's Prairie Valley, and take in the mountains and views of Okanagan Lake from the Trout Creek Bridge, a major feature of the original line.

CHOICES: The KVR offers regular excursions over a six-mile route. The 90-minute trip winds through Prairie Valley and its scenic vistas. A century-old steam locomotive, No. 3716, or a backup diesel engine supplies the power. You can ride in two 1940s vintage passenger coaches or three open-air cars. Special events are scheduled throughout the year and include Easter, Mother's Day, and Christmas trains. About a dozen train robbery and barbecue events take place.

WHEN TO GO: The KVR operates on a varied schedule mid-May through Canadian Thanksgiving in October. Spring and fall excursions run Saturday through Monday. In summer, Thursday and Friday excursions are added.

GOOD TO KNOW: Summerland is situated in the Okanagan Valley amid lush orchards and vineyards, and the valley is home to more than 50 wineries.

WORTH DOING: Take a side trip into nearby Penticton and tour the former CP ship SS *Sicamous*. This steel-hulled sternwheeler was built in 1914 as a multipurpose vessel that provided first-class passenger service as well as delivering cargo and daily mail.

DON'T MISS: The Trout Creek bridge, at the current turnaround point south of Summerland, sits 238 feet above the canyon floor and provides spectacular views.

GETTING THERE: Air service is scheduled into and out of Kelowna, about an hour's drive to the south. The Prairie Valley station is located off Highway 97.

Rocky Mountaineer

LOCATION: 1755 Cottrell Street, Vancouver
PHONE: 800-665-7245 or 604-606-7245
WEBSITE: rockymountaineer.com
E-MAIL: reservations@rockymountaineer.com

Rocky Mountaineer

This premier rail tour company offers more than 40 different rail outings through British Columbia and Alberta. In addition to its signature Vancouver to Banff route, the company has initiated service to Seattle on its Coastal Passage route.

CHOICES: Rocky Mountaineer offers two-day (or longer) all-daylight trips over five routes. On First Passage to the West, you follow the route of early explorers over the Rockies from Vancouver to Banff, Lake Louise, or Calgary in Alberta. On Journey through the Clouds, you experience coastal mountains, Fraser Canyon, Hell's Gate, Pyramid Falls, and Mount Robson on the journey from Vancouver to Jasper, Alberta. The Rainforest to Gold Rush route takes you from Whistler through Gold Country to Quesnel for an overnight stay and then along the Fraser River to Jasper. The Coastal Passage provides passengers with a three-day trip from Banff or Jasper to Seattle. The Whistler Sea to Sky Climb is a 3.5-hour trip between Vancouver and Whistler, British Columbia, along the Sea to Sky corridor, with scenic views of waterfalls, forests, and mountains.

WHEN TO GO: Excursions run between April and October.

GOOD TO KNOW: The Jasper and Banff/Lake Louise/Calgary trains are combined between Vancouver and Kamloops. Trains operating on the former British Columbia Railway north of Greater Vancouver arrive and depart from the vicinity of the former BCR station in North Vancouver.

WORTH DOING: Go for the gold and take advantage of the fancy digs and pampering with GoldLeaf service. It is a cruise train, after all. On Canadian Rockies routes, GoldLeaf service features bi-level dome coaches with full-length windows. You can also try SilverLeaf service, which is featured in a single-level, glass-domed coach.

DON'T MISS: Except for the Whistler Sea to Sky Climb, trips run both eastbound and westbound, and either direction offers spectacular scenery.

GETTING THERE: Air service is available to Vancouver and Calgary. Scheduled motor coach service connects Jasper, Banff, and Whistler to the outside world. VIA Rail Canada provides service to Jasper and Vancouver.

West Coast Railway Heritage Park

LOCATION: 39645 Government Road, Squamish
PHONE: 800-722-1233 or 604-898-9336
WEBSITE: wcra.org
E-MAIL: info@wcra.org

John Godfrey

Heritage Park provides a home to the West Coast Railway Association's large collection of locomotives and rolling stock. Located in a beautiful 12-acre mountain valley setting, the museum offers visitors a chance to learn about railway history from 1920 to 1960 in Canada's westernmost province.

CHOICES: The park features a variety of railway stations and other buildings. You are also able to see railway equipment in various stages of restoration in the 1914 PGE car shop. The collection of more than 90 vintage railway cars and locomotives includes cabooses, snowplows, a restored 1890 business car, and the only surviving Pacific Great Western steam engine. A mini train ride circles the park.

WHEN TO GO: The park is open year-round, except for Christmas and New Year's Day. Summer months provide the least likelihood for an encounter with the area's famous "wet sunshine." The park holds various special events including days out with Thomas the Tank Engine and the *Polar Express*.

GOOD TO KNOW: The West Coast Railway Association also operates the Locomotive 374 Pavilion in Vancouver, which houses historic CP locomotive 374. The locomotive, built in 1886, brought the first transcontinental passenger train into the city.

WORTH DOING: Incorporate a visit to the museum with a scenic drive along the Sea to Sky Highway for a nice day-long family outing. The Sea to Sky Highway travels through five different biogeoclimatic zones, from coastal rain forest to mountain forest. This predominantly two-lane road goes from Vancouver to Whistler.

DON'T MISS: The park's 21,000-square-foot roundhouse displays various exhibits including Royal Hudson No. 2860, one of the last Royal Hudson locomotives built for the Canadian Pacific Railway by Montreal Locomotive Works in June 1940.

GETTING THERE: From Vancouver, it is about an hour's drive north on Highway 99 along spectacular Howe Sound, North America's southernmost fjord, to Squamish. Turn left on Industrial Way until Queens Way and then turn right and follow the signs.

MANITOBA

Prairie Dog Central Railway

LOCATION: Prairie Dog Trail, Winnipeg
PHONE: 866-715-2348 or 204-832-5259
WEBSITE: pdcrailway.com
E-MAIL: info@pdcrailway.com

Mark Perry

This railway's 36-mile round trip over the former CN Oak Point Subdivision from the north side of the Manitoba capital to the town of Warren offers a glimpse into prairie railroading of the past.

CHOICES: The train takes a leisurely trip through rural Manitoba, and you can choose to travel in either open-vestibule or closed-vestibule coaches. The wooden coaches, built between 1901 and 1913, are fully restored and air-conditioned—when the windows are open. Power is provided by steam locomotive No. 3, ex-BNSF GP9 No. 1685, or diesel No. 4138, which was built in 1958 for the Grand Trunk Western Railroad. Many options are available throughout the season including train robberies, historical-themed trains, and Halloween trains. You can also ride in a caboose or be an engineer for a day.

WHEN TO GO: Trains operate on select weekend days during May and June, and they maintain a regular weekend schedule July through September. Special runs also operate on Victoria Day, Canada Day, and other select holidays.

GOOD TO KNOW: Ex-Winnipeg Hydro 4-4-0 No. 3 was built in 1882 by Dubs in Scotland and is one of the oldest operable engines in North America. The railway's station, constructed in 1910 by the Canadian Northern Railway, is a Canadian Heritage Railway Station. It was moved from St. James Street to its present location in 2000 and renamed Inkster Junction Station.

WORTH DOING: During the stopover at Grosse Isle, take time to examine the displays of local crafts and home-baked goods. Grosse Isle is home to the 72-mile Prime Meridian Trail, a recreation and conservation trail built on an abandoned rail line.

DON'T MISS: Secure a ticket in either combine No. 104 or coach No. 105. These beautifully maintained relics are rolling time machines to another century.

GETTING THERE: Inkster Junction is located immediately north of Winnipeg's airport on Prairie Dog Trail. It is on the north side of Inkster Boulevard between Route 90 and Sturgeon Boulevard.

Winnipeg Railway Museum

LOCATION: 123 Main Street, Winnipeg

PHONE: 204-942-4632

WEBSITE: wpgrailwaymuseum.com

E-MAIL: wpgrail@mts.net

Mark Perry

The Winnipeg Railway Museum takes visitors back to the historical first days of railroading across the vast western Canadian prairies. The museum's two tracks, located under the train shed at VIA Rail Canada's Union Station, host a variety of equipment, exhibits, and displays for all to enthusiasts enjoy.

CHOICES: The museum operates in the train shed of the grandiose Canadian Northern 1911-built Union Station. It contains various displays of both vintage steam and diesel locomotives, railbuses, passenger coaches, freight cars, cabooses, and many other Canadian railway artifacts. A pair of restored vintage fire trucks that came from nearby railway shops are displayed. Various spreaders, snow dozers, and other equipment round out the collection.

WHEN TO GO: The museum is open year-round. It is open daily May through October. During March, April, November, and December, it is open Monday, Thursday, Saturday, and Sunday. During January and February, it is open Monday and Thursday.

GOOD TO KNOW: Located in the heart of downtown Winnipeg, Union Station is still actively used by VIA Rail Canada's passenger trains. The CN's busy two-track Rivers Subdivision runs right next to the train shed.

WORTH DOING: A historic gathering place for centuries, the fantastic shopping, dining, and entertainment development is Winnipeg's number-one tourist attraction. Formerly, The Forks was a CNR rail yard, and the remaining historic railway buildings have been well preserved and upgraded. Railway equipment is preserved on the grounds, and a pristine CNR F unit is displayed inside the Children's Museum.

DON'T MISS: The museum features some notable railway equipment on display including the first steam engine in Manitoba, Canadian Pacific's wood-burning Baldwin *Countess of Dufferin*.

GETTING THERE: Winnipeg is 85 miles north of the North Dakota border on Highway 75. VIA Rail operates a cross-country passenger train from Vancouver and Toronto that stops in Winnipeg. James Armstrong Richardson International Airport makes it easy to fly in and out of the city.

NEW BRUNSWICK

New Brunswick Railway Museum

The museum contains more than 20 pieces of rolling stock that includes locomotives, passenger cars, freight cars, maintenance-of-way equipment, and cabooses. Some of the cars are open for viewing. The museum also displays a speeder car, telegraph office, and smaller artifacts. It is open June through September.

LOCATION: 2847 Main Street, Hillsborough
PHONE: 506-734-3195
WEBSITE: nbrm.ca
E-MAIL: nbrailway@nb.aibn.com

NEWFOUNDLAND

Railway Coastal Museum

The Railway Coastal Museum is housed in the restored 1903 Riverhead station and contains a large collection of items relating to Newfoundland's rail and coastal boat services. You can walk along the platform where passengers boarded the *Newfie Bullet* and examine the rolling stock displayed in the train park. The museum is open year-round.

LOCATION: 495 Water Street West, St. John's
PHONE: 866-600-7245 or 709-724-5929
WEBSITE: railwaycoastalmuseum.ca
E-MAIL: info@railwaycoastalmuseum.ca

Railway Society of Newfoundland Train Site

The society maintains a collection of narrow gauge rolling stock from the Newfoundland Railway. Several trains are displayed including the *Newfie Bullet*, once Newfoundland's fastest passenger train. Steam locomotive No. 593 is displayed with a representative selection of cars. A snowplow train is also featured. You can walk through all the railcars. The museum is open daily during the summer.

LOCATION: Marine Drive and Station Road, Corner Brook
PHONE: 709-634-2720 (in season)
WEBSITE: cornerbrook.com

NOVA SCOTIA

Orangedale Railway Museum

The museum was originally built in 1886 as a Queen Anne-style station. The ground floor retains the original appearance of the agent's bay and waiting rooms. The second floor has been restored as the station agent's living quarters. The museum also displays a diesel switching locomotive, snowplow, caboose, and several railcars. It is open late June into October.

LOCATION: 1428 Main Street, Orangedale
PHONE: 902-756-3384
WEBSITE: museevirtuel-virtualmuseum.ca
E-MAIL: orangedale.station@gmail.com

Sydney & Louisburg Railway Museum

The museum features rolling stock, artifacts, and photographs relating to the Sydney & Louisburg Railway. Housed in an 1895 S&L station, the museum also contains historical exhibits about Louisburg. An original freight shed and roundhouse also contain displays. You can also view Nova Scotia's oldest passenger coach. It is open June through September.

LOCATION: 7330 Main Street, Louisburg
PHONE: 902-733-2720
WEBSITE: museevirtuel-virtualmuseum.ca

ONTARIO

Chatham Railroad Museum

Housed in a retired 1955 Canadian National baggage car, the Chatham Railroad Museum includes interactive exhibits and photos on local as well as national and international railroad history. Located across from the VIA rail station, the museum is open Tuesdays through Sundays during the summer.

LOCATION: 2 McLean Street, Chatham
PHONE: 519-352-3097
WEBSITE: chathamrailroadmuseum.ca
E-MAIL: crms@mnsi.net

Fort Erie Railroad Museum

This museum site features the restored Grand Trunk's Ridgeway station, which houses historic furnishings, telegraph equipment, tools, and other artifacts. Canadian National Railway steam engine No. 6218, a 4-8-4 Northern type, is the museum's centerpiece. Also on display are a fireless engine, a CN caboose, and other equipment. The CN's B-1 station that monitored traffic over the International Railway Bridge is also on site. It is open June to August.

LOCATION: 400 Central Avenue, Fort Erie
PHONE: 905-871-1412 or 905-894-5322
WEBSITE: museum.forterie.ca/website/museumweb.nsf
E-MAIL: museum@forterie.on.ca

Komoka Railway Museum

Kamoka's restored Canadian National station houses a collection of artifacts and photos dedicated to rail history in the area. It includes tools, lanterns, and a tiny flag stop station. Also on display are a 1913 Shay locomotive and a steel-sided baggage car. The museum is open Friday through Monday during summer and on Saturdays the rest of the year.

LOCATION: 133 Queen Street, Komoka
PHONE: 519-657-1912
WEBSITE: komokarailmuseum.ca
E-MAIL: station-master@komokarailmuseum.ca

Memory Junction Museum

Memory Junction features several structures including an 1857 Grand Trunk station, a baggage shed, and an unloading depot. A rare N-4-a locomotive is on display along with a wooden, outside-braced 1913 boxcar and other railcars. The museum includes local historical and railway artifacts.

LOCATION: 60 Maplewood Street, Brighton
PHONE: 613-475-0379
WEBSITE: brighton.ca
E-MAIL: re.bangay@sympatico.ca

Muskoka Heritage Place

Muskoka Heritage Place contains the Muskoka Museum, Pioneer Village, and *Portage Flyer*, a restored 1902 steam train that takes you on a short trip to the past. A diesel engine may also run. After boarding at the train station, you travel along the Muskoka River to Fairy Lake. The train station doubles as a museum with exhibits focusing on local steamships and locomotives. You can enjoy the entire site or just ride the *Portage Flyer*.

LOCATION: 88 Brunel Road, Huntsville
PHONE: 888-696-4255 or 705-789-7576
WEBSITE: muskokaheritageplace.org
E-MAIL: form on website

Northern Ontario Railroad Museum & Heritage Centre

This museum emphasizes railroading history in northern Ontario and includes additional exhibits on mining and lumbering. Artifacts are displayed in the Museum House, which was used by the Canadian National as a superintendent's residence. In nearby Prescott Park, it displays a U-1-f bullet-nosed steam locomotive, a wooden CNR caboose, and other equipment. Its newest acquisition is a hot metal car.

LOCATION: 26 Bloor Street, Capreol
PHONE: 705-858-5050
WEBSITE: normhc.ca
E-MAIL: info@normhc.ca

Port Stanley Terminal Rail

Excursion trains depart from a historic station next to the King George lift bridge. Early diesel locomotives pull open and closed coaches that have been converted from cabooses. Regular one-hour excursions run to Whytes Park. A variety of special trains run during the season, and some travel the entire line into St. Thomas. You can view the fleet of equipment in the yard just north of the station.

LOCATION: 309 Bridge Street, Port Stanley
PHONE: 877-244-4478 or 519-782-3730
WEBSITE: pstr.on.ca
E-MAIL: form on website

Railway Museum of Eastern Ontario

This museum is housed in a restored 1914 Canadian Northern Railway station that contains artifacts relating to the Canadian Pacific, Grand Trunk, Canadian National, and other railways. The national historic site displays a 1912 steam locomotive, a CP diesel, passenger cars, a CN snowplow, and a unique dental car. It is open May through December.

LOCATION: 90 William Street West, Smiths Falls
PHONE: 613-283-5696
WEBSITE: rmeo.org
E-MAIL: info@rmeo.org

School on Wheels Railcar Museum

This car was one of seven railway schools that served children and adults along northern Ontario railways. When touring the car, you will walk through the classroom and living quarters and view historical videos, children's activities, artifacts, and photos. It is open Thursdays through Sundays and holiday Mondays Victoria Day weekend through September.

LOCATION: 76 Victoria Terrace, Clinton
PHONE: 519-482-3997
WEBSITE: schoolcar.ca
E-MAIL: cnrschoolonwheels@gmail.com

Toronto Railway Museum

The museum features a variety of railroad components including the John Street roundhouse, an interlocking tower, and operational turntable. In addition to viewing historic rail equipment and displays, visitors can check out the cab of a steam locomotive, tour Roundhouse Park, and ride on a miniature railway.

LOCATION: 255 Bremner Boulevard, Toronto
PHONE: 416-214-9229
WEBSITE: trha.ca
E-MAIL: info@trha.ca

Waterloo Central Railway

The railway operates excursion trains through southern Ontario behind a 60-ton diesel locomotive. The railway's restored steam engine may also run. You can take the entire 12-mile round trip or detrain at St. Jacobs, where you can look around, and take a later train back. The railway also operates various special trains throughout the year.

LOCATION: 10 Father David Bauer Drive, Waterloo
PHONE: 519-885-2297 (in season)
WEBSITE: waterloocentralrailway.com
E-MAIL: form on website

York-Durham Heritage Railway

The railway operates excursions and special trains between Stouffville and Uxbridge. Diesel locomotives pull passenger coaches built between the 1920s and the 1950s. The Uxbridge station, which was built in 1904, contains displays of rail artifacts. There are numerous special events, and extra trains run in fall. Caboose rides are also available.

LOCATION: 6176 Main Street, Stouffville
PHONE: 905-852-3696
WEBSITE: ydhr.ca
E-MAIL: info@ydhr.ca

Algoma Central Railway

LOCATION: 129 Bay Street, Sault Ste. Marie
PHONE: 800-242-9287 or 705-946-7300
WEBSITE: agawacanyontourtrain.com

Algoma Central Railway/CN

The Algoma Central Railway offers the chance to ride into unspoiled Canadian wilderness from Sault Ste. Marie north into Ontario as far as the spectacular Agawa Canyon or to the end of the railroad at Hearst. Either way, you will not go away disappointed.

CHOICES: You can ride the tour train to Agawa Canyon and back, or you can ride the entire railroad—almost 300 miles one way—to the end of the line at Hearst. Or, best of all, you can do both: ride the canyon train out and then catch the regular passenger train to Hearst and back. Going to the canyon, you'll see mixed forests, mountain lakes, and streams, and past the canyon, there are boreal forests, muskegs, and moose. The railway also offers winter snow trains and wilderness adventure trains.

WHEN TO GO: The railroad runs year-round. Fall bookings can be intense so plan ahead. The average daily temperature stays below freezing during December, January, and February.

GOOD TO KNOW: The tour train is usually packed, but the regular passenger train is more relaxed. You'll stop at only the canyon on the tour train, but the regular train pauses to let fishermen, hunters, and other outdoor types get off at just about any point. It's a lot of fun to see what people will load onto the baggage car.

WORTH DOING: There is much to do in Sault Ste. Marie, such as strolling along the boardwalk, visiting a casino, or touring the locks. Winter activities include skiing and snowboarding.

DON'T MISS: For scenery viewing, ride one of the railroad's two dome cars. Find a good vantage point at mile post 19, where the railroad crosses the Montreal River on a huge curving trestle perched atop a dam. For a wilderness experience, you can camp out overnight in a caboose at Agawa Canyon.

GETTING THERE: Sault Ste. Marie is located at I-75 and Highway 17. Signs show the way to the depot, which is located downtown.

Canada Science and Technology Museum

LOCATION: 1867 St. Laurent Boulevard, Ottawa
PHONE: 866-442-4416 or 613-991-3044
WEBSITE: sciencetech.technomuses.ca
E-MAIL: cts@technomuses.ca

Jim Wrinn

The museum's rail collection contains 1,000 artifacts that range from photos to locomotives and dates back to the early days of Canadian railway history. Other exhibits focus on Canadian inventions, communications, and space technology.

CHOICES: Locomotive Hall showcases four locomotives, but other equipment is displayed throughout the museum and outdoors in Technology Park. Technology Park also includes a lighthouse, radar antenna, and Atlas rocket. During the summer, on Wednesdays and Sundays, you can take a 10-minute ride in vintage railcars. Operated by volunteers of the Bytown Railway Society, the Shay locomotive usually pulls a century-old business car and a caboose.

WHEN TO GO: The museum is open year-round but is closed most Mondays during winter. It also closes down for about four days for its annual cleaning. Look for new exhibits and special events throughout the year.

GOOD TO KNOW: For a small fee, you can try the museum's space simulator. Missions include trying to save a colony on Mars and flying toward a comet on a collision course with Earth.

WORTH DOING: In Ottawa, the country's capital, there are numerous attractions and activities. Sites to see include the Rideau Canal, Canadian War Museum, and National Gallery of Canada. You can even watch the changing of the guard at Parliament Hill.

DON'T MISS: In Locomotive Hall, you'll find four unique engines: CNR No. 40, built for the Grand Trunk Railway in 1872 and Canada's oldest mainline steam locomotive, Canadian Pacific No. 926, which spent 50 years hauling freight and passenger trains between Winnipeg and Calgary, CNR No. 6400 with its distinctive semi-streamlined design and painted olive green, and CP No. 2858, one of five preserved CP Hudsons.

GETTING THERE: The museum is located about 10 minutes southeast of downtown Ottawa. Exit Highway 417 at St. Laurent south and turn left on Lancaster Road.

Credit Valley Explorer

LOCATION: 49 Townline Road, Orangeville
PHONE: 888-346-0046
WEBSITE: creditvalleyexplorer.com
E-MAIL: info@creditvalleyexplorer.com

John Godfrey

The *Credit Valley Explorer* offers a scenic round trip between Orangeville and Brampton over a route that was completed in 1879. The ride, aboard 1950s rail coaches, takes you through rolling hills and deep valleys, over the Credit River, and across a 1,146-foot-long trestle bridge.

CHOICES: The regular three-hour excursion departs Orangeville and travels through the Caledon Hills, Cataract, and the forks of the Credit River to Inglewood and Brampton before returning. Tours include meal service with complimentary refreshments, interpretive commentary, and a mile-by-mile printed guidebook.

WHEN TO GO: Scenic excursions operate year-round, and different times of year offer different experiences. Late spring and early summer give you a chance to see the countryside before the foliage becomes dense. Autumn is busy, and the trains are full, but the fall colors are spectacular.

GOOD TO KNOW: You can take a walking tour through Orangeville's historic downtown or examine the unique Art Walk of Tree Sculptures.

WORTH DOING: The Hills of the Headwaters is a great area for experiencing the great outdoors, no matter what the season. Hiking trails abound, and you can also fish, golf, and ski in a variety of locations.

DON'T MISS: Most mid-day trips stop in Inglewood, so you can explore this quaint rural community.

GETTING THERE: Orangeville is about an hour's drive from Toronto in southern Ontario. Trains depart from the railway yard on Town Line Road. From Highway 10, take Broadway to Town Line Road and turn left. Follow Town Line Road to the entrance.

Elgin County Railway Museum

LOCATION: 225 Wellington Street, St. Thomas
PHONE: 519-637-6284
WEBSITE: ecrm5700.org
E-MAIL: thedispatcher@ecrm5700.org

John Godfrey

The railroad has been a part of life in St. Thomas since 1856. Over the years, a total of 26 railways have passed through town, helping it garner the moniker of the Railway Capital of Canada. Located in the former Michigan Central locomotive shops, the Elgin County Railway Museum helps preserve and display the railway heritage of St. Thomas and the surrounding area.

CHOICES: As a working museum, equipment restoration is ongoing, and you can occasionally catch a glimpse of the volunteers in action. The museum displays a variety of equipment including locomotives, cabooses, and passenger cars. Highlights are a CP diesel locomotive, a CNR Hudson, a Grand Trunk Western caboose, a Pullman sleeper, and an electric-powered car that transported children to school in the 1920s. In St. Thomas, the BX interlocking tower is available for touring during special events.

WHEN TO GO: The museum is open year-round. It is open Tuesday through Sunday between Victoria Day and Labor Day weekends. The rest of the year, it is open Wednesdays through Saturdays, and closed the last week of December. Thomas the Tank Engine stops by in July. It also hosts a Railway Nostalgia Weekend in June.

GOOD TO KNOW: A short drive from the regional center of London, St. Thomas is a small town with all services. Its Iron Horse Festival coincides with the museum's Railway Heritage Day.

WORTH DOING: Combining a visit to the museum along with a ride on the nearby Port Stanley Terminal Rail makes for an interesting day of exploring the preserved rails of southern Ontario.

DON'T MISS: The museum celebrates the Canadian railway on Railway Heritage Day, which is usually held in August. During the celebration, short train trips often operate.

GETTING THERE: VIA Rail Canada offers scheduled passenger service through London to the north. If driving, the museum is two hours from Toronto, two hours from the U.S. border at Detroit, Buffalo, or Niagara Falls, and one hour from Sarnia and Port Huron. Once in St. Thomas, you will find the museum on Wellington Street between Ross Street and First Avenue.

Halton County Radial Railway

LOCATION: 13629 Guelph Line, Milton
PHONE: 519-856-9802
WEBSITE: hcry.org
E-MAIL: streetcar@hcry.org

Halton County Radial Railway

Canada's preeminent trolley museum brings the streetcar era to life with the help of the largest collection of operable streetcars in the country. Its streetcars, radial cars, and work cars operate over a rebuilt portion of a long-abandoned interurban railway.

CHOICES: Streetcars, such as Toronto Transit Commission No. 2894, travel over a short track on a 20-minute ride through a hardwood forest. The railway features four display barns filled with 75 pieces of equipment that, in addition to streetcars, includes freight cars, passenger coaches, buses, and a locomotive or two. Most of the streetcars were built in the early 20th century.

WHEN TO GO: Streetcars operate on weekends from May to October and daily during July and August. A number of special events are incorporated into the operating season and some center on spring wild flowers, autumn color, Halloween, and Christmas.

GOOD TO KNOW: Admission includes unlimited streetcar rides and access to the exhibits displayed in the carbarns and Rockwood Station, which was built in 1912 for the Grand Trunk Railway. You can also enjoy a picnic lunch on the railway's grounds.

WORTH DOING: On Labor Day weekend, steam fans can take in Milton's steam-era event that features steam-powered equipment in action, a parade of tractors and antique autos, and tractor pulls.

DON'T MISS: After a long day of streetcar riding, reward yourself with ice cream from the ice cream shop. Share a romantic streetcar ride under the stars and enjoy ice cream together on the Ice Cream and Starlight evening.

GETTING THERE: Milton is 25 miles west of Toronto on Highway 401. From Highway 401, take Exit 312 and go north on Guelph Line until you reach the museum. It is also the the terminus of Toronto's Milton commuter train line.

Polar Bear Express

LOCATION: 200 Railway Street, Cochrane
PHONE: 800-265-2356 or 705-272-5338
WEBSITE: ontarionorthland.ca
E-MAIL: form on website

Ontario Northland's *Polar Bear Express* transports you to the shores of James Bay and the edge of the Arctic.

CHOICES: The *Polar Bear Express* provides passenger excursions between Cochrane and Moosonee on James Bay. You can take a day trip, with several hours for exploring the area, or stay over and return on a different day. The train features a family car to keep young travelers busy. It makes flag stops along the way.

WHEN TO GO: The *Polar Bear Express* operates Mondays through Fridays.

GOOD TO KNOW: In Cochrane, the Station Inn provides handy overnight lodging on the upper floors of the train station. The *Polar Bear Express* features a canoe car for storing canoes for anyone planning a paddling adventure.

WORTH DOING: On the *Polar Bear Express* layover, be sure to take one of the side trips to the island of Moose Factory, a former Hudson's Bay Company fur-trading settlement. If you want to see polar bears close up, you can visit the Polar Bear Conservation and Education Habitat, a polar bear rehabilitation facility, in Cochrane, where you can see the bears in natural habitat and even swim alongside them (with a window in between).

DON'T MISS: The dome car aboard the *Polar Bear Express* provides the most panoramic scenic views.

GETTING THERE: Cochrane, North Bay, and Toronto are connected by bus and train service. VIA Rail connects Toronto with Quebec and Ontario locations, and Amtrak connects Toronto with southwest Ontario and New York. Scheduled air service is available to Toronto and to Moosonee.

South Simcoe Railway

LOCATION: Mill Street West, Tottenham
PHONE: 905-936-5815
WEBSITE: southsimcoerailway.ca
E-MAIL: info@southsimcoerailway.ca

South Simcoe Railway

The South Simcoe Railway operates over four miles of former Canadian National trackage through rolling countryside approximately an hour north of Toronto. Excursions are powered by a 1948 diesel locomotive or steam locomotives No. 136, which was built in 1883, or No 1057.

CHOICES: Regular excursions from Tottenham to Beeton and back take about an hour. As the train rolls through Beeton Creek Valley, the conductor provides an informative commentary. Passengers ride in restored 1920s steel heavyweight coaches. Special trains include the Easter Express, Halloween Adventure, and Santa Claus Express.

WHEN TO GO: The railway runs multiple trips on Sundays and on holiday Mondays between Victoria Day weekend and Canadian Thanksgiving. It also operates Mondays and Tuesdays from the third week of July to the third week of August as well as on select Saturdays in October.

GOOD TO KNOW: The town of Tottenham has a variety of quaint shops and eateries. Across the road from the railway is Tottenham Conservation Park, which offers swimming, camping, fishing, and hiking.

WORTH DOING: For a unique combination rail-water excursion, the RMS *Segwun*, the oldest operating steamship in North America, sails July and August on the Muskoka Lakes, about a two-hour drive north to Gravenhurst.

DON'T MISS: Take one rail trip and then follow one of the others for some great photos. The engine faces south into the sun, and the relatively slow pace of the train makes it easy to follow.

GETTING THERE: No public transit is available to this neck of the woods. From Highway 400, take Highway 9 west nine miles to Tottenham Road and turn right. Continue into downtown Tottenham and turn left onto Mill Street to reach the station.

PRINCE EDWARD ISLAND

Elmira Railway Museum

The museum offers a look at railroading on the island in the early 1900s. It features a station house with a re-created station master's office and waiting room as well as displays and artifacts. A miniature train operates around the museum, and various special events take place on the outdoor stage, which was built from the base of a flatcar. The museum is open June through September.

LOCATION: 457 Elmira Road, Elmira
PHONE: 902-357-7234 or 902-368-6600
WEBSITE: peimuseum.com
E-MAIL: elmira@gov.pe.ca

QUEBEC

Exporail

LOCATION: 110 St. Pierre Street, St. Constant
PHONE: 450-632-2410
WEBSITE: exporail.org
E-MAIL: info@exporail.org

Jim Wrinn

The largest collection of railway equipment in the country is well worth a stop for anyone interested in Canadian railways and rail transit. Locomotives, rolling stock, and streetcars from many parts of the country tell of the evolution of both industries.

CHOICES: The museum's collection boasts 160 railway vehicles. Special events and exhibits are scheduled throughout the year geared toward modelers and transit enthusiasts. The museum has several train ride options. A streetcar runs daily between May and October. On Sundays May to October, you can take a short ride on a passenger train. The main building contains only a portion of the collection, and you can explore the rest of the site from stops along the streetcar loop. You'll be able to see Barrington Station, a restored, rural flag stop station from southwestern Quebec.

WHEN TO GO: The Canadian Railway Museum is open daily between mid-May and the beginning of September. During September and October, it is open Wednesday through Sunday. The remainder of the year, the museum is open on weekends, for spring break, and around Christmas.

GOOD TO KNOW: Locomotive No. 4489, the *Dominion of Canada*, is on loan to the National Railway Museum in York, England, to commemorate the 75th anniversary of the official world speed record by a steam locomotive. It will return in 2014.

WORTH DOING: There is much to see and do in Montreal. You can discover centuries of history in Old Montreal and explore Olympic Park.

DON'T MISS: An observation pit in the Grand Gallery allows you to view the undersides of both a steam locomotive and diesel engine (CP No. 2850 and CN No. 6765).

GETTING THERE: The museum is located 12 miles from downtown Montreal. Amtrak's *Adirondack* connects the city with the rest of its network in Albany, N.Y. CIT Roussillon provides bus service near the museum and AMT provides commuter rail.

Orford Express

LOCATION: 806 Minto Street, Sherbrooke
PHONE: 866-575-8081 or 819-575-8081
WEBSITE: orfordexpress.com
E-MAIL: info@orfordexpress.com

Jim Wrinn

After boarding at the restored Sherbrooke station, this train takes you on a scenic trip to Eastman along the shores of a river and several lakes, all in view of Mount Orford. The train uses the tracks of the Montreal, Maine & Atlantic Railroad, which is normally a freight-only line.

CHOICES: For the 3.5-hour trip to Eastman, you can sit in one of two rebuilt RDC cars or a refurbished former Northern Pacific dome car. Interiors of the cars feature rich wood, carpeting, and comfortable seating. Brunch, lunch, and dinner are dining choices. Along the way, informative videos and narration add food for thought. The return trip features a stop at Merry Point in Magog, where you can enjoy the panoramic view. For anyone looking for a just a scenic train ride, L'Escapade is a non-dining option. Specials include a train ride combined with a cruise on Lake Memphremagog and a trip from Magog to Bromont.

WHEN TO GO: The train runs from mid-May through December. The brunch train operates on Sundays. The lunch and dinner trains operate on slightly different spring/fall, summer, and winter schedules. More trains run in summer and a few less run in winter. In summer, lunch service runs Wednesday through Sunday, and dinner trains run Thursday through Saturday.

GOOD TO KNOW: The train began as the project of a Roman Catholic priest, Donald Thompson, who partnered with a businessman to create the train. You'll see him on the video narration as well as in person as the conductor or engineer.

WORTH DOING: In downtown Sherbrooke, view the large Fresco Murals on various buildings. You can also take a guided tour in an antique automobile through the North Ward and its beautiful Victorian homes.

DON'T MISS: Make sure to check out the railroad's FL9 streamlined passenger diesel locomotive, the only one in Canada.

GETTING THERE: Sherbrooke is about a two-hour drive east from Montreal.

Train of Le Massif de Charlevoix

LOCATION: 4300 Sainte Anne Boulevard, Québec City
PHONE: 877-536-2774
WEBSITE: lemassif.com
E-MAIL: info@lemassif.com

Train of Le Massif de Charlevoix

Along 75 miles of the Charlevoix Railway, this train takes you from Montmorency Falls provincial park in Quebec City to the riverside towns of Baie-Saint-Paul or La Malbaie along the scenic north shore of the St. Lawrence River.

CHOICES: From spring through fall, Le Massif offers one-day trips to Baie-Saint-Paul or La Malbaie as well as a gourmet dinner train. Both trips offer four optional tours that you can take during the stopover in Baie-Saint-Paul. You can meet area food producers and restaurateurs, go kayaking, take a guided tour of the area, or visit a museum. Winter trains allow you to ski or take part in other outdoor activities. You can also combine excursions with a lodging package.

WHEN TO GO: Beginning in May, most summer trains operate Thursday through Sunday. Some also depart on Wednesday. Winter trains run on weekends. The fall colors are usually spectacular in early October, while in early spring, the passenger count is usually lighter. It may take some extra planning for a stay in Quebec City. For cruise ships along the St. Lawrence, the city is a popular destination during summer and fall. Also, many workers in the province are on vacation the last two weeks of July.

GOOD TO KNOW: Quebec is the only fortified city in North America north of Mexico. It features two miles of walls, gates, and fortifications to explore.

WORTH DOING: Take in Montmorency Falls from Parc de la Chute-Montmorency. The falls can be seen by cable car or on foot. It is 272 feet high, 98 feet higher than Niagara Falls.

DON'T MISS: Seats on the right side of the train heading east from Montmorency offer virtually unimpeded views of the St. Lawrence River.

GETTING THERE: Quebec City's Jean Lesage International Airport is served by a number of airlines. VIA Rail and intercity buses call at the city's venerable downtown Palais Station. The train station is about a 30-minute drive east from the airport and 15 minutes from downtown.

SASKATCHEWAN

Rusty Relics Museum

Rusty Relics Museum portrays pioneer life in Saskatchewan. Housed in Carlyle's 1910 station, its collection features several buildings, machinery, and artifacts. Railway items include a caboose, a jigger, a tool shed, and a working telegraph. It is open Monday through Friday June through August.

LOCATION: 115 Railway Avenue West, Carlyle
PHONE: 306-453-2266 or 306-453-2363
WEBSITE: museevirtuel-virtualmuseum.ca
E-MAIL: rustyrelicsmuseum@gmail.com

Saskatchewan Railway Museum

This seven-acre museum contains more than 10 buildings, including a station, express shed, interlocking tower, and tool sheds, from the Canadian National, Canadian Pacific, Canadian Northern, and Grand Trunk Railways. On display are a variety of freight cars, passenger coaches, streetcars, cabooses, and a CPR S3 diesel locomotive. You can take a guided tour or explore the museum on your own during the summer season.

LOCATION: Highway 60, Saskatoon
PHONE: 306-382-9855
WEBSITE: saskrailmuseum.org
E-MAIL: srha@saskrailmuseum.org

Western Development Museum

The WDM in Moose Jaw focuses on transportation, and it displays a passenger coach, Canadian Pacific station, and CPR locomotive 2634. It also offers train rides pulled by a Vulcan steam engine, the only operational steam locomotive in the province. The museum is open Tuesday through Sunday.

LOCATION: 50 Diefenbaker Drive, Moose Jaw
PHONE: 306-693-5989
WEBSITE: wdm.ca
E-MAIL: moosejaw@wdm.ca

Southern Prairie Railway

LOCATION: 401 Railway Avenue, Ogema
PHONE: 855-459-1200 or 306-459-1200
WEBSITE: southernprairierailway.com
E-MAIL: sprailway@yahoo.ca

Southern Prairie Railway

Located in southern Saskatchewan, this new operation offers excursions across the prairies, not unlike the ones early settlers would have taken.

CHOICES: Trains leave from a restored Canadian Pacific station, and several uniquely themed excursions are available. The Heritage Train runs west along an old CP branch line to Horizon, where tour guides take you through a grain elevator. On your return, you can visit the Deep South Pioneer Museum (admission is included with your ticket). A stargazing train allows you to view the stars in the dark skies.

WHEN TO GO: Trains operate Saturday and Sunday from first weekend in June to mid-October. On Saturday mornings, you can ride to Pangman for a farmers market. On select dates, dinner trains offer a one-of-a-kind, steak-and-potatoes, pitchfork fondue meal.

GOOD TO KNOW: The CP train station was built in 1912 and moved 150 miles from Simpson, Saskatchewan. The train features a 1922 Pullman passenger coach and a 1945 GE diesel locomotive.

WORTH DOING: About an hour's drive south of Ogema, you'll find the Big Muddy Badlands, with its cone-shaped hills, steep cliffs, caves, and unique weathered formations, highlighted by Castle Butte.

DON'T MISS: The Deep South Pioneer Museum features 30 buildings that re-create a pioneer village. The museum also includes more than 150 tractors and pieces of farm equipment.

GETTING THERE: Ogema is about 90 minutes south of either Moose Jaw or Regina and about four hours northwest of Minot, N.D.

YUKON

Copperbelt Railway & Mining Museum

Located in copper country, the museum's exhibits focus on the area's mining and rail history. You can take a ride through the 10-acre park on a passenger car pulled by a diesel mining engine. The museum is open daily mid-May until early September, and the train ride runs every 30 minutes.

LOCATION: Mile 919 on the Alaska Highway, Whitehorse
PHONE: 867-667-6198
WEBSITE: yukonrails.com
E-MAIL: copperbelt@northwestel.net

Whitehorse Waterfront Trolley

In downtown Whitehorse, you can ride a restored 1925 trolley along the city's waterfront. The trolley departs from Rotary Peace Park and travels to Spook Creek. Along the way, you can stop at the MacBride Museum of Yukon History, White Pass & Yukon depot, visitor information center, and SS *Klondike* National Historic Site. You'll also hear stories about the area's history. The trolley operates daily mid-May through September.

LOCATION: 1127 First Avenue, Whitehorse
PHONE: 867-667 6355
WEBSITE: yukonrails.com
E-MAIL: mchrs@northwestel.net

Index

D

E

F

N

O

S

T

Advertiser Index

321

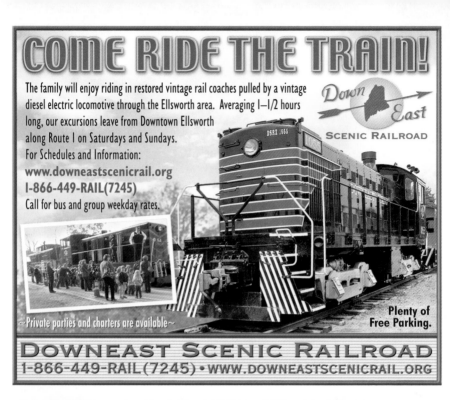
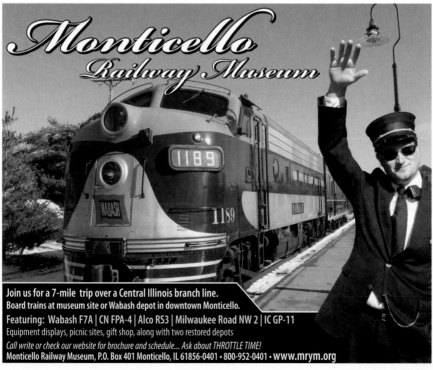

ALL ABOARD!
MID-CONTINENT RAILWAY MUSEUM
Celebrating 50 Years of Providing Living Railroad History

RIDE INTO THE PAST! Take a 55-minute, diesel-powered, 7-mile round-trip journey through rural Wisconsin countryside aboard railcars dating back nearly 100 years! Choose from coach seating, caboose, or even join the engineer in the locomotive!

DISCOVER the rich history of railroading through our museum filled with restored locomotives, railcars & more! Mid-Continent strives to recreate the shortline way of life during the Golden Age of Railroading, between 1880 and 1916. With over 125 pieces of rolling stock, many restored, Mid-Continent is a *must see* railroad destination!

REMEMBER your experience with a visit to the railroad gift shop, located in our restored 1894 C&NW depot.

OPEN DAILY from June 1-Sept. 2
OPEN WEEKENDS May 4-27 & Sept. 7-Oct. 20
DEPARTURES at 11am, 1pm & 3pm*
Museum Hours: 9:30am-5pm on days trains operate
*Departure times may differ during special events

Also join us for these special events:
- Mothers Day weekend: May 11 & 12
- 50th Anniversary Celebration: June 1
- Autumn Color™ weekends: Oct. 4-5-6 & 11-12-13
- Pumpkin Special™: Oct 19-20
- Santa Express™: Nov. 30-Dec.1
- Snow Train™: Feb. 14-15-16, 2014

First Class Trains, Brunch Tains and Dinner Trains offered during select special events. For more information on these and other events call or visit our website!

1963-2013
50 Years
at NORTH FREEDOM

Located 1 hour from Madison and only 30 minutes from Wisconsin Dells, the Waterpark Capital of the World!
E8948 Museum Rd., North Freedom, WI 53951
For info & reservations call **1-800-930-1385**
or visit **www.midcontinent.org**

THERE'S A GREAT SEAT

SANTACRUZRAILWAY.COM
Santa Cruz, CA

MTHOODRR.COM
Hood River, OR

COLORADOTRAIN.COM
Alamosa, CO

The Pacific Coast has long used rails for mining and logging but now passengers can enjoy the serenity of coastal beaches and sunset rides in vintage cars.

- Dining cars with fresh regional menus
- Wine Trains
- Special events and themed trains

Journey through the lush green forests of the Columbia River Gorge to the valley's fertile vineyards and orchards overlooked by the striking snow capped peak of Mt. Hood.

- Spring Blossoms and Fall Foliage excursions
- Sunday Brunch and Western Train Robberies
- Murder Mysteries

The Rocky Mountains that define this state shape every curve of this railroad. Steep passes, tunnels and wildlife let you see a colorful Colorado behind a 100 year-old steam engine.

- Summer weekends feature outdoor mountaintop concerts
- Rails & Ales Brewfest, Photographer's Train
- Wine Trains, holiday trains and more

from the PACIFIC *to the* ATLANTIC

Photo: Robert Kissel

ANY TIME OF YEAR

TSRR.COM
Rusk and Palestine, TX

SNCRR.COM
Saratoga Sprigns, NY

CAPETRAIN.COM
Buzzards Bay, MA

Dubbed a "Texas Treasure", these historic rails travel through rolling hills and piney woods with wildlife sightings while sampling the service of true southern hospitality.

- Lunch and Dinner Trains
- Holiday theme trains
- Full campground facilities

The Adirondacks offer four seasons of beauty best seen along breathtaking waterway vistas in heritage cars with exceptional service and classic rail dining.

- Fall Foliage rides
- Snow Train to winter resorts
- Holiday theme trains

Travel to the hidden beauty of the Cape through marshes and dunes alive with sea birds where just around the bend the views offer glimpses of the open sea bay and picturesque island villages.

- Brunch and Dinner Trains
- Murder Mysteries
- Holiday theme trains

IOWA PACIFIC
PASSENGER RAILS

VISIT OUR WEBSITES FOR EVENT INFORMATION AND OUR E-NEWSLETTER

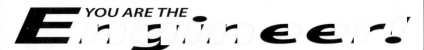

Lose track of time.

There's something amazing about trains. The familiar whistle has always promised adventure. The gentle rock of the rails has set the rhythm of our lives. Experience it all again at the Colorado Railroad Museum.

Stroll the Museum's 15-acre railyard with over 100 narrow and standard gauge steam and diesel locomotives, passenger cars, cabooses, Galloping Geese and G-scale garden railway.

Watch as Colorado railroad history is brought back to life in our Roundhouse restoration facility with working Turntable.

Visit the 1880s-replica Depot Museum housing thousands of rare artifacts, along with the Denver HO Model Railroad Club's operating model layout that depicts Colorado mountain railroading.

And take home a memory from our Depot General Store featuring thousands of train gifts for every railfan.

• •

RIDE THE RAILS SATURDAYS
Open daily from 9:00 AM – 5:00 PM

Minutes from Downtown Denver

303-279-4591 or 800-365-6263
17155 W. 44th Avenue, Golden, Colorado 80403

Colorado RILROAD Museum.org

SCFD
Scientific & Cultural
Facilities District
Making It Possible.

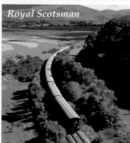

VACATIONS BY RAIL℠

Experience over
30 EXCITING TOURIST TRAINS WITH
VACATIONS BY RAIL

Durango & Silverton Train

Top 5 Escorted Train Vacations

- America's Parks & Monuments with Mt. Rushmore – 11 Day Tour
- Great Parks of the Southwest – 11 Day Tour
- Colorado Rail Adventure – 8 Day Tour
- Autumn in New England – 8 Day Tour
- New England's Fall Colors & Scenic Trains – 10 Day Tour

Browse Vacations By Rail's complete collection of rail vacations online at www.vacationsbyrail.com

Mention Tourist Trains Guidebook and receive up to **$50.00 off per person** on your rail vacation!

VACATIONS BY RAIL℠

The trusted authority on rail vacations in the United States, Canada, Europe & Beyond.

www.vacationsbyrail.com • 1-877-929-7245 (toll-free)

Ride the Playground

Txt "trains2" to 304.782.0400 for Rides, Rooms & More!

Enter keycode "trains2" on our website for Rides, Rooms & More!

50+ Scenic Miles
of Historic Railroad...

The Cass Scenic Railroad State Park and the Durbin & Greenbrier Valley Railroad combine to make Pocahontas County the land of historic trains. It's a showcase for the restoration and operation of historic railroads, attracting tens of thousands of riders and railroad enthusiasts each year. Come join the fun.

PocahontasCounty®
WEST VIRGINIA
NaturesMountainPlayground.com

WVTOURISM.COM
West Virginia
Wild and Wonderful
800-225-5982

For more info visit:
NaturesMtnPlayground.com/trains2
or call:
800.336.7009

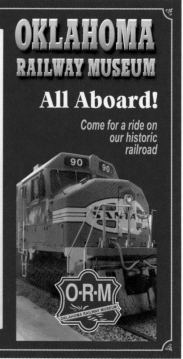
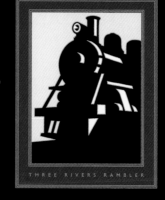

Explore America's Railroad Heritage

X 4017   X 4017

UNION PACIFIC
4017

Open Now – January 2014

An exclusive exhibit of
The Christopher Railroad
China Collection

National Railroad Museum

ELGIN COUNTY & ST. THOMAS, ONTARIO, CANADA
Railway Capital of Canada

**Historical Sites
Museums
Jumbo the Elephant
Family Attractions
& Events**

St. Thomas' railway heritage is sure to delight visitors of all ages. Explore various museums and monuments, multiple railway themed festivals and events, and exciting railway attractions. Take a ride on the Port Stanley Terminal Rail, visit the annual "Day Out with Thomas" event or tour the local craft brewery. No trip to St. Thomas is complete without a visit to the Jumbo monument to see the most famous elephant that ever lived!

**1-877-GO-ELGIN ext.168
www.elgintourist.com/railways**

RAILWAY
CAPITAL
of Canada

5 Ways to Experience the

Railways

of St. Thomas & Elgin County

1

2

Railway City Brewing Co.

Visit Railway City Brewing Company for a tour and sample their Iron Spike beer, or try the popular Dead Elephant Ale, a tribute to Jumbo. St. Thomas' own microbrewery also features seasonal brews inspired by Elgin's local bounty.

3

Port Stanley Terminal Rail

Climb aboard the Port Stanley Terminal Rail, located in the village of Port Stanley. You'll travel along the rail bed of one of Ontario's oldest railways and the longest running tourist operation in Elgin.

Elgin County Railway Museum

Visitors to the Elgin County Railway Museum have the opportunity to see firsthand the inner workings of a real locomotive shop. View an impressive collection of artifacts, including several locomotives and various pieces of rolling stock.

Canada Southern Railway Station

Travel back to a time when railway ruled St. Thomas with a visit to the historic Canada Southern Railway Station. Tours are available of this impressive Italianate style building, built between 1871 and 1893, and currently undergoing an extensive restoration.

4

5

Jumbo the Elephant Monument

Jumbo, star of the Barnum & Bailey Circus, was said to be the largest elephant ever held in captivity. He was tragically killed in 1885 after being struck by a locomotive in St. Thomas; 100 years later, the city dedicated a 38 ton life-sized statue in his honour.

For more information, call 1-877-GO ELGIN x168 or visit www.elgintourist.com/railways

60th ANNIVERSARY
ILLINOIS RAILWAY MUSEUM
1953 - 2013

9911-A

Burlington Route

AMERICA'S LARGEST

RAILWAY MUSEUM

See and Ride Our Time Machines!

- Over 400 Railroad & Transportation vehicles operating & on display!
- Ride trolleys, interurbans, and coaches on our railroad!
- Explore the displays in car barns and open railyards

Hours of Operation:

Sundays: April - October:
10:30 a.m. to 5 p.m.
Saturdays: May - October:
10:30 a.m. to 5 p.m.
Weekdays: Memorial Day - Labor Day:
10 a.m. to 4 p.m.

Free Parking & Picnic Area!

All Aboard!

UNION, ILLINOIS IN MCHENRY COUNTY
Call 1-800-BIG-RAIL visit: www.irm.org
7000 Olson Rd., Union IL 60180 (Take I90 to Hwy 20 Exit— Follow the Signs)

ILLINOIS RAILWAY MUSEUM

Houghton County Historical Museum

53102 Hwy M-26
Lake Linden, Michigan

Coordinates: 47.187007,-88.412782
www.houghtonhistory.org

Phone & office hours : (906) 296-4121, Mon. and Fri. 9:30am - noon.

* Railroad Opportunities *

Engineer for a Day – 4 hours of operation.

2013 Annual Locomotive Pass:

> Drive a steam locomotive for $10 each trip -no passengers
> Free Cab Rides
> Free (Grand)Parent Pass: children at regular rate.

Family Pass: parents and children ride free.

Grandparent Pass: grandparent & adult guest free, children at regular rate.

UPGRADED

All Aboard!

Experience the same rugged landscapes that inspired the Group of Seven to create some of Canada's most notable landscape art as you enjoy one of the most popular rail excursions in North America.

This one-day wilderness tour will transport you 114 miles north of Sault Ste. Marie, Ontario, over towering trestles, alongside pristine northern lakes and rivers and through the awesome granite rock formations and mixed forests of the Canadian Shield enroute to an hour and a half stopover in beautiful Agawa Canyon park.

The tour train has also undergone extensive upgrades designed to make your experience more enjoyable. From bigger windows and all new tinted glass to an informative GPS triggered tour narration available in 5 languages and locomotive mounted cameras that relay the view of the engineers back to the numerous flat screen monitors installed in all of the coaches.

It's all aboard and 're-experience' the world famous Agawa Canyon Tour Train.

AN HOUR NORTH OF THE MACKINAC BRIDGE

TOURS DAILY: June 25th to October 14th, 2013
Departs: 8:00 am · Returns: 6:00 pm

Algoma Central Railway – Passenger Sales
129 Bay Street, Sault Ste. Marie, ON P6A 6Y2

1-800-242-9287   www.agawacanyontourtrain.com

Museum of Transportation

3015 Barrett Station Road
St. Louis, MO 63122

The St. Louis Museum of Transportation houses *'one of the largest and best collections of transportation vehicles in the world,'* **according to the Smithsonian Institution.**

Visit us soon!

358

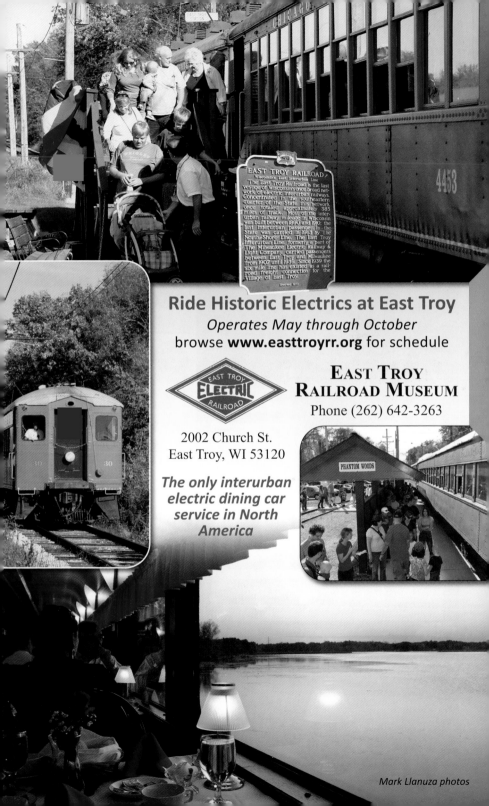

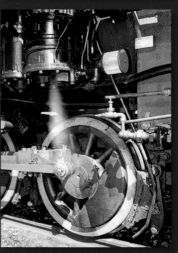

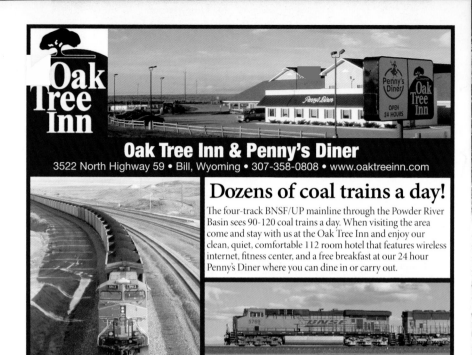

Come and ride the trains of the.....

Boone & Scenic Valley Railroad & Museum

Now Open - James H. Andrew Railroad Museum & History Center

EXCURSION TRAINS
Sats. in May at 1:30 p.m.
Memorial Day weekend -
October 31
Sun. - Fri. at 1:30 p.m.
Saturday at 1:30 and 4 p.m.
DAY OUT WITH THOMAS™
Late September
SANTA EXPRESS™
Late Nov. - Dec.

DINNER TRAINS
Saturdays at 5:30 p.m.
April - November
Fridays at 5:30 p.m.
June - October
DESSERT TRAINS
Sat. at 12:30 p.m.
June - October
PICNIC TRAINS
Sun. at 12:30 p.m.
Late May - October

1-800-626-0319 • www.scenic-valleyrr.com
Boone & Scenic Valley Railroad & Museum
225 10th Street, Boone, IA

Folkston Funnel
Funnel Street, Downtown Folkston, GA

The "Folkston Funnel" is CSXT's double track line which serves as the main artery for ninety percent of the railroad traffic into and out of Florida. From the Train Viewing Platform visitors can watch upwards of 60 trains a day pass through this charming southeast Georgia town. The platform is equipped with scanner, fans, electricity, internet, & floodlights for night train watching. Diagonally across the street is the restored Train Depot, home to our Train Museum, featuring the "Cookie" William's Model Train Room. Don't miss the new radio exhibit & museum gift shop. The Depot has a covered pavilion perfect for a picnic or cookout. There are plenty of open areas for taking pictures or video. If you love trains, you'll love Folkston.

Save the Date
"ANNUAL RAIL WATCH"
April 6, 2013

For more information visit our website at
www.folkston.com or call **912-496-2536.**

365

this is the Scenic Ra